REPUBLIC OF SHADE

REPUBLIC OF SHADE

New England and the American Elm

THOMAS J. CAMPANELLA

Yale University Press

New Haven and London

Frontispiece: Temple Street, New Haven, Connecticut, c. 1865 (Courtesy of the New Haven Colony Historical Society)

Set in Adobe Garamond type by Amy Storm. Printed in the United States of America by Thomson Shore

Library of Congress Cataloging-in-Publication Data
Campanella, Thomas J.
Republic of shade: New England and the American elm / Thomas J. Campanella
        p.   cm.
Includes bibliographical references (p.   ).
ISBN 0-300-09739-5 (alk. paper)
1. American elm—New England. 2. American elm—United States. I. Title.
SB413.A54 C36 2003
635.9'77345—dc21   2002151147

A catalogue record for this book is available from the British Library.

The paper in this book meets the guidelines for permanence and durability of the Committee on Production Guidelines for Book Longevity of the Council on Library Resources.

10   9   8   7   6   5   4   3   2   1

In memory of Irene Lee,
1932–2001

And the great elms overhead
Dark shadows wove on their aerial looms
Shot with golden thread

—Henry Wadsworth Longfellow

CONTENTS

ACKNOWLEDGMENTS

To me, as a child of New York City, elm trees were magical emissaries from the countryside. My parents would point them out on summer road trips through the Finger Lakes, the Adirondacks, or Vermont. Peering out of the Rambler's rear window, I learned to watch for their telltale form, a gushing fountain of limbs and leaves. But by this time—the early 1970s—many of the elm trees I spied along the roadsides and pastures were already lifeless hulks. The elms were dying. Before long, I was told, they might all be gone, dwindled from billions to none like the passenger pigeon a century before.

But there was another place in my childhood world where there would always be elms. In a quiet alcove at the American Museum of Natural History, I had come upon an illuminated painting of elm trees on a Vermont farm. Part of a diorama titled "The Elm in Northeastern United States," the image left an indelible impression in my mind. Perhaps it was because I knew that, even as the trees vanished from the summer landscapes of my youth, I could always take the subway from Brooklyn and visit my farmstead elms as they flourished in the dusky Hall of North American Forests.

Many years later, as a graduate student in urban and landscape history, I was awakened again to the enduring power of the American elm. I had just published an author's query in the *New York Times Book Review,* asking readers for recollections and memories about elm trees. The response was overwhelming. Week after week I received letters—more than a hundred in all—from addresses across the United States. My respondents ranged from cooks and shopkeepers and nursing home residents to poets and Ivy League professors. They sent me photographs from family albums, yellowed newspaper clippings, extracts of diaries and snippets from love letters; they sent poems and eulogies and sermons. And all for a *tree!*

A majority of my letter writers were elders, men and women who—like the protagonist in John Cheever's *Oh, What a Paradise It Seems*—were "old enough to remember when the horizons of his country were dominated by the beautiful and lachrymose wine-glass elm tree." The writers armed me with a popular mandate for this book: the American elm was something of paramount significance for the people of the United States, and of New England in particular. Incredulous that no one had told the story of this remarkable tree, I set out to do it myself.

I have accumulated a great pile of debts along the way. First among the many individuals who deserve thanks are Lawrence Vale, Leo Marx, and Gary Hack, who supervised this project when it was still a doctoral dissertation. Robert Cook of the Arnold Arboretum gave me an opportunity to complete the manuscript as a Mercer Fellow there. Sheila Connor, Phyllis Andersen, Peter Del Tredici, and Karen Madsen provided insights about trees and the cultural landscape of New England. My teachers Leonard Mirin, John Stilgoe, Dennis Frenchman, and Lois Craig provided early encouragement, as did Sam Bass Warner, Jr. (who also attempted to play Hewitt's "Old Elm Tree" on the piano). Matthew Potteiger inspired my interest in landscape studies years ago while I was still an undergraduate.

I also thank Tom Zetterstrom—a gifted photographer of trees and founder of Elm Watch—for information about recent efforts to bring the elm back to New England. John Hansel, founder of the Elm Research Institute, shared with me insights from his nearly four decades of advocacy on behalf of the American elm. Denny Townsend of the U.S. National Arboretum in Glenn Dale, Maryland; Bruce Carley of Acton, Massachusetts; Bill Chittick of the Bristol Tree Society, Bristol, Rhode Island; Jim Ozanne of the Greenrange Elm Project, Whiting, Vermont; Roger Holloway of Riveredge Farms in Atlanta; Bob McCarthy, tree warden of Williamstown, Massachusetts; and Bill Monroe of Cincinnati, Ohio, all provided me with invaluable information and sources for the conclusion of my book. So did Oscar Stone, Jim Ingram, Bill Hubbard of Winthrop, Massachusetts, and the late Paul Walgren, a legendary arborist who cared for Yale University's trees for nearly half a century.

Many collections were consulted in the writing of this book, and I am grateful to the many archivists and librarians who aided my research: Brenda Milkofsky and Wes Christiansen, Wethersfield Historical Society; Carol David of the Arnold Arboretum Library; Martha Noblick and Penny Leveritt, Historic Deerfield, Inc.; Suzanne Flynt and Mary Hawks of the Pocumtuck Valley Memorial Association, Deerfield, Massachusetts; Marilyn Aarrestad, Shenipsit State Forest, Connecticut; the staff of the Sterling Memorial Library, Yale University; Bill Barry, Maine Historical Society; Roxanne Roy, Historical Society of Cheshire County, New Hampshire; Maggie Humberston and Cynthia Murphy, Local History Library of the Springfield Museums; Kathleen Rawlins and the staff of the Cambridge Historical Commission; Robert Egleston, New Haven Colony Historical Society; and Philip Abbott, New Hampshire Historical Society.

Judy Metro, my original editor at Yale University Press, deserves thanks for taking this project on when it was still in a formative stage. My subsequent editors, Patricia Fidler and Michelle Komie, each helped carry the project to completion, as did Phillip King and John Long. A grant from the Graham Foundation provided financial support in the early research stage.

I owe the deepest debt of gratitude to my friends. I thank especially Jean Riesman, who shared a tiny student office with me for several years at MIT, and who never lost faith in this subject or its handler. I thank also Deborah Howe, C. Adair Smith, Sabine Hrechdakian, and Betsy Bates, all of whom commented on rough drafts. Tunney Lee, Uwe Brandes, Andrew Kaplan, Roy Strickland, Vishaan Chakrabarti, Joshua Stein, Minakshi Amundsen, Brent Ryan, Allie Southworth, Tess Oliver, Ranjan Nambiar, Peter Gorer, Arun Rewal, Vara Lipworth, Amy Brown, Jeanne Cresse, and Yelena Lembersky all brought joy and happiness into my life during the writing of this book, and played no small role in bringing about its completion.

Finally, I have been blessed with a wellspring of love and support from my parents, Mario and Rose Ann Campanella. It is to them that I owe this and all my work.

INTRODUCTION: "THE GLORY OF NEW ENGLAND"

The American elm, once the best-known and most popular tree in the United States, has a history all its own. Unlike the bison or the passenger pigeon, the elm flourished at the interface of nature and culture—for a time, at least. The tree was a token of the native forest that yielded to domestication with grace and dignity, a fragment of wild nature planted curbside from coast to coast.

Elm culture in America first took root in New England, but it soon spread to nearly every corner of the United States. Borne by the "westward transit of New England culture" that has defined so many of our national traditions—from Thanksgiving to the Cape Cod house—the practice of planting elms sped along the Great Lakes to Michigan, Wisconsin, and the northern Midwest, and from there across the plains and the Rockies to the Pacific Northwest.[1] Sapling trees found purchase in distant soils, carried in prairie schooners and even square-riggers bound for Oregon via Cape Horn.[2] The trees were set out to shade tender homesteads on the treeless plains, or simply to serve as a keepsake of a life and landscape left behind. The range of the American elm slowly expanded until it spanned the continent.

By the 1920s, the tree had become an almost universal element of the American urban landscape. A survey in 1937 revealed that more than 25 million American elms embowered the cities, towns, and suburbs of the nation. Sacramento had as many elms as did New Haven, Connecticut; Dallas had six times as many elms as Boston, and Dubuque, Iowa, had more trees than elm-rich Springfield, Massachusetts.[3] *Ulmus americana* had become truly worthy of its name. Collectively, America's elms formed the most expansive urban forest ever planted, a verdant parasol soaring above the quotidian, casting it in a dappled and flattering light. And in the process, the trees defined one of America's most storied and archetypal places—Elm Street.

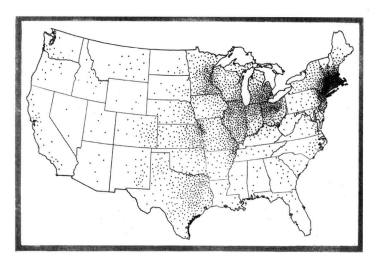

"America's elms shade the nation." Each dot represents ten thousand shade tree elms, showing clearly the concentration in New England, the wellspring of elm culture in America. (Joseph Edgar Chamberlain, "To Arms for the American Elm," American Forests 40:5, May 1934)

If the American Dream had a home, it would be tucked beneath the sunshot canopy of Elm Street, USA. Few towns proud of their place in the national tapestry could not direct a visitor to their version of this American tradition. Even Fifth Avenue in New York had Elm Street aspirations. On a midnight walk in 1939, E. B. White came upon none other than Nelson Rockefeller presiding over the planting of a series of seventy-foot elms by Rockefeller Center. "I think elm-birth is the prettiest fairy tale in the city's wonderbook," he wrote, "for the big trees are delivered at night . . . arriving furtively in the marketplace and sliding into position for early risers to discover on their way to work."[4]

The universal appeal of Elm Street—"one of the glories of world urbanism," as the urbanist Andrés Duany put it—was not only due to the splendid visual and spatial effects of the flanking trees, but because Elm Street delivered the elusive ideal of a *rus in urbe*—the countryside in the town. Long before Central Park, Americans attempted to forge an urban pastoral by endowing their city streets with this harbinger of the countryside and its "rural values." The effect was often magical: as Charles Dickens observed of New Haven in 1842, streetside elms brought about "a kind of compromise between town and country; as if each had met the other half-way, and shaken hands upon it."[5]

Even as Elm Street made its way across the United States, no region in the country possessed a greater concentration of the namesake tree than New England. And nowhere in the American experience would a tree of any kind more deeply penetrate the soul of a people than the Yankee elm. It was amid the whitewashed steeples and prim greens of innumerable New England towns that evolved an extraordinary union between mankind and tree, a verdant republic of shade that stretched from Connecticut to northern Maine. It was unlike anything in the world.

But the age of the Yankee elm proved fleeting. Elm Street was doomed by the very popularity of its namesake tree. A century after Dickens visited, the elms of New Haven were under siege, ravaged by a deadly interloper known as Dutch elm disease. By the 1960s, the pathogen had virtually extirpated the tree from the New England landscape and was moving swiftly westward. Americans had planted elms in an almost unbroken chain across both New England and the continent. In the process they created a profoundly unstable ecological condition, a vast sylvan monoculture that guaranteed its own demise. Though *Ulmus americana* survives today, Elm Street endures largely in name and memory alone. By the 1980s some 77 million American elms had been lost to Dutch elm disease. It was an ecological calamity that changed the face of the American nation. And nowhere was this loss more visible, more keenly felt, or more deeply mourned than in New England.

The urbanist and historian Spiro Kostof once lamented that "Elm Street has yet to find its scholar." What follows is the long-neglected story of this American icon and its namesake tree. It is a story about transformations—of a wayside weed into a tool of "village improvement"; of a woodland tree into a symbol of a region and its people; of a local practice into a national institution known as Elm Street.

A Death in Deerfield

On August 15, 1853, the *Gazette and Courier* of Deerfield, Massachusetts, reported that "one of the majestic old elms in Deerfield street . . . had arrived to such a state of decay as to render its removal necessary." Deerfield elected to give it an honored burial. Doing so was no simple task, for this was a gargantuan plant. A ditch was dug around the base of the tree, severing the roots and "leaving a ball of earth about twelve feet in diameter." Rigging was then fastened to the limbs, and "with powerful purchase" the mighty elm was eased to the ground. Its great ball of roots was upended now, but still very much attached. After it was cut apart from the trunk, the great stump "returned back to its mother earth for its final burial."[6]

But the old tree did not go quietly into the night. Its felling and interment drew a crowd of Deerfield citizens who gathered about "to commemorate this interesting event." Leaders of the community stood on the stump and eulogized the sylvan deceased in turn. Dr. Stephen West Williams rarely made public speeches, but he could not "pass over the occasion of this event in silence." He had for years instructed pupils beneath the tree, which had come to be known as the Literary Elm. "I love trees in villages," Williams confessed, "altogether with a greater love than any other objects in nature." He ventured further: "I can hardly refrain from saying that I should feel but very little worse to have every house in Deerfield street burnt to the ground than to have every tree in it destroyed."[7]

These were strong words. During the seventeenth century Deerfield had been burned to the ground by Native Americans infuriated at the usurpation of their land; many settlers had died in the attack. Recalling such a calamity was no joking matter. But in 1853 elms were profoundly important to Deerfield. The trees were not only elemental to the community's identity; they were a key part of its economy. Deerfield's renowned beauty was featured on many a tourist's itinerary, and this beauty was largely attributable to its magnificent elms. As Williams informed the assembly, "I have heard many . . . strangers and travelers speak of the beauty of this village, principally on account of these trees, as unsurpassed by any other village in the United States."[8] The loss of a Deerfield elm was a tragedy indeed.

The "interesting event" closed with a benediction by the Reverend Nathaniel Whitman. "I shall speak as moved by the occasion which has called us together," he began, and proceeded to address the audience as a medium "through whom the spirit of the departed sends to you the counsels of age and the exhortations of experience." Animating this "ancient settler," Whitman rhapsodized on the history of Deerfield and its founding generation. He exhorted those gathered to uphold the intellectual and moral ideals of their ancestors; to "go forth in the spirit of the olden times, to deeds of goodness—to enterprises of improvement." Bonded for a moment, man and tree held forth: "I was sent to you on a mission of mercy. . . . But now my mission is accomplished . . . and the spirit of the olden times is here to honor my exit. My earthly ties are severed, I am about to descend to my final resting place, amidst the benedictions of the grateful, the joys of the hopeful, and the songs of the tuneful." And perhaps with a final, leafless sigh, "I sink to rest with peace."[9]

The Yankee Elm

"In the beginning," writes Thomas J. Schlereth, "was not the word, nor the thing, but the plant."[10] Linked with human affairs since the dawn of time, flora—from the lotus to the tulip and the rose—have come to bear rich cultural associations. As the largest and most imposing members of the vegetable kingdom, trees have found notable service in this regard—all around the world. Smaller plants may feed and sustain us, but in trees we see ourselves. We appreciate the symmetry

Wind-thrown elm, Wapping, Massachusetts, August 1890 (Courtesy of the Pocumtuck Valley Memorial Association, Memorial Hall Museum, Deerfield, Massachusetts)

of human and sylvan life. In the seasons of a tree we find a map of our own lives. Trees, Simon Schama writes, satisfy our longing "to find in nature a consolation for our own mortality."[11] It is hardly surprising, then, that few of the world's cultures lack an arboreal component; in many, trees play a central role.[12]

No tree has loomed larger in American history than the American elm, and nowhere more so than in New England. The naturalist Charles Sprague Sargent put it best. "In no other part of the country," he wrote in 1890, "is there a tree which occupies the same position in the affection of the people as the Elm does in that of the inhabitants of New England."[13] Native to the eastern half of the United States, *Ulmus americana* flourished as New England was settled and cultivated by European colonists. Elms were often spared the ax as cultivators cleared the land of its forest cover, and elm seeds sprouted vigorously along fencerows and waysides. Tall and distinctive in form, elm trees soon gained a commanding presence in the pastoral landscape of colonial New England.

They also began to collect a range of historical and sentimental associations. Colonists planted elms as domestic ornaments, to shelter a home from lightning and storms, or to mark weddings or the birth of a child. Wayside elms often emerged as totemic centerpieces in towns and villages—a late echo of pre-Christian tree worship in a God-fearing land. Other elms were assigned specific historical associations, commemorating persons or events of significance. Occasionally such elms evolved into monuments of national importance, as was the case with the legendary Washington Elm at Cambridge, Massachusetts. Long before marble and granite graced the Yankee commons, elm trees served as vessels of collective memory. As one writer put it in 1856, an aged elm was like a "witness upon the field of history," a timepiece in a fresh and unstoried land.[14]

However commonplace, field and wayside elms were still largely an occasional element in New England at the beginning of the nineteenth century. But in the 1830s, a "new craving for spatial beauty" swept across the Yankee states, yielding America's first environmental movement.[15] Village improvement societies were organized, beginning in western Massachusetts, to beautify the civic spaces of town and village. These groups engaged in a wide range of activities to enhance the attractiveness of their public lands, but first and foremost they planted trees— *elm* trees. In doing so, they changed the face of New England, and forged one of the most powerful images of place in America—the elm-tufted Yankee town.

Like the whitewashed steeple or the village green, the American elm became a symbol of New England throughout the United States. So dominant was its presence that few depictions of the region in literature and the arts failed to account for the tree. From the modest etchings of village greens by itinerant artists like John Warner Barber to the popular lithographs of Currier and Ives and the softly sentimental photographs of Samuel Chamberlain, elm trees were ubiquitous. And the tree moved pens like no other. Scores of writers, both local and from afar, struggled to capture the beauty, grandeur, and symbolism of the American elm, and to fathom its grip on the native imagination. Henry David Thoreau, Anthony Trollope, Charles Dickens, Oliver Wendell Holmes, and Henry James were among the many literati to write about the elm; many others, from Henry Wadsworth Longfellow and Nathaniel Hawthorne to Edith Wharton and Eugene O'Neill, evoked the tree in poems, novels, and plays.

Charles Joseph Latrobe, a visiting Briton who toured New England in the 1830s, remarked simply that the American elm was "the glory of New England." Other writers were more effusive. "The Elms of New England!" gushed the firebrand abolitionist Henry Ward Beecher: "They are as much a part of her beauty as the columns of the Parthenon were the glory of its architecture." For Beecher, elm trees were "tabernacles of the air" that transformed the lowliest street into a splendor of leaf and limb. Speaking on behalf of all New Englanders, Beecher admitted, "We had rather walk beneath an avenue of elms than inspect the noblest cathedral that art ever accomplished." Nathaniel Parker Willis would have agreed. To the popular romantic poet, the famous elms of New Haven were "an unhewn cathedral, in whose choirs / Breezes and storm-winds, and the many birds / Join'd in the varied anthem."[16]

Children gathered beneath the Town Street elms in Deerfield,
c. 1868 (Courtesy of the Pocumtuck Valley Memorial Association,
Memorial Hall Museum, Deerfield, Massachusetts)

Henry David Thoreau was more grounded in his estimation of elms, but no less entranced. Indeed, no Yankee writer penned more words of praise to the tree. To the poet of Walden Pond, elms consecrated the landscape. "When I see their magnificent domes, miles away in the horizon, over intervening valleys and forests," he wrote, "they suggest a village, a community." Thoreau imagined the "rural and domestic life passing beneath," for a great elm was "the vignette to an unseen idyllic poem." In other elms, he read stoicism and perseverance. The trees "adjourn not night nor day," he wrote; "they stand for magnificence; they take the brunt of the tempest; they attract the lightening that would smite our roofs, leaving only a few rotten members scattered over the highway."[17]

But Thoreau's elms could be radical too. At the tip of his pen, the trees were transformed into a political symbol that bore Thoreau's moral outrage over slavery. Following passage of the Fugitive Slave Law and the 1854 Kansas-Nebraska Act (which cleared the way for the extension of the South's "peculiar institution" into territories not yet granted statehood), Thoreau spoke out publicly against slavery.[18] His elms became allegories for the abolitionist movement, particularly the Free Soil Party, which formed in response to the apathy of politicians over the expansion issue.[19] Thoreau implored the abolitionists to remain true to their principles, and to take a lesson from the elms. For the trees, "free-soilers in their own broad sense . . . send their roots north and south and east and west into many a conservative's Kansas and Carolina, who does not suspect such underground railroads—they improve the subsoil he has never disturbed—and many times their length, if the support of their principles requires it. They battle with the tempests of a century. . . . Yet they never adjourn; they steadily vote for their principles, and send their roots further and wider." Thoreau prophesied that the elms (and the Free Soilers) would, in the end, "acquire new States and Territories, while the old dominions"—a reference to Virginia and the pro-slavery South—would "decay, and become the habitation of bears and owls and coons."[20]

On most days, however, the Concord elms were simply Thoreau's sylvan soul mates. In January 1856, Thoreau observed the felling of one such friend. The tree, measuring more than fifteen feet in circumference, had made creaking noises in a recent storm, and neighbors feared the great plant was about to fall. "I have attended the funeral of this old citizen of the town," Thoreau confided to his *Journal*; he spoke "a few words of eulogy . . . remembering the maxim *de mortuis nil nisi bonum* (in this case *magnum*)." But only Thoreau had come to bid the great tree farewell. "How have the mighty fallen!" he lamented. "No longer will our eyes rest on its massive gray trunk, like a vast Corinthian column by the wayside; no longer shall we walk in the shade of its lofty, spreading dome." Indeed, the woodsmen "have laid the axe . . . to one of the king-posts of the town."[21]

Thoreau was not alone in his worship of the American elm. His Concord neighbor Nathaniel Hawthorne considered the tree "a great deal more stately" than its English cousin. Anthony Trollope, too, appreciated "the beautiful American elm, whose drooping boughs have all the grace of the willow without its fantastic melancholy." No other tree, wrote Henry Ward Beecher in 1868, "unites, in the same degree, majesty and beauty, grace and grandeur, as the American Elm." The "weeping elm" of New England, waxed an anonymous writer in an 1864 edition of the *Hampshire Gazette*, was indeed "a nobler tree than any of nature's other favorites." "The boasted oak of England," he wrote, "the straight, poverty-stricken English elms, the Norwegian pine, the stately royal palm, king of palms, the noble cedar of Lebanon, the tall Italian cypress, the sacred olive with its thousand associations, all yield the crown to the wondrous power, grandeur and grace of those forest glories . . . which stand, here and there, in solitary grandeur scattered over your meadows, proud monuments to the appreciative taste of the yeoman ancestors."[22]

The Knight Elm in Newburyport, Massachusetts, 1927 (Photograph by E. H. Wilson; courtesy of the Photographic Archives of the Arnold Arboretum, Harvard University)

Oliver Wendell Holmes, Boston's poet-physician and man-about-town (and country, too), expressed a depth of affection for the Yankee elm that was matched by few writers. He was born in 1809 within sight of the Washington Elm in Cambridge, and the trees were among his earliest memories. "When I first rolled my infant eyes toward the glare of the western sky," he wrote toward the end of his life, "four green masses, each of them 'a forest waving on a single stem' . . . printed themselves on my retina through my blinking eyelids." Elms "entered into my young life," recalled Holmes, "as truly as the milk that made its blood."[23]

Holmes struggled to capture the beauty and lyric grandeur of the elm, deploring the plodding descriptions of science. "Just think of applying the Linnaean system to an elm!" he exclaimed. "Who cares how many stamens or pistils that little brown flower, which comes out before the leaf, may have to classify it by? What we want is the meaning, the character, the expression of a tree." To Holmes, no tree could match the American elm in grandeur and beauty. Apple trees (for which he expressed a fatherly affection) were but common "fruit peddlers" compared to the mighty elm, which "dealt only with the sunbeams." To truly understand the Yankee mind required an appreciation of the American elm, for this tree came "nearer to having a soul," Holmes explained, "than any other vegetable creature among us." "Nobody knows New England," he wrote in 1891, "who is not on terms of intimacy with one of its elms."[24]

Holmes was prone to hyperbole, but this time he got it right. Well into the twentieth century, the New England landscape was embowered with columns of elms, on its streets, parks, commons, and village greens. The tree was one of the quintessential symbols of the region. Other species may have been more commercially valuable or more useful, but the elm was rooted in the Yankee soul. "We have dwelt beneath their sheltering boughs since we were born, we have walked beside long avenues of their stately boles," wrote W. E. Ekblaw in 1935. "We have made New England glorious and famous throughout our land by planting these lordly trees."[25] Even in death the Yankee imagination longed for the elm. Solomon Sanborn's sweetly macabre last will and testament, written in 1871, recorded his wish to be "composited for fertiliser to contribute to the growth of an American elm, to be planted in some rural thoroughfare, that the weary wayfarer may rest, and innocent children may play beneath its umbrageous branches rendered luxuriant by my remains."[26] From cradle to grave, elm trees bore the very identity of the New England people.

I

A PROSPECT OF ELMS

In the European imagination, the New World was Eden recovered, and Eden was covered with trees. North America appeared like a leafy apparition across the Atlantic. Travelers' descriptions of the new land were often fantastic, and stories of this green and bountiful paradise, slumbering since creation, moved many an Elizabethan pen to verse (including that of William Shakespeare, whose *Tempest* allegorized the New World's promise of terrestrial elysium). Unlike the long-trampled landscapes of Europe, here was a virgin realm still "cloathed with infinite thick woods," as John Josselyn described Connecticut in the 1670s.[1] These forests were believed to bear the mark of the creator, with soil unstirred by the hand of man. Europe's reaction was a mix of piety, lust, and wonder. "Who can describe the feelings," pondered the vicomte de Chateaubriand, "that are experienced on entering these forests, coeval with the world, and which alone afford an idea of the creation, such as it issued from the hands of the Almighty."[2]

Encounters

The myth of the New World as Eden recovered was seductive indeed, but it bore only a passing resemblance to reality. Human hands had in fact long shaped the landscapes of the New World, and this was especially the case in those parts of New England first settled by the Puritans. Rather than a howling wilderness of trees, the newcomers discovered landscapes extensively altered by America's native peoples. William Wood, writing in 1634, was among the first to record accurately the true state of the New England landscape: "And whereas it is generally conceived that the woods grow so thicke, that there is no more cleared ground than is hewed out by labour of man," he wrote, "it is nothing so"; for there were "divers Acres . . . cleare," and a man could "ride a hunting in most places of the land."[3]

The native inhabitants of New England were America's first landscape planners, and fire was the tool they used to alter the environment. An Englishman, Thomas Morton, noted this practice while touring southern Massachusetts in 1622. The natives, he wrote, "are accustomed . . . to set fire of the country in all places where they come; and to burn it, twize a yeare, vize at the Spring, and at the fall of the leafe."[4] Firing profoundly altered the spatial character of the countryside, creating a "very beautifull, and commodious" mosaic of field and woodland —landscapes that reminded Morton of hunting parks in his native England.[5] "A traveler emerging from the forest," diarist Timothy Dwight later wrote of the fire-cleared meadows, "naturally concludes that it is the commencement of a settled country."[6] Indeed it was.

The woods were fired for a variety of purposes. Burning freed the land of its woody mantle, clearing it for seasonal camps and the cultivation of maize, squash, pumpkins, and other crops. Firing yielded "fresh and sweet pasture for the purpose of alluring the deer," Dwight noted, and also created an abundance of border zones between forest and grassland—an ecological niche that provides rich habitat for a variety of flora and fauna.[7] After being scorched with flames, the land would spring forth in new abundance, providing tribespeople with a ready supply of rabbit, fox, quail, and a variety of medicinal and food plants, such as blackberry and raspberry.[8]

The native inhabitants of the land were selective in their burning, but even where fire had its way, the flames did not affect the landscape equally in all places. Some woodland habitats proved more combustible than others. While the drier uplands burned readily, the moist bottomlands—where the ground was perpetually wet or even inundated for many months of the year—rarely succumbed.[9] As Wood reported in 1634, such low grounds were preserved from fire "by the wetnesse of the soile."[10] Thus certain forest types—and, in turn, certain trees—were favored. Those of the dry uplands were diminished, while trees of the moist bottomlands flourished.

As a result, the largest, oldest trees in a particular region could almost always be found in the soggy bottomlands. Thomas Morton made this point, in a roundabout way, in his 1637 treatise *New English Canaan:* "Hee that will looke to finde large trees, and good tymber," advised Morton, "must not . . . finde them on the upland ground; but must seeke for them . . . in the lower grounds where the grounds are wett when the Country is fired." Bottomland trees were safe from flames, which, due to the presence of water, "have no power to doe them any hurt."[11] Here towered the primeval woods reported so breathlessly in Europe, where mighty trees flung their limbs skyward, safe from man.

Descriptions of the woody bottomlands of colonial New England are rare, but we can be certain these forests were home to some true arboreal giants. Button-wood *(Platanus occidentalis)*, common along rivers and streams, was a tree of tremendous girth. Virgin maples, beeches, birches, and other hardwoods would have outclassed almost anything in Europe at the time. But the largest and most visually impressive tree of the New England bottomlands was a new species of *Ulmus*, a genus European botanists were well acquainted with.

The tree was loftier, more graceful, and larger than its Old World relatives, and the European botanists simply named it *Ulmus americana*.[12] "Common in moist land and swamps," wrote the American naturalist Manasseh Cutler in 1783, the American elm reached its greatest development in precisely those lower grounds that had been spared by fire.[13] There, in the boggy intervales of colonial New England, *Ulmus americana* grew virtually unmolested. Often it dominated the woodland scene—"a great fountain of dark and brilliant green above its humbler companions of the forest."[14]

The New World contained a bounty of flora unknown to science, and its gradual unveiling was one of the defining events of the Enlightenment. Of the many new plant species discovered across the Atlantic, few made as lasting an impression as the American elm. Its entry into the annals of Western science was deceptively quiet, however. John Clayton, a physician and amateur botanist in the Virginia colony, was the first to describe the tree.

Clayton's connections to some of Europe's leading botanists of the time assured that the specimens he sent back would at least be seriously considered. Among the men for whom Clayton collected was J. F. Gronovius, a friend and patron of the great Swedish botanist Linnaeus. Gronovius used Clayton's speci-mens to write the first book on North American flora, *Flora Virginica*, which he published in 1739.[15] Seeds of the new elm found their way to nurserymen across the Atlantic, and by 1750 the species was under cultivation in English gardens.[16]

But it was Luigi Castiglioni, a Milanese patrician with a passion for trees, who was the first European to write about the aesthetics of the American elm. Cas-tiglioni traveled extensively throughout North America during the 1780s, record-ing its sylva in a travelogue titled *Viaggio negli Stati Uniti dell'America settentrionale* (1790).[17] Castiglioni's object was utterly pragmatic: to identify species of potential commercial use to his native Italy. Yet he had a ken for arboreal grandeur. "It is remarkable for the beauty of its branches," he wrote of the American elm, "which are numerous, very wide-spreading and pendant almost like those of the

African willow." Castiglioni was also the first to note the elm's great potential as an urban amenity and a street tree. Its unique architectural properties would, he reasoned, make the tree "preferable to the European for making avenues and other ornamental plantings."[18]

François André Michaux, a French contemporary of Castiglioni's, was equally enthusiastic about the new elm's beauty. Michaux treated the tree at length in his classic *Histoire des arbres forestiers de l'Amérique septentrionale* (translated into English as *The North American Sylva*). Michaux was born in France in 1770 into a life of plants. His father traveled to North America to study its forests on behalf of the French government in 1785.[19] With the endorsement of Thomas Jefferson, Michaux senior embarked on a remarkable series of journeys from the Bahamas to Hudson Bay, accompanied by his young son François. After the elder Michaux's death in Madagascar, François carried on his father's work, publishing his three-volume masterpiece in 1802.[20]

Michaux saw many trees in his day, but none earned the high marks he gave the American elm. Although Michaux observed the tree to range "over an extensive tract of the North-American Continent," he found that the elm attained its greatest physical development in New England.[21] Michaux devoted the requisite paragraphs in his book to the elm's leaf, petiole, flower, and seed, but what truly impressed the Frenchman was the tree's beauty and formal grandeur. Many of the specimens Michaux found possessed trunks four or five feet in diameter, with a bole that "ramified" (branched) into several massive limbs before climbing to a height of one hundred feet or more.

From this towering crown tumbled "long, flexible, pendulous branches, bending into regular arches and floating lightly in the air." If the burly buttonwood matched the elm in girth and "amplitude of its head," the American elm offered "a more majestic appearance . . . owing to its great elevation, to the disposition of its principal limbs, and to the extreme elegance of its summit." To Michaux, the American elm was a masterpiece of sylvan architecture, or as he memorably put it, "the most magnificent vegetable of the temperate zone."[22]

Triumph of a Weed

Long before the arrival of the botanizing Europeans, elm trees were widely used by native peoples. Tough, stringy elm bark found service among the Huron in Ontario for covering longhouses, while cups and bowls were crafted from limbs. The Iroquois used bark to construct canoes and to manufacture rope. Among the Algonquin, sections of fresh elm bark were used to store food. Medicinal applications were equally extensive. Among the Penobscot, an infusion of bark

Pl.126

Bessa del. *Gabriel sc.*

1. *2.*

White Elm.
Ulmus Americana

The American elm, or white elm, as portrayed in François André Michaux's The North American Sylva, *1810 (Courtesy of the Library of the Gray Herbarium, Harvard University)*

was used as an antihemmorhagic, to cure "bleeding at the lungs." The Mohegans used infusions of inner bark for colds and coughs, while the Iroquois mashed elm twigs and root bark to treat internal bleeding and control menstruation. They also developed a bark compound to facilitate childbirth, and to treat symptoms of "summer disease."[23]

American elm also found a place in the materia medica of the colonists, as did a closely related tree known as slippery elm.[24] Joseph Strong of Philadelphia, an army surgeon in the 1790s, experienced "the most happy effects" by applying poultices of elm bark to gun-shot wounds. Strong also prescribed elm poultice for "old ill-conditioned ulcers and fresh burns," and found that an infusion of elm bark alleviated diarrhea and dysentery—a treatment no doubt adopted from native medical practice. Strong treated one soldier "who had lost his way" and survived for ten days on little more than sassafras and the mucous substance produced by boiling elm bark.[25]

But the uses for forest trees by the European settlers of New England differed fundamentally from those of the native peoples. To the newcomers, forests were an impediment to settlement and agricultural development, and trees were a resource to harvest at will. In the colonial period, much of the forest cover that escaped burning by Native Americans fell to the settler's ax—mainly to prepare land for cultivation. At first, pioneers favored the fields opened earlier by Native Americans, as these required relatively little effort to bring under cultivation. Many of the first New England villages, such as Plymouth, Massachusetts, were in fact located on such land.[26] But these places had supported human occupancy for generations, and their soil was often depleted of nutrients. The quest for fertile land, combined with the burgeoning European population, forced settlers to begin clearing the long-slumbering bottomlands.

Expanding outward from the compact villages of the seventeenth century, European settlement began to spread into the fertile valleys of the Connecticut, Housatonic, and Merrimac rivers. To aid the search for good new land, settlers looked closely at vegetation, and at trees in particular. Folk wisdom suggested that "the larger the trees and the more luxuriant the growth, the better the soil."[27] Pioneer settlers in New England understood that elms, among the largest trees in the landscape, signaled deep, rich alluvial soil. Elms and good farmland were paired in the native imagination, an association carried over from the Old World. In the British Isles, folk knowledge assured tillers that "a good elm never grew on bad ground," and that "tall elms and fat cows" went hand in hand.[28]

In spite of "miasmas" associated with low, wet ground (and the very real risk of malaria), valley bottomlands became favored sites for agriculture.[29] In preparing these so-called intervales for agriculture, colonial husbandmen adopted many of the practices used earlier by the Native Americans. "The rotational clearing and widespread burning practiced by the Indians," writes forest historian Michael Williams, "were not eliminated but were often replaced by more extensive and thorough clearing and burning, so that areas never touched by fire . . . were now affected"—including the "wet bottomlands."[30]

In Hatfield, Massachusetts, colonists cleared the heavily wooded swamps and "boggy meadows," and continued the Indian practice of annual burning.[31] Clearing the bottomland forests, removing centuries-old trees, was a Herculean task even for the ablest of settlers. In the southern colonies, large trees were removed by girdling the bark and waiting months for the tree to die. In New England, colonists simply felled trees with an ax.[32] Felling a large tree required an immense investment of time and effort on the part of the farmer—one worth making only if the tree was truly an obstacle to cultivation, or commercially valuable enough to make removal pay. Elms were neither, so they were typically left to live.

The commercial harvesting of timber and forest products often occurred in unison with agricultural clearing. Farmers, in the process of preparing land for cultivation, supplied much of the wood upon which the timber economy of New England was based.[33] In this economy, not all trees were equal. Elm was of limited practical use, and thus of little commercial value—though not entirely. Elm was used for crafting hubs for cart and carriage wheels, for yokes and saddletrees, and for flooring and cooperage.[34] Occasionally the wood was used for shipbuilding, in the manufacture of blocks and keels. The bark of the tree was used for ox whips and chair bottoms, and "when macerated in water and rendered supple by pounding" could be twisted into rope.[35]

But elm wood, tough and fibrous, was no friend of the carpenter. It took forever to dry, and its elongated cellular structure made planing difficult. Elm was "not admitted into the construction of houses or of vessels," noted Michaux, "except occasionally in the District of Maine for keels, for which it is adapted only by its size."[36] Compared with oak, maple, and other species, elm was essentially a trash tree. Even in a later age, with improved woodworking technology, elms were still considered "the most useless piece of vegetation in our forests."[37] Because big elms were hardly worth the sweat of felling them, farmers commonly let them remain in their fields and hedgerows; they were "allowed to escape the axe."[38]

Elms escaped for other reasons, too. The tree was considered relatively inoffensive by farmers, and even somewhat useful. Field elms were often left standing to provide shelter for livestock—and were often planted for that reason. Agricultural writers in the nineteenth century verified the old colonial wisdom of keeping field and pasture elms. The trees not only rendered land "more congenial to the growth of grass and grain, and the health of pasturing animals," but were thought to have a positive microclimatic effect. "It is, indeed, astonishing," reasoned the *New England Farmer*, "how much better cattle thrive in fields, even but moderately sheltered, than they do in an open, exposed country." Big field elms not only afforded livestock "protection from the keen winds of spring and autumn" but were even believed to communicate "a degree of warmth, or softness, to the air."[39]

Trees on farms threatened crops by blocking the sun, and of course the main reason for clearing land was to open it to the light. But elms were hardly offensive in this regard. The absence of low-spreading limbs and the great elevation of the tree's crown allowed sunlight to easily reach the ground below; the shadow cast by an elm swung quickly though its arc, with minimal impact on plants growing below. Moreover, elm leaves were small, and light could still pass through the crown; rarely did an elm produce the killing shade cast by a maple or an oak. The *New England Farmer* assented, advising cultivators to avoid the opaque shade of oaks and chestnuts in favor of "trees with lofty stems, and large heads," such as the elm.[40]

Old elm trees were also spared the ax because they were often used as boundary markers. "Indian deeds" and other instruments of conveyance in colonial New England included precise descriptions of the land. Property lines were perambulated or "bounded" using natural landmarks, such as rock outcroppings, streams, and trees prominent for their great size and age.[41] Such specimens were transformed into legal instruments. As the molestation of boundary markers was a severe and punishable offense, such landmark trees gained protection from the ax and were assured a lasting place in the landscape.[42]

But *Ulmus americana* hardly required such legal assistance to secure its place in the settled landscape. The fertile intervales favored by farmers were, after all, the tree's chosen ground. Purging the elm from the Connecticut and Housatonic bottomlands would likely have been a difficult task even if economic factors favored such action. For the tree germinated easily, sprouted vigorously, and sped to maturity faster than a busy farmer could swing an ax in protest. In pasture, field, and hedgerow, elms shot skyward with little help from humans. As tenacious and fast-growing as a weed, the tree quickly gained a foothold in the pastoral landscape.[43]

Inadvertently favored by the cultural practices of both the Native Americans and the European colonists, the elm gradually gained a commanding presence in the New England landscape. Michaux remarked on the elm's amplified position in the wake of agricultural development: "In clearing the primitive forests," he wrote, "a few stocks [of elm] are sometimes left standing; insulated in this manner it appears in all its majesty."[44] In time, this remnant of the native forest emerged as the very essence of Yankee pastoralism.

In few places did the American elm gain more prominence in the landscape than in the fertile valleys of the Housatonic, Merrimac, and Connecticut rivers. The floodplain of the Connecticut was almost unmatched as elm habitat, and it became the hearth of elm culture in America. A rich and well-watered land, its deep alluvial soils sustained, in the words of Oliver Wendell Holmes, "a race of giants."[45] The Connecticut's valley was settled early in the seventeenth century, and its venerated river towns—Deerfield, Northampton, Hatfield, Longmeadow, and others—later became some of the first communities in America to plant elms along their streets.

The pastoral vale, and its luxuriant elms, was early praised by men and women who appreciated the spatial beauty of the cultivated landscape. "No watery glades thro richer vallies shine," Joel Barlow wrote of the Connecticut in his 1787 *Columbiad*, "Nor drinks the sea a lovelier wave than thine."[46] Adam Hodgson, an Englishman who visited America in the 1820s, concluded that the Connecticut was no less than "one of the finest portions of the cultivated regions of America." He was particularly impressed by "some of the finest American elms we have observed in the country," and by the manner in which these trees stood like sentries "singly in the fields." Liberated from the surrounding forest, the elms had "power to expand," tossing their limbs over hedgerow and meadow.[47]

Charles Joseph Latrobe, another Briton who toured the United States, had a similar reaction in 1832. "The valley of the Connecticut river," he wrote in *The Rambler in North America*, "struck us as one of the most lovely we had ever beheld." Ancient specimens of "weeping elm" were among the many "beauties with which nature has decked the verdant, fertile, and park-like shores of that pastoral stream."[48] Margaret Hunter Hall, accompanying her husband on a trip through the United States in the 1820s, described a view of the Connecticut plains as "one of the most beautiful prospects I ever saw"; the river's flanking meadows were made especially winsome by the "very picturesque trees . . . scattered over them."[49]

Artists, too, praised the Connecticut, and it eventually became a favored subject of the Hudson River school of landscape painters. "The imagination can scarcely conceive," wrote Thomas Cole in his *Essay on American Scenery* (1835), "Arcadian vales more lovely or more peaceful than the valley of the Connecticut"; there, waters born in the wilds of New Hampshire descended into a "luxuriant valley . . . glancing through the green expanse of elm-besprinkled meadows."[50] Cole's *Oxbow*, featuring the river and its elm-rich flanks, remains one of the formative paintings of the nineteenth century. Like Cole, Albert Bierstadt found inspiration there for some of his best work, including *Mount Ascutney from Claremont, New Hampshire*, and *Moat Mountain, Intervale, New Hampshire*.

Field elms in the Connecticut Valley, as seen in Albert Bierstadt's Mount Ascutney
from Claremont, New Hampshire, *1862 (Courtesy of the Fruitlands Museums,
Harvard, Massachusetts)*

Well into the twentieth century, the Connecticut Valley, graced by its spreading
field elms, remained perhaps the most compelling image of Yankee pastoralism.
Few writers better captured the halcyon beauty of the scene than Berkshire
author Walter Prichard Eaton. In *Green Trails and Upland Pastures*, he evoked
"the picture of a green intervale, of browsing cattle, of a winding stream with
vervain and wild cucumber on the banks, and now and then, rising like graceful
green fountains or like great vases on slender stems, the noble elms—the wardens of the peaceful landscape." To Eaton, riverbank elms were like "figures by
Botticelli arrested in a stately dance." They were especially beautiful at dusk,
"when the shadows are creeping like long amethyst fingers over the grass." Then,
the trees appeared to rise above the intervale "in radiant lightness against the
west, every detail of their lovely symmetry outlined sharply against the sky."[51]

These Arcadian scenes did not remain solely in verse and on canvas; they were
recalled again and again as Americans built towns and cities across the nation.
The custom of planting elm trees along streets was at its core an effort to endow
urban life with the placid beauty of New England's valley landscapes.

The colonists who settled New England came from a culture intimately familiar
with trees—and elms in particular. The early colonial settlers were predomi-
nantly emigrants from England and the forest-rich precincts of northern Europe,
descended from a long line of forest-dwelling people. This intimacy with trees
deeply influenced the place that forests occupied in their culture. As landscape

Albert Bierstadt, Moat Mountain, Intervale, New Hampshire, *1862, with elm trees as a prominent feature (Courtesy of the Currier Gallery of Art, Manchester, New Hampshire)*

historian J. B. Jackson put it, northern Europe's "old vernacular culture of trees" was carried by the early colonists to North America.[52] There, the Old World pagan fear of woods was transplanted, and even briefly flourished.

In premodern Europe, the forest was the antipode of civilization, the bewildering domain of ogres, elves, and fairies.[53] The expanding umbra of Christianity in the Middle Ages encouraged the conversion of heathen forests into plowed fields and pious settlements, a transformation of landscape that implied an analogous transformation of the soul. In New England too, forested wilds were quickly cleared—for cultivation and timber, to be sure, but also because they were considered a threat to the moral order. Consuming the great mantle of trees was crucial to the spiritual welfare of the embryonic settlements.

Yet even as this wholesale clearing of the forest was occurring, an ethos of the individual tree was beginning to take form. The Indo-European peoples who settled the forested continent of premodern Europe brought out of Asia fruit and other trees, and established a culture of tree planting even as the woods themselves were looked upon as frightful places. Trees were planted in medieval northern Europe for a variety of practical purposes, and in time many species acquired symbolic value.[54] The early New England colonists carried with them this cultural legacy, in which the forest was an object of fear, but individual trees were still things of great value and utility. And elms in particular had a long and rich history of cultural service in the Old World, especially in England.

English Traits

Although it differed in important respects from the Old World species, the American elm was similar enough to have been immediately recognized by the English transplants. Thomas Morton and others found much of New England hauntingly reminiscent of the English countryside, both in its spatial composition as well as in its flora and fauna. As geographer Carl Sauer has written, "It would be impossible . . . to cross an ocean anywhere else and find as little unfamiliar in nature on the opposite side."[55] The New England landscape's inherent similarity to that of old England facilitated the transference of many cultural practices, including the embrace of certain kinds of trees. By the seventeenth century, the "Atlantic landscape" of England and the northern European countries had effectively been transplanted to North America.[56]

In many parts of the Old World, elms had seen cultural service for centuries and were an important feature of the countryside long before the colonization of North America. In England, the elm was second only to the oak in cultural significance. There are some thirty species of elm found in the British Isles, but only the Wych elm *(Ulmus glabra)* is native. Of the non-native species, English elm *(Ulmus minor* var. *vulgaris,* or *Ulmus procera)* is most prevalent. It was introduced to the British Isles during the Roman occupation, but in time the tree's foreignness faded as it evolved into one of the arboreal icons of England.[57] English elm was most common in the southern and eastern counties, and a close relative, *Ulmus minor* var. *minor,* or field elm, prevailed in East Anglia and the eastern counties of Essex and Kent.[58] Elms were thus a feature in the landscapes of just those regions of the British Isles that produced many of the early settlers of the Massachusetts Bay Colony. East Anglia, in particular, was "the original source of much of the New England population."[59]

In contrast to *Ulmus americana,* the English elm had great practical utility. Among the earliest known uses of elm in England was for archer's bows. The foliage of the tree long served as animal feed, a practice dating back at least as far as ancient Greece; boiled elm leaves may have even been fed to children. In the medieval period, elm found numerous medicinal applications, and its wood was used for mouldboards, timber framing, floorboards, bell headstocks, coffins, gunstocks, and bridge piles. John Evelyn's *Sylva* of 1664 noted that elm wood served well for making pipes, ladles, rails and gates, "blocks for the hat maker," trunks, dressers, "shovelboard tables of great length," as well as "most of the ornaments appertaining to the orders of architecture." The wood was also extensively used for water mains in the seventeenth and eighteenth centuries, and the tree was often planted specifically for this purpose.[60]

But utility was just one facet of the elm's place in English culture. The tree was also an established visual presence in the vernacular culture and countryside of England. Elms were objects of worship and veneration from the earliest period of English history. They marked the sites of May Day dances, fertility rites, and other pagan rituals. Elms later became associated with early Christian cults, and may have even played a liturgical role. Suicides and executed felons were required to be buried with a stake of elm driven through their hearts, and the tree was believed to have magical properties that were useful as a prophylactic against witchcraft.[61]

Elm was also a hallmark of settlement, planted about the domiciles of the earliest permanent habitations, and as an amenity in villages from the late Middle Ages onward.[62] Specimen elms adorned many village crossroads and greens, and this practice was later recalled in New England. Elm groves, or spinneys, dating from the Middle Ages were a common feature of English villages in Cambridgeshire and elsewhere.[63] Elms were a common hedgerow tree in the British Isles, particularly after the enclosure movement of the fifteenth and sixteenth centuries. As would later occur in the Connecticut River valley and elsewhere, cultural disturbance favored elms in the English countryside. "The more land was enclosed," writes Gerard Wilkinson, "the more hedges were made and the modern habitat of elms increased."[64]

As the place of origin for many of New England's early settlers was a place of elms, it is likely that English precedent played a significant role in the subsequent cultural embrace of the American elm in the New World. The somewhat similar uses of elm wood in England and the United States suggest that cultural transference was at work. It follows that aesthetic and even symbolic uses may have been similarly imported. Such cultural influences likely operated at a number of levels simultaneously, both conscious and subconscious. Little or no evidence remains to establish clear links of any kind, however. For example, no documentary material proves that the practice of leaving field and hedgerow elms was informed by recollections of the English countryside or the remembered landscape of enclosure. But such may well have been the case.

In settling an alien land, artifacts with even a passing resemblance to those of home would have struck a resonant chord. As New Englanders began planting trees to adorn their domestic environments or to beautify their villages and towns, English ghosts guided their hand. "The people who settled the shores of Massachusetts Bay," Charles Sprague Sargent wrote, "brought with them the remembrance of the Elm-trees which were such an important and conspicuous feature in the country where they had been bred."[65] New Englanders possessed a natural affinity for the elm, a plant that recalled their ancestral landscape. In time they came to favor it above all other trees.

2

DOORYARD AND COMMONS

Settlement favored the American elm. A tenacious and adaptable tree, it flourished in the wake of clearing and agricultural development. The ubiquity of the tree, combined with the familiarity of elms to the colonists from the Old World, helped endear the tree to the European immigrants who settled New England. In time, these men and women began planting sapling elms for the purposes of shelter and ornament.

Shelter and Totem

The close association of home and elm began in the earliest settlement period. The ground surrounding large elms was often selected as a sheltered place to erect a house. Ephraim Foster, an early settler of Ipswich, Massachusetts, built his home under a big elm in 1678.[1] While the house sheltered the inhabitants, the spreading limbs of the big tree sheltered the house. The umbrageous form of the elm seemed to embrace whatever lay beneath its limbs. "The general impression," wrote the folk-wise *New England Farmer* in 1843, "is that the elm is a very great protection to a building, if standing near it." "As a dooryard tree," Donald Culross Peattie later wrote, "it hangs above the roof like a blessing—clean of branches under the crown but shading the roof like a second air chamber above it."[2] A domicile elm was also thought to offer protection during thunderstorms—at least as effective, the *Farmer* opined, "as a well constructed lightning rod."[3]

But colonial homesteaders planted trees for sentimental value, too. Whipstock elms, often dragged from a neighboring swamp, were set out as dooryard ornaments to celebrate the establishment of a home, or to commemorate family events such as a birth, betrothal, or marriage. A pair of "bridal elms" was often

An old house elm near Newburyport, Massachusetts, 1927 (Photograph by E. H. Wilson; courtesy of the Photographic Archives of the Arnold Arboretum, Harvard University)

set out to mark nuptials. Naturalist and plant hunter Ernest H. Wilson suggested that this practice may have originated with the legend of Baucis and Philemon, who passed their lives "in love and concord" and wished that death would visit them both in the same hour. "The prayer was granted," Wilson related, "by the two being transformed into leafy trees and as the bark closed over their bodies they bade each other farewell."[4]

Many celebrated landmark elms of nineteenth-century New England had begun as bridal trees in the colonial era. The Pratt Elm of Concord, Massachusetts, well known to Emerson and Thoreau, was one of a bridal pair set out around 1700. For generations the two trees "grew in silence and obscurity," wrote the naturalist Lorin L. Dame, "till they overtopped their fellows and found themselves famous."[5] In Northampton, the Jonathan Edwards Elm was said to have been planted by the great theologian and orator on the occasion of his wedding to Sarah Pierpont.[6] Another bridal tree was the storied "Old Elm of Newbury" in Massachusetts. Transplanted in 1713 by Richard Jaques from his sweetheart's girlhood home, the tree gradually passed into legend. "The twig took root; and as time flew by," wrote the poet Hannah Gould,

> Its boughs spread wide, and its head grew high;
> While the priest's good service had long been done,
> Which made the youth and the maiden one;
> And their young scions arose and played
> Around the tree in its leafy shade.[7]

Not all house elms were nuptial in origin. Trees were also transplanted as gifts or tokens of friendship. A famous pair of elms in Natick, Massachusetts, began as a gift from Native Americans in 1722. As told by the *New England Farmer*, "a deputation of Indians . . . one bearing two Elm trees on his shoulder," sought permission from the minister Oliver Peabody to plant the brace of saplings before his house, "as a mark of their regard, or as the *Trees of Friendship*."[8] The Natick trees survived well into the nineteenth century, longer even than the tribe that bestowed them.

The Pierpont Elms of New Haven, planted in 1686 in front of the home of the Reverend James Pierpont, were similarly a gift, from a poor farmer named William Cooper. Having little to contribute toward the furnishing of the pastor's house, he gave instead a vigorous pair of sapling elms. By the early nineteenth century the building had vanished, but the elms endured — "to speak forth," as Charles Upham Shepard put it in 1838, "the humble charity of a poor but virtuous man."[9]

A pair of old bridal elms in South Chelmsford, Massachusetts, 1925
(Photograph by E. H. Wilson; courtesy of the Photographic Archives of
the Arnold Arboretum, Harvard University)

Whatever their provenance, homestead elms became endeared to New England, evoking an aura of mellowed age and domestic tranquillity. "Of wide circumference, rooted before the door," Nathaniel Hawthorne's Pyncheon Elm in *The House of the Seven Gables* is just such a tree, a venerable giant coeval with the old house it shelters. "It had been planted by a great-grandson of the first Pyncheon, and, though now fourscore years of age, or perhaps nearer a hundred, was still in its strong and broad maturity, throwing its shadow from side to side of the street, overtopping the seven gables, and sweeping the whole black roof with its pendent foliage. It gave beauty to the old edifice, and seemed to make it a part of nature."[10]

In time, the aged house elm—hoary and pendulous—became part of the romanticized image of New England domestic life. Towering over a rural homestead, such elms imparted "an air of comfort and ease to the humblest cottage," the *New England Farmer* wrote.[11] The dooryard tree came to symbolize the tranquil pleasures of the home life; indeed, a homestead without a sheltering elm was like a parlor without a hearth. Few understood this better than Henry David Thoreau. Spying from afar the expansive dome of an elm near Carlisle, Massachusetts, Thoreau imagined the "quiet rural and domestic life passing beneath it." For the bard of Walden Pond, a great elm was "the vignette to an unseen idyllic poem." "Homestead telegraphs to homestead through these distant elms seen from hilltops," wrote Thoreau. "I fancy I hear the house-dog's bark and lowing of the cows asking admittance to their yard beneath it. The tea-table is spread; the master and mistress and the hired men now have just sat down in their shirtsleeves."[12]

To many observers of Yankee culture, it was this domestic role that most endeared the elm in the native imagination. Charles Sprague Sargent wrote of the New Englander's attitude toward the American elm, "No other tree is so associated in his mind with the idea of home," and he called the tree "the most remarkable feature of the domestic New England landscape."[13] So cherished was the companionship of elms that when the aged Hannah Williams elm by the Champney House in Deerfield, Massachusetts, finally came down in 1885, the house itself was moved back on the property so "that it might hold the same relation to a younger elm."[14]

Evoking a tree-tossed image of domestic life, a writer in the *New England Farmer* suggested, "There is not a more lovely object than an ancient elm, with its glossy leaves stirred by the wind at eventide, with the hum of insects sounding from its branches, and the troops of children frolicking about its trunk."[15] Recalling "summer days of youth under the lovely shade around the paternal domicile," a later writer reflected that "such reminiscences of our purer days deserve to be fondly cherished, and should never be obliterated by the sterner

A homestead elm in Conway, New Hampshire, 1930 (Photograph by E. H. Wilson; courtesy of the Photographic Archives of the Arnold Arboretum, Harvard University)

pursuits" of later life. The sheltering elm exerted "a delightful moral influence," he reasoned, "and thus becomes, as it were, a cherished member of an affectionate family. Its longevity renders it an abiding friend of succeeding generations— a silent but most interesting witness of the advent and departure of children, and children's children—while its aged trunk remains an emblem and a precious memorial of a long line of venerated ancestry."[16]

The Hannah Williams Elm on the Champney estate in Deerfield. The old tree fell in 1885, causing the owners to relocate the house to be near another tree. (Photograph by J. W. Champney; courtesy of Historic Deerfield, Deerfield, Massachusetts)

If elms stood as guardians of the domestic scene and keepsakes "of venerated ancestry," they also early assumed a civic role in many a New England village. This was particularly the case with large, indigenous trees close to the center of a settlement. Saints of circumstance, these aged specimen elms served as community totems. They recalled pagan rituals of tree worship in the Old World, particularly the pre-Christian symbolism of the tree of life. The totem elms of New England also harkened back to the *rolands* of early Europe. Rolands marked the center of *landschaften*, the pattern of fields and clustered dwellings that distinguished the settled, agricultural landscape from the surrounding wilderness.[17]

Although commonly a stone or a timber staff, the roland was sometimes a great single tree, about which dwellings were clustered. In the British Isles, these tree rolands were often elms. By the medieval period, they had become commonplace on village greens or at the junction of roads.[18] May Day fertility rites would take place around such trees, a practice that survived well into the modern era. Early Christian missionaries understood the power of these symbols: they often pressed the pagan symbol into the service of Christ by supplanting the roland with a crucifix. As John R. Stilgoe put it, the roland was the "objectified essence" of the settled landscape.[19] The ancient custom of roland worship found its way to New England in the form of lofty elms located at or near the center of town. Such trees symbolized the conversion of forest wilderness into the spatial order of settlement. They served as a hub of town life and the focal point of ritual and celebration in the community. Sometimes they even defined the community's very identity.

The Pittsfield Elm

Pittsfield, Massachusetts, was known around the world for the mighty elm that stood at its center. By the time the region was settled in the early eighteenth century, the tree was already more than two hundred years old.[20] The elm was saved from the ax by Captain Charles Goodrich, who directed construction of a cart path around the tree in 1752.[21] In clearing the Pontoosuc intervale, early settlers spared the elm, inspired by its "peculiar beauty and magnificent proportions."[22] So powerful a presence was the tree that the first white settlers in the area chose to build their homes within its orbit. "All village affairs gravitated to the elm," a later writer reflected; "public and business buildings circled it in homage."[23]

The Pittsfield Elm was indeed a sight to behold, "fairer than any work of man's hand."[24] On a visit to the town in 1838, Nathaniel Hawthorne described the sylvan giant as having the "loftiest and straitest stem that ever I beheld."[25] Its soaring bole rose 70 feet before parting into limbs, and held aloft a "leafy coronal" that brushed the sky 128 feet above the town.[26] Far below its crown, community life unfolded.

Beneath it boys play their games of cricket and bass, . . . the swain whispers there his soft tale to the ruddy-cheeked lass he loves; the school-girls circle round it, in their soft-toned merriment; fourth of July brings to it crowds of mimic, noise-loving

The Pittsfield Elm, c. 1807 (Courtesy of the Berkshire Athenaeum, Pittsfield, Massachusetts)

Staffordshire pearlware platter depicting the Pittsfield Elm, by James and Richard Clews, 1825 (Courtesy of Historic Deerfield, Deerfield, Massachusetts)

heroes, whose shots, and bruises, and unceasing crackings, the old tree, dressed in gay pennons and waving flags, receives upon his rough sides, like a hearty, hale veteran. . . . The grave go there to meditate, and the gay to dance; strangers stand and admire the broad base and erect trunk of the unmatched elm; it is the hunting party's rendezvous to count their game; the lawyer holds his petty court and the itinerant minstrel his gaping crowd beneath its broad branches; while its deep shadows are alike sought, and alike grateful, to the youth and the man of eighty years.[27]

The Old Elm was an integral part of quotidian life, but it hosted events of significance as well. Tories were upbraided beneath its limbs in the days before the Revolution, and there "Fighting Parson" Thomas Allen rallied the Berkshire Minutemen to plan their assault on Fort Ticonderoga in New York.[28] It was to the trunk of the Pittsfield Elm in 1809 that Elkanah Watson tied a pair of Merino sheep that had been smuggled out of Spain. The strange animals attracted so much attention that Watson was encouraged to expand his idea to a larger scale, thus inaugurating the agricultural fair in America.[29] A decade or so later, Lafayette was feted beneath the limbs of the Pittsfield Elm, during his much-celebrated tour of America in 1824.[30] It was in the shadow of the Old Elm that the Thirty-seventh Massachusetts Regiment was blessed by the preacher John Todd before heading south to Civil War.[31]

The Pittsfield Elm towered over the town, physically and figuratively, and its fame traveled far and wide. In 1825 an English pottery maker—the James and Richard Clews Factory of Staffordshire—chose the Pittsfield Elm to decorate a series of platters and plates. English dinnerware intended for the American market in this period usually featured architectural or urban scenes from major port cities, natural wonders like Niagara Falls, or technological feats such as the Erie Canal.

The Pittsfield Elm, c. 1826 (Courtesy of the Berkshire Athenaeum, Pittsfield, Massachusetts)

Subject matter was calculated to flatter national pride and appeal to the widest possible market. That Pittsfield was selected is testament to the renown of the Old Elm, for images of small rural American towns were rare in Staffordshire pottery.[32]

But as a living thing, Pittsfield's leafy roland would not be around forever. By the 1830s, the tree was visibly dying. Storms had torn at it for centuries, and in 1841 a tremendous lightning bolt scarred the length of its trunk—"a stroke of the elements," one writer lamented, "which caused great sorrow in a multitude of hearts."[33] Herman Melville, who worked on *Moby-Dick* in Pittsfield in the early 1850s, evoked this scar in the "slender, rod-like mark, lividly whitish" on Captain Ahab's face. "It resembled that perpendicular seam sometimes made in the straight, lofty trunk of a great tree," Melville wrote, "when the upper lightning tearingly darts down it, and without wrenching a single twig, peels and grooves out the bark, from top to bottom, ere, running off into the soil, leaving that tree still greenly alive, but branded."[34]

Broken, branded, and shorn of its limbs, the "central gem" of Pittsfield was finally laid to rest in 1864, "amid the tears of the sternest men."[35] Wielding the ax was a man with the ironic name of Sylvanus Grant. An African-American woods-man, his felling of the Pittsfield Elm made him something of a local celebrity. (As late as 1943, decades after Grant's death, his ninety-six-year-old widow was profiled in a local newspaper as the "wife of the man who felled the Old Elm.")[36] The wreckage of the tree itself was auctioned off, its scraps carved into bric-a-brac, an armchair, and picture frames to hold portraits of the tree itself.

Tree of Liberty

One of the most potent symbols of political resistance during the American Revolution was an elm, a totem tree in seventeenth-century Boston that gained worldwide fame as the Tree of Liberty. The freedom fighters of Massachusetts used the pulpit and the printing press to spread their gospel of self-determination. But in the "department of silent propaganda," wrote Arthur M. Schlesinger, "no single venture paid richer dividends than the Tree of Liberty."[37] Its life began inaus-piciously enough, as a tree set out in 1646 by an innkeeper named Garrett Bourne.

Bourne's house was located on the old Neck—the narrow isthmus that once linked the Shawmut peninsula to mainland Massachusetts, close to what is today Washington Street. His house was later expanded into a tavern, and it was a pop-ular meeting place for the Sons of Liberty. The passage of the hated Stamp Act in 1765 triggered an avalanche of ill-will toward the British government. On an August night that year, a crowd gathered under the "wide-spreading branches" of Bourne's tree to demonstrate against the tax and to harry one Andrew Oliver into resigning his post as stamp officer.[38]

The next morning an effigy of Oliver was found hanged from a limb of the elm, along with a likeness of the devil himself (peering out of a huge boot and clutching a copy of the Stamp Act).[39] The king's agent wisely resigned, but a symbol of resistance was born. The "harmless elm" became endowed with symbolic power (or as one uncharitable loyalist put it, the tree had become "consecrated as an Idol for the Mob to worship"). In September 1765, the tree's new status was confirmed with a copper plate nailed to the trunk bearing the words "The Tree of Liberty."[40] (The tree also served a parallel life as an urban amenity: at one point the Sons ordered the elm pruned, after which a local newspaper reported that "the Tree is now become a great ornament to the street.")[41]

"Liberty Tree" *(F. S. Hassam,* Liberty Tree, Liberty Hall, *1891)*

Detail of a British cartoon depicting colonists administering tea to a tarred-and-feathered tax collector beneath the Liberty Tree (Walter Muir Whitehill and Norman Kotker, Massachusetts: A Pictorial History, *1976)*

In spite of the tree, the Stamp Act went into effect as planned on November 1, 1765. The patriots were outraged, and fresh demonstrations were scheduled for the Liberty Tree. New effigies were hoisted into its limbs—this time of British prime minister George Grenville and the author of the Act itself, John Huske. Another placard appeared:

> But if some Brethren I could Name,
> Who shar'd the Crime, should share the shame,
> That glorious Tree tho' big and tall,
> Indeed would never hold 'em all.[42]

When the Act was finally repealed the following May, a citywide celebration was held and again the Liberty Tree played a central role. In preparation for the event, known as the Great Illumination, the tree was decorated with flags and bunting, and so many lanterns were hung on its limbs that "the sailors in charge," reminisced one antiquarian, "could not find another twig to bear another light."[43] Paul Revere had designed an obelisk that was specially constructed for the occasion. Covered with oiled paper and lighted from within, the glowing phallus was decorated with poems and illustrations about tyranny, freedom, and love of liberty. One panel bore a likeness of the Liberty Tree, "with an eagle feeding its young, in the topmost branches, and an angel advancing with an aegis."[44]

In the prelude to Revolution, neighboring towns and provinces adopted Liberty

A drawing of Paul Revere's Liberty Pyramid, an obelisk erected to celebrate repeal of the Stamp Act in May 1766. The drawing shows the Liberty Tree in the second panel from the right. (M. A. DeWolfe Howe, Boston Common, *1910)*

Trees of their own. These were not always elms. The citizens of Braintree, Massachusetts, selected a buttonwood to bear their patriotic burden, as did those of Newport, Rhode Island. Providence, Rhode Island, chose a big elm. On the occasion of its consecration on July 25, 1768, an orator (speaking from a platform built among the limbs) invoked "that Liberty which our Forefathers sought out, and found under Trees, and in the Wilderness."[45] Even Harvard College had a "rebellion elm." About it students rallied to protest unpopular rules foisted upon them by their superiors — Stamp Act protests in miniature. According to Samuel Eliot Morison, students assembled at the tree in 1768 "to pass resolutions and organize resistance" against imagined acts of oppression.[46] "The spirit of Liberty," remarked an acerbic Thomas Hutchinson (then lieutenant governor of Massachusetts and an infamous Tory), has "spread where it was not intended."[47]

Some Liberty Trees were not even living. Dedham, Massachusetts, was among the first to erect an artificial "Pillar of Liberty" — a log set on a granite plinth and crowned by a likeness of William Pitt, the member of Parliament popular in the colonies for having opposed the Stamp Act. New York substituted a stick for a tree as well. Near the present-day site of City Hall, New York patriots erected numerous "Liberty Poles," most of which were quickly pulled down by the British troops.

A particularly massive timber was later raised, complete with iron hoops to prevent cutting, but in January 1770 the redcoats succeeded in removing that, too, an action that touched off a series of scuffles between citizens and soldiers. The fifth and final Liberty Pole was erected with great fanfare a month later; the tremendous pine mast was decorated with a gilded vane inscribed "LIBERTY." As in Boston, the patriots frequently gathered beneath the Liberty Pole to commit—in one Tory's view—"*idolatrous* and *vociferous* Acts of Worship, *to a Stick of Wood*."[48]

The Boston tree saw action again in 1773, when the flames of rebellion were fanned by the East India Company's newly granted monopoly of the American tea market. It was only after repeated failed attempts to intimidate local company agents under the elm (by subjecting them to a "Tree Ordeal") that the colonists resorted—famously—to dumping the herb into the harbor: the celebrated Boston Tea Party of December 1773. The tea squabbles, and the punitive "Intolerable Acts" passed by Britain in response, produced a new crop of Liberty Poles. These "hated tokens of insurgency" appeared in rapid succession in towns across Massachusetts and Connecticut, and even as far south as Savannah, Georgia.[49]

In the end, the potent symbolism of the Liberty Tree proved fatal for Bourne's old dooryard elm. As fighting broke out in April 1775, British soldiers and sympathizers set their eyes on the seditious symbol and, in a "vandal act" that August, succeeded in cutting it down.[50] One of the offending soldiers was reportedly killed as the great tree crashed to the ground ("one of those prophetic emblems," a writer mused in 1838, which required "but little superstition to clothe with supernatural importance").[51] Having stoked the flames of rebellion, the good elm was now reduced to fourteen cords of firewood.

No scion ever sprouted from the Liberty Tree's hallowed root, but the spirit of the elm lived on, spreading far and wide. Each of the thirteen original American colonies designated a Liberty Tree or built an artificial equivalent. One of these, a tulip poplar at Annapolis, Maryland, survived until Hurricane Floyd necessitated its removal in 1999. Incredibly, the wood of the four-hundred-year-old tree was simply trucked off to a landfill. Most of it was later rescued and used to craft a series of limited-edition guitars, one of which was played by singer-songwriter Livingston Taylor during a celebration in August 2002 of the Boston tree that began it all.

The Liberty Tree tradition proved extraordinarily portable, moving on to Europe after American freedoms were secure. In France, the Liberty Tree became one of the symbols adopted by the Jacobins. This practice may have found its way across the Atlantic via Tom Paine, who had been in Paris on the eve of the French Revolution, and had earlier penned a verse to the Liberty Tree ("A fair budding branch from the gardens above . . .").[52] It may have also arrived by way of Lafayette, who was well acquainted with the Boston tree, and the cause of *liberté*. Lafayette's return to the site of the Liberty Tree was in fact one of the high points of his celebrated 1824 tour of America.

For the occasion, a new Liberty Pole and a grand ceremonial arch were erected, draped with French and American flags. The pillars of the arch were decorated with flowers, "elm garlands," and bunting in red, white, and blue, and from its center hung a scroll bearing a gilded inscription: WASHINGTON AND LAFAYETTE. A REPUBLIC NOT UNGRATEFUL. Tablets were affixed on either side, one of which bore Thomas Dawes's eulogy to the old elm:

> Of high renown, here grew the tree
> Of elm, so dear to Liberty;
> Your sires, beneath its sacred shade,
> To Freedom early homage paid.
>
> This day with filial awe surround
> Its root that sanctifies the ground,
> And by your fathers' spirits swear
> The rights they left you'll not impair.[53]

On August 23 the aged Lafayette made his way to the site, greeted by "the densest crowd ever seen in Boston." Among the many gifts presented to him that day were relics of the Tree of Liberty itself—a tiny piece of root, and a section of the trunk "showing the bark, the sap, and the heart."[54]

Meet Me by the Elm

The civic centrality of the elm in many New England communities persisted well into the late nineteenth—and even the twentieth—century. Wethersfield, Connecticut, came of age "in the shadow of the Great Elm."[55] The massive tree was a communal centerpiece, as well as one of the largest American elms in the United States.[56] It began humbly enough, stuck in the ground in the 1750s by a boy who yanked the tree from a nearby meadow as a whip to drive home his cows. By the end of the nineteenth century, the Wethersfield Elm was described as "perhaps the most magnificent tree east of the Rockies," and it drew admirers from around the country. More, it helped identify Wethersfield both to its inhabitants and to the world outside; the town and its tree were intimately bound together.[57]

Like Wethersfield, the Massachusetts towns of Winchester, Medfield,

Unionville, and Wrentham also possessed a "representative elm" at the center of town.[58] An elm tree marked the center of Harvard Square in Cambridge for much of the nineteenth century. Keene, New Hampshire, had an "Auction Elm," and Litchfield, Connecticut, had a "Sign-Post Elm." Legal notices were posted on the "calm flank" of this tree, and beneath it the sheriff sold off confiscated property.[59] The great Hatfield Elm, a remnant of forest clearing in the 1670s, served as a centerpiece from the earliest days of that town's settlement.[60] Its role is recalled in the Hatfield town seal, where it remains in spite of the big tree's passing.

Sheffield in western Massachusetts also identified itself with an elm tree. Venerated by the first settlers for its grandeur and beauty, the Sheffield Elm served in lieu of a meetinghouse during the 1730s. In later years, festivals and orations were held beneath the tree. So expansive was the Sheffield Elm that five hundred people—nearly all of Sheffield's population—could gather together under its canopy.[61] The tree itself was the subject of occasional fetes. For such an event in 1896, a song was specially commissioned to honor the arboreal citizen. In a scene evoking Old World rites of tree worship, Sheffield children (dressed all in white) circled the base of their big tree, singing,

> Father of elms, we offer thee,
> The homage of true loyalty;
> Dear Sheffield, was but a baby sprite
> When first thy branches met the light.
>
> CHORUS: We'll rally round the brave old tree,
> Emblem of all that's good and free.
>
> You've known our woes, also our joys,
> Our winsome lassies, sturdy boys
> How well you know a lover's tread,
> Or silent anguish of our dead.
>
> Did'st thou that gallant deed inspire,
> Which fills each breast with sacred fire;
> The deed we celebrate today,
> Whilst Nature smiles in sweet array.
>
> Father of elms! long may you stand,
> A joy and wonder in our land;
> A rallying spot for meetings gay,
> With speech and song on a summer's day.[62]

The Wethersfield Elm in 1924, Wethersfield, Connecticut (Photograph by E. H. Wilson; courtesy of the Photographic Archives of the Arnold Arboretum, Harvard University)

The centrality of elms was not restricted to towns. The Commonwealth of Massachusetts itself had its center marked by an elm—the famous Central Tree of Rutland.[63] And long after Harvard's "rebellion elm" disappeared, another took its place in the civic life of the college. Known as the Class Elm, the tree was a Harvard landmark throughout the nineteenth century. Bedecked with garlands, the tree served as the hub of Class Day festivities.[64] This rite of passage was a hearty bacchanal that preceded the more formal commencement. With punch and cider flowing freely, students gathered about the Class Elm to dance and listen to poems and oratory.[65]

The Symmetry of Icons

The great solitary "central elms" that loomed over the Yankee commons were, in the iconography of New England, sylvan counterpoints to the whitewashed steeple of the meetinghouse. Thrusting heavenward, steeple and elm graced the Yankee scene with loft and verticality. The sheer height and mass of a mature elm made it one of the only objects in the landscape to match the visual dominance of New England's ecclesiastical architecture. Steeple and elm were, until very late in the nineteenth century, the loftiest objects in the landscape — the dual icons of Yankee space. Such symmetry was perhaps nowhere more sharply rendered than at Pittsfield, where the great elm surpassed even the meetinghouse as the chief visual and symbolic element in the townscape. During Lafayette's visit in 1824, the icons were literally bound together. For the occasion, an immense American flag was draped from a rope secured at one end to the spire of the meetinghouse and at the other to the lowermost limb of the Pittsfield Elm (itself some seventy feet high).

Class Day festivities beneath the Class Elm at Harvard College, by Winslow Homer, 1858 (S. B. Sutton, Cambridge Reconsidered, *1976)*

The Hatfield town seal, which includes the iconic church spire and elm tree (Daniel White Wells and Reuben Field Wells, History of Hatfield, Massachusetts, *1910)*

Henry David Thoreau well understood the symbolic function of elm trees in the New England landscape; spire and elm were, for this sharp-eyed chronicler of Yankee space, cohabitants of the skyline. The big trees pressed themselves into his memory as effectively as the tallest steeple. From a hilltop prospect, big elms could be seen "as far, at least," wrote Thoreau, "as a white spire"—even if the spire was of greater height. Such elms were "so lifted up in the horizon" that they appeared "like portions of the earth detached and floating off by themselves into space." Lofty elms, spied from afar, played tricks on Thoreau's eye. One elm, several miles north of Concord, appeared to be closer than it actually was: "Perhaps it looms a little," mused the naturalist. From a Concord hilltop in 1857, Thoreau caught sight of the Baptist church in North Tewksbury—some fourteen miles

The symmetry of icons, as seen in an engraving showing Petersham, Massachusetts, by John Warner Barber, c. 1840.

A gathering of Methodist ministers beneath the Great Elm of Boston Common in 1866
(J. W. Hamilton, Memorial of Jesse Lee and the Old Elm, *1875)*

away. The steeple was braced by its peers of verdure, a pair of big elms "in the horizon on the right of it."[66]

Like the meetinghouse or the church and its white spire, New England's totem elms were beacons of meaning in the landscape. Mircea Eliade has written in *The Sacred and the Profane* that we "found" the world by investing it with religious significance, and fix sacred space with signs and totems.[67] The embryonic settlements of the early colonial period were surrounded by vast tracts of wilderness; from the perspective of the newcomers, this "unknown, foreign, and unoccupied territory," still shared "in the fluid and larval modality of chaos."[68] Out of such disarray emerged the spatial—and moral—order of settlement, an order objectified by the meetinghouse and its upthrust steeple. "Like Jacob's ladder," writes John R. Stilgoe, "the New England meetinghouse existed as a hierophany, an axis linking earth with Heaven."[69] Such civic totems as the Liberty, Sheffield, and Pittsfield elms were secular counterpoints to the meetinghouse, leafy Jacob's ladders reaching for the light. If the meetinghouse spire was the architectural objectification of Yankee space, the totem elm was its sylvan counterpart.

3

THE WITNESS TREE

Such elms as the Tree of Liberty and the Sheffield, Wethersfield, and Pittsfield elms served as totemic objects in the civic and political lives of their communities. But in the early years of the nineteenth century, these and other New England elms came to be increasingly celebrated for their age and associations alone. Antiquity—particularly if it extended far enough back to antedate European arrival (and, therefore, history as Americans imagined it)—was now a valued commodity in itself. Such a shift in attitude toward the past came as part of a larger quest for cultural validation in the early nineteenth century.

The Pleasures of Antiquity

In breaking the chains of colonialism, America in effect unhitched itself from the Old World's burdened past, and from history itself. On the American horizon was self-reliance, a bright morning circumstance untarnished by the "catalog of errors" that occluded European skies.[1] To the Western mind, here was a fresh, new land; and here the human project could begin again. This was more than the boosterism of an upstart people. European intellectuals, too, believed that the New World offered freedom from the past, the chance to bring about a new Golden Age and restore "a prelapsarian state of grace."[2] In Elizabethan England, the popularity of pastoral poetry was due partly to florid accounts of the New World. Arcadia was suddenly more than just a literary conceit; as Leo Marx has written, it now gained "a note of topographic realism."[3] In Shakespeare's *Tempest*, Gonzalo envisioned an ideal society in which the sum total of "calculated human effort"—history itself—is denied. To Gonzalo, man was "happiest in the beginning," for the "record of human activity is a record of decline."[4]

Lacking cathedral ruins and crumbling castles, the American scene was unburdened by the shards of the past; or, as Goethe wrote, "undisturbed . . . by useless remembering."[5] William Tudor, in 1819, mused, "Our picturesque objects of an artificial kind are vastly fewer than those in older countries." While he admitted that the "total absence of ruins deprives us of what is an abundant source of associations in Europe"—a particular deficiency for artists—Tudor balanced this by arguing the inherent pathology of the Old World, and the detritus scattered about it. "The landscape," he wrote of ruins, "is better without them." For "these grisly, hideous remains conjure up the ideas of baronial oppression, feudal slavery, and monkish delusion; that in those mouldering dungeons were formerly immured the victims of priestly or lordly tyranny; and those ruined walls once protected a few lawless despots, who carried on a petty but cruel warfare for personal revenge, and held a wretched peasantry in abject dependence; . . . and awaken painful recollections in the midst of the most smiling scenery." The American scene was a "happy region of freedom . . . encumbered with no mark or trophy of despotism" and unburdened by monuments to "a period of anterior degradation." Indeed, "whereever the eye turns," concluded Tudor, "it beholds the unpolluted soil of liberty."[6]

But in spite of these florid assertions, Americans longed for just such keepsakes of their own. Before his ink had dried, William Tudor himself admitted that "if this ranting will not do, I must frankly give up the point, and acknowledge our want of this class of objects."[7] The landscape, impoverished of relics and ruins, offered precious little evidence to affirm the supposed grandeur of the American project. The lack of an artifactual past seemed to diminish native efforts, to render them transparent in the eyes of time. Americans feared that theirs was a hustling, superficial culture, one without depth or durability—one that, moreover, was rapidly sweeping away whatever legacy it did possess. "The axe of civilization is busy with our old forests," one critic lamented in 1847. "What were once the wild and picturesque haunts of the Red Man, and where the wild deer roamed in freedom, are becoming the abodes of commerce and the seats of manufactures; . . . even the primordial hills, once bristling with shaggy pine and hemlock, like old Titans as they were, are being shorn of their locks, and left to blister in cold nakedness in the sun."[8]

If architectural ruins of great age were scarce in America, those of natural origin were in great abundance. Nature would supply the very "class of objects" necessary to endow the landscape with temporal depth. New England was among the first regions of America to be settled by Europeans, and it was one of the first to seek in the landscape affirmation of its historical identity. In doing so, New Englanders turned to the elms the founding generation had planted or spared when clearing the land. The young nation might have no piles of marble, but it certainly had its "old Titans"—trees that were of prodigious antiquity, or at least appeared that way.

The wayside giants of New England, old elms left behind by the first settlers or planted as bridal pairs and dooryard trees, acquired new symbolic power in the early nineteenth century. Like marble scattered on the Appian Way, the aged elm served as a yardstick of cultural time; or, as Orville Dewey wrote of the great Sheffield Elm, "as a witness upon the field of history."[9] Aged elms became the Yankee equivalent of Old World ruins, a point the Reverend Nehemiah Adams made in 1838 when he wrote that an old elm "is to antiquity with us what a pyramid is in Egypt."[10] Andrew Jackson Downing could only agree. "If we have neither old castles nor old associations," he wrote, "we have at least, here and there, old trees that can teach us lessons of antiquity, not less instructive and poetical than the ruins of a past age."[11]

Trees were ideal for such service. Not only were they grand and inspiring natural objects, but they also conformed to the cycles of human life. Trees embodied not the melancholia of twilight but the bright light of life itself. Subtle processes of growth and decay are continually at work in a tree, transforming and renewing it so that successive generations may know it as a unique entity. By this process, every age comes to possess a moment in the life of the plant.

To Charles Joseph Latrobe, the English author of *The Rambler in North America*, published in 1835, the senescent elm was what endowed the Connecticut Valley landscape with its "air of comparative antiquity." Such an arboreal relic ("sole survivor of the original forest, and boundary-mark of the first colonists") was the hallmark of "long and steady cultivation." Along the Connecticut River, old elms helped "throw a degree of interest over the country," wrote Latrobe, "which contrasts agreeably with that air of rawness and newness which is imprinted upon the works of man in other portions of the continent" (and which, he added, "is so opposed to anything like poetry and sentiment").[12]

As the pace of life quickened, keepsake trees became more and more meaningful. They should be cherished, urged one writer in 1841, "as a bit of antiquity not to be slighted in these days of mushroom things."[13] And indeed they were. In 1853, five hundred workers at the Amoskeag Manufacturing Company in New Hampshire petitioned its proprietors to spare an elm that was to be felled for a new mill building. The "beautiful and goodly tree" should be saved, they argued, simply because the elm harkened back to a time "when the yell of the red man and the scream of the eagle were alone heard on the banks of the Merrimack, instead of two giant edifices filled with the buzz of busy and well-remunerated industry." The aged elm served a crucial role: it was "a connecting link between the past and present."[14]

As with the Amoskeag tree, the mystique of such relics derived in large part from their presumed aboriginality. Antiquity amplified the mystique of an elm. To Nehemiah Adams, such trees were "like the pillars of Hercules, bounding the unknown ages which preceded the arrival of the Pilgrims."[15] They were looked upon as keepsakes from a mythic prelapsarian age, legacies antedating the deluge or the fall of man. But even if an elm was in truth no aged relic, it could very well appear to be—and that was usually good enough. The American elm is a fast-growing tree that achieves "scale" quickly and often looks much older than it actually is. In as little as a century an elm could achieve height and massiveness enough to be taken for a tree twice its age.

In the early nineteenth century, Americans hungered for artifacts that would grant them a sense of historical legitimacy. And the early maturity of the elm was particularly useful in this regard, for even a relatively young elm could impart to the landscape an air of antiquity. Oliver Wendell Holmes understood the value of such trees in endowing upstart Yankee villages with an element of age. "A life of between two and three centuries seems a long one in a new country like ours," he wrote, "and 'the old elm' is often the most ancient monument of a New England village."[16]

Ancient wayside elms were a presence in many New England communities throughout the nineteenth century. The Great Elm at Springfield, among the oldest and largest trees in New England, towered over the southwest corner of Court Square and was "thought to be a natural growth in that place."[17] Winthrop, Massachusetts, was similarly proud of its ancient Gibbons Elm. In 1912, a crowd of three thousand people attended a farewell ceremony for the three-hundred-year-old tree, an arboreal elder that had "witnessed so much of the history of the town." A poem entitled "The Old Elm" was commissioned for the occasion, and the event itself was described as "one of the most remarkable gatherings ever held in honor of a tree."[18]

Relic on the Common

But it was nearby Boston that possessed the most celebrated antique elm in New England—the Great Elm of Boston Common. Occupying a spot by the old Frog Pond, close to the center of the Common, the elm remained unchallenged by other vegetation for much of its life. The Great Elm became the subject of songs, poems, and children's stories, and at least one patriotic ballad was written in its honor—John Hill Hewitt's "Old Elm Tree."[19] The Great Elm drew into its orbit events of great and small importance. As Lorin Dame put it in 1890, "whatever took place anywhere on the Common . . . gravitated into the history of the big elm."[20] The tree was frequented by the Sons of Liberty, who "caused

The Great Elm at Springfield, c. 1860 (Courtesy of the Connecticut Valley Historical Museum, Springfield, Massachusetts)

*Title page of the published sheet music for
"The Old Elm Tree," by John Hill Hewitt, 1842 (Courtesy of
the Special Collections Department, Alderman Library,
University of Virginia)*

it to be illuminated with lanterns on evenings of rejoicing and on festal occasions."[21] Later generations held elections and recruited soldiers in its shade, and paused there to listen to orators and firebrands of every stripe.

The Great Elm clearly served a civic function in Boston, but the tree was celebrated mainly for its antiquity. Thought to have antedated the arrival of the Puritans, the Great Elm was venerated as a vegetable patriarch, presumed to be the oldest living object in the city. "It is known by the most ancient surviving inhabitants of Boston," wrote J. C. Warren in 1855, "as THE GREAT TREE."[22] Certainly it looked the part. The tree was gnarled and picturesque even in the

The Great Elm on Boston Common, c. 1813 (The Polyanthos, *June 1813*)

early nineteenth century, having "braved the storms and gales of centuries."[23] Like New England's other aged trees, the Great Elm was "a witness upon the field of history"—a living chronometer that linked the aboriginal age to the modern era.

"No citizen now living can remember" a time when the Old Elm "was not venerable for its years and its history," John W. Hamilton wrote in 1875. "No monument stands in the city that is older," he added; "no family Bible has a record of its age. Before Washington or Winthrop the tree was. And before Blaxton bought ground of the Indians, and Trimountaine or Shawmutt were the names of Boston; when Chickatabut was chief Sachem, and sat with his council in the shade of the trees, the great elm stood forth in the sun, hospitable then as now."[24] Such associations moved many a would-be bard to verse. "When first from Mother Earth you sprung," wrote an anonymous Boston poet (with considerable artistic license),

> Ere Chaucer, Spenser, Shakespeare sung,
> Or Puritans had come among
> The savages to loose each tongue
>   In psalms and prayers.
> These forty acres, more or less,
> Now gayly clothed in Nature's dress,
> Where Yankees walk, and brag and guess,
> Were but a howling wilderness
>   Of wolves and bears.[25]

Poets were perhaps expected to rhapsodize like this, but science swooned with equal abandon. "This tree," wrote Warren, then president of the Boston Society of Natural History, "we must venerate as a visible relic of the Indian Shawmut; for all its other native trees and groves have been long since prostrated; the frail and transient memorials of the Aborigines have vanished; even the hills of Tri-mountain cannot be distinguished." Indeed, only "this native noble elm" remained to link the present with the ever-receding past.[26]

The true nature of the Great Elm's age and origins was a matter of endless speculation among Boston antiquarians. While some accounts claimed that the tree was set out by one Hezekiah Henchman in 1670, it appears to have been even older than that.[27] The John Bonner Map of 1722 depicted the elm as a spec-imen of considerable size, hardly a tree only 50 years old (even an elm did not achieve such splendor so quickly). A limb that fell in 1860 was determined to itself be 190 years old, which would have made the tree decades older still. On the other hand, it is unlikely that the tree was alive much earlier than 1640, making it old by American standards, but hardly a relic of the Deluge.

It is also impossible, then, that the Great Elm could have been used as a hanging tree by the Puritan oligarchy, as many antiquarians claimed. If witches and Quakers met their end dangling from a tree on the Common, it was certainly not the tender whipstock that became the Great Elm. And a good thing, too, M. A. DeWolfe Howe pointed out, as this "might have made the Great Elm and Tyburn Tree synonyms of shame."[28] As aged as it was, the Great Elm was no more than a late child of the aboriginal landscape. The real miracle is that the sapling tree managed to escape the molars of the "Cattell" and other livestock that were set loose on the Common each morning.

Decrepitude in later years magnified the aura of the Great Elm. The predations of storms pruned the tree into a living wreck, and with each limb laid low the tree truly began to evoke a classical ruin. The demise of the Great Elm actually began at an early date. A needlepoint work from 1755 depicted a hole in its trunk large enough to accommodate a small boy. (The cavity was eventually repaired with clay and a canvas tarpaulin, and in time new growth erased all traces of the wound.)[29] In 1832 a powerful storm knocked several principal limbs to the ground; still partially attached to the tree, these were then bolted back into place.[30] By the middle of the nineteenth century, the Great Elm's days were numbered.

On the night of June 29, 1860, "a storm of no ordinary character" swept into the city, ripping several limbs off the Great Elm. Boston awoke the next morning to rumors that the icon had fallen. Scores made their way to the Common, scram-bling for a fragment of the tree—"the choicest of the relics of the olden time."[31] Yet the Great Elm had life in it still, and in the following weeks no expense was

The Great Elm on Boston Common, c. 1850 (M. A. DeWolfe Howe,
Boston Common, *1910)*

spared to save the battered hulk. The end came on a blustery winter night in 1876. Gale-force winds on the evening of February 15 rocked its crown, and at precisely 7:17 P.M. the tree "fell with a crash, which sounded like the report of a cannon." It came to earth with such force as to "splinter the trunk in every imaginable manner." News of the Great Elm's fall spread rapidly. The *Boston Herald* reported that, within hours, the Common "was crowded with relic hunters, who began an attack upon [the tree]. These 'curious' people crowded upon the trunk, and, with knife in hand, were not long in gratifying their found desire by getting such souvenirs as they most prized. On the departure of each successive squad its place was filled by fresh arrivals." In this way, "a good deal of the tree, in fact about all of the smaller limbs and branches, were taken away before the police could prevent it."[32]

It is not likely that Boston's poet laureate Oliver Wendell Holmes was among the people jostling for a fragment, but he did pen some verse in eulogy:

> The darkened skies, alas! have seen
> Our monarch tree laid low,
> And spread in ruins o'er the green,
> But Nature struck the blow;
> No scheming thrift its downfall planned,
> It felt no edge of steel,
> No soulless hireling raised his hand
> The deadly stroke to deal.[33]

Three months later, in May 1876, a new tree was planted on the site of the vanished relic—the "Centennial Elm." Beneath it was buried a time capsule, a small metal box containing an "appropriate inscription," a list of Boston luminaries of the day, and coins and sundry other articles.[34] The new tree found purchase in the soil, but not in the minds of Boston's self-conscious aristocracy. Transplanted from a Dorchester nursery, the Centennial Elm lacked the requisite pedigree. Then, some years later, an offshoot of the Great Elm was revealed to be growing on the Common. It had been quietly set in the ground in 1873 by two policemen who removed "a small shoot growing from the roots" of the old tree. On Arbor Day, 1889, Mayor Thomas Hart officiated a ceremonious replanting of this tree, to a more honored spot closer to the site of the Great Elm. An inscribed tablet was to be placed nearby, but Hart left office shortly after, and "the whole matter was forgotten." It was not until 1909 that an affidavit signed by the policemen was discovered in the offices of the city auditor, verifying that a "true scion" of the Great Elm indeed flourished on Boston Common.[35]

Other Yankee elms acquired more fixed and specific historical associations. If a relic tree such as Boston's Great Elm was a keepsake of antiquity in general, name-bearing monument elms recalled precise events and people of significance. The great size, beauty, and grandeur of an old elm—along with its aura of durability and timelessness—made the tree an ideal candidate for the commemoration of hale deeds and great souls. Elms bore memory well, a point Donald Culross Peattie captured when he wrote, "If you want to be recalled for something that you do, you will be well advised to do it under an Elm."[36]

Monument elms were important landmarks in many nineteenth-century New England villages and towns—and cities, too. They were among the first symbols of collective remembrance to occasion the landscape—"repositories of memory" that endowed quotidian space with historical depth and richness.[37] Long before granite or marble found a place on the New England common, elm trees remembered. Indeed, some monument elms became so famous in their own right that they eventually gained stone tablets of their own. Most of New England's early monument elms were linked, in some large or small way, with the Revolution. These trees served a civic purpose, reminding citizens to whom they owed their freedom. "We need such monitors in our public places," urged Samuel Adams Drake, "to arrest our headlong race, and bid us calmly count the cost of the empire we possess."[38]

For the most part, monument elms gained their historical value serendipitously. Many became, in time, objects of veneration themselves. A few had been planted by the person or persons whose memory they bore. Jonathan Edwards set out the tree that would became his sylvan monument. Before departing their native Litchfield, Connecticut, in 1862, a unit of Union volunteers planted a long row of elms along the Harris Plain—a "last gift to their home district" that, by the end of the Civil War, had sadly become their own memorial.[39] But most monument elms were more tenuously linked to the souls they celebrated.

By the middle of the nineteenth century, the New England landscape boasted scores of monument elms. Nearly every town or village could point to such a tree when queried about its local history or distinguished sons. The Cushing Elm of Hingham, Massachusetts, set out in 1729, was an old house tree bearing the name of its planter. The elm later sheltered a company of Cohasset soldiers, who offered prayers under its limbs during the siege of Boston. The big tree—"a marvel of strength and symmetry"—was ever after linked to the patriots, a living monument to "the illustrious dead."[40]

A stately elm growing near a site distinguished by a great event often assumed the task of bearing its memory. Monument elms often gained their status in association with a house of historical significance, and sometimes the tree even drew fame away from the building itself. The Marlboro Elm in Massachusetts grew along the road near the house of a Tory sympathizer who had been shot during the Revolution (a musket ball had lodged in one of the beams).[41] But as the house changed hands through the years, it lost much of its historical aura. Gradually the kernel of meaning migrated from the building to the tree. In effect, it relocated to a more public spot, an object judged more fit to bear collective memory than a stranger's house.

At Kennebunk, New Hampshire, a big elm recalled Lafayette's celebrated American tour of 1824. It stood on the grounds of a house in which Lafayette

The Cushing Elm of Hingham, Massachusetts, 1925 (Photograph by E. H. Wilson; courtesy of the Photographic Archives of the Arnold Arboretum, Harvard University)

The Lafayette Elm, Kennebunk, New Hampshire, in 1926 (Photograph by E. H. Wilson; courtesy of the Photographic Archives of the Arnold Arboretum, Harvard University)

had been a guest, but in time the tree itself became the chief repository of the event's memory. Deerfield, Massachusetts, had a surfeit of monuments both sylvan and stone, and often these were paired. As one observer described it, "there is hardly a spot in historic Deerfield marked by a monument which is not also marked, at no great distance, by an old tree." In time, the relationship between the two was inverted. The Deerfield trees—"witnesses of the events commemorated by tablets"—drew attention away from the chiseled stone in their shadows.[42] As the eulogies of August 1853 demonstrated, elms loomed large in the Deerfield scene.

Not all monument elms recalled heroes and events of the Revolution. The Boxford Elm of Essex County, Massachusetts, celebrated a historic encounter between colonists and local tribesmen. Near the site of the tree in 1701 a meeting was held in which the purchase of town land was arranged. In a somewhat dubious transaction, the colonists acquired title to considerable acreage in exchange for two shillings in silver and "Rum and vittles enouf." The tree that eventually bore the memory of the event was not planted for another fifty years. Yet, as it aged, it struck an appropriately senescent attitude and was anointed the repository of the town's creation myth.[43]

Often the work of assigning memory to trees fell to the antiquarian. Lamenting the poverty of monument elms in New Haven, Henry Howe took it upon himself to christen some of his own. "At this late date," he wrote in 1883, "we must try to make amends, and as we describe in course our most noble trees, we shall suggest names for each by which they shall hereafter be known." Before Howe began his project, New Haven had only one name-bearing elm. A local poet-eccentric named Jerry Ailing (known as "the Milton of Hamden Plains") dragged a sapling elm into town on the day of Benjamin Franklin's death in 1790. In exchange for some rum, he gave the tree to Thaddeus Beecher, a local shopkeeper who suggested that Ailing plant the elm next to the village pump.[44] Whether this was an act of commemoration or simple serendipity, the tree came to be known as the Benjamin Franklin Elm.

Howe the antiquarian added a number of others to his sylvan register, in the process snipping freely at the broadcloth of history. One behemoth by the African Congregational Church was known locally as the African Church Elm ("We call it a good pious tree," he wrote, "and after enjoying the Sabbaths of seventy-five years right under its wings, we presume it to be well grounded in orthodoxy"). Regardless, Howe renamed the tree in honor of John Wesley, the founder of Methodism, whose first flock in New Haven had earlier occupied the site. Another elm—an "imperious, cloud-climbing individual" on Grove Street— Howe christened in the name of Nathan Beers, a patriot of the American Revolution who had lived nearby; in Howe's view, the tree perfectly manifested the "sweetness and moral grandeur" of Beers's character.[45] Other memory-bearing elms were named after "representative men" in New Haven society—merchants, bankers, educators, and other luminaries of the local empyrean.

New England's monument elms were a patrician institution. Reflecting the gender dynamics of nineteenth-century society, women were rarely represented by an elm. One of the few name-bearing elms dedicated to the memory of a woman was at Hatfield, Massachusetts. The great soprano Jenny Lind—the "Swedish Nightingale" who took midcentury America by storm—toured western Massachusetts in 1852, spent her honeymoon in Northampton, and performed there at the town hall. At nearby Hatfield she sang beneath an elm, a tree that was afterward known as the Jenny Lind Elm.[46]

General Washington's "Memorial Pile"

When it came to monument elms, none had greater purchase in the New England imagination than those associated with George Washington—and if local legend is to be believed, Washington was often in the shade of elm trees.

The Benjamin Franklin Elm in New Haven, Connecticut, c. 1860
(Collections of the Library of Congress)

Beneath the Holliston Elms, Washington allegedly rested on his return from Boston in 1789.[47] The Great Elms at both Wethersfield and Springfield were said to have sheltered the great man, and they were often referred to by his name. At Palmer, Massachusetts, stood yet another Washington Elm, which, according to tradition, witnessed *two* passages of the national hero—in 1775 and in 1789.[48]

Yet none of these trees could match the status of the Washington Elm at Cambridge—the greatest of all Yankee name-bearing elms, and the most famous tree in America by the end of the nineteenth century. Until the tree's destruction in October 1923, the Washington Elm was among the most popular landmarks in the Boston area. Luminaries of every rank—from princes to presidents—made an obligatory stop at the tree. Its image was carried on hotel chinaware, furniture upholstery, postcards, stereographs, and even a United States postage stamp. The Washington Elm was the subject of many songs, rhymes, Decoration Day speeches, and patriotic verse. It was most memorably venerated in James Russell Lowell's poem "Under the Old Elm."

> Historic town, thou holdest sacred dust,
> Once known to men as pious, learned, just,
> And one memorial pile that dares to last;
> But Memory greets with reverential kiss
> No spot in all thy circuit sweet as this,
> Touched by that modest glory as it passed,
> O'er which yon elm hath piously displayed
> These hundred years its monumental shade.[49]

The Washington Elm of Cambridge in 1839, from an engraving by John Warner Barber

The Washington Elm, c. 1861 (Courtesy of the Cambridge Historical Commission)

Three months after the firefights at Lexington and Concord signaled the beginning of the Revolution, Washington was summoned to Massachusetts, where he was to assume command of the Army of the United Colonies. He arrived at Cambridge on July 3, 1775, and, after reviewing the troops on Cambridge Common, was placed in their command. Myth and fact have long blurred the true nature of the day's events. The "traditional" version of the story holds that Washington assumed his command with great drama and gravitas, "beneath the wide-spreading branches of the patriarch tree" that would later bear his name.[50] Wheeling about on his stallion, Washington drew his sword, pointed it toward heaven, and "resolved . . . that it should never be sheathed till the liberties of his country were established."[51] If American independence stirred to life beneath the Tree of Liberty, it took up arms beneath the Washington Elm—at least according to legend.

Oddly, this rousing event was not always associated with the Washington Elm, and for many decades the tree was accorded only passing interest. The coupling of the tree to Washington's actions at Cambridge was largely a manufactured one, an "invented tradition" of the nineteenth century. According to Eric Hobsbawm, invented traditions—usually based partly in truth—seek to "establish continuity with a suitable historic past." They often appear during periods of change, when a "rapid transformation of society weakens or destroys the social patterns for which 'old' traditions had been designed."[52] In the case of the Washington Elm, the seeds of the tradition had long been planted but did not germinate until a situation arose that appeared to destabilize the old order and the sanctity of the past itself.

In Cambridge, that moment came along in the 1840s. The town's population, which was fewer than thirty-five hundred from 1765 to about 1820, nearly doubled ten years later—and doubled again by 1845.[53] This was a period of massive immigration, driven by the industrial development of East Cambridge. Culminating with the founding of the City of Cambridge in 1846, the convulsive growth appeared to threaten the Anglo-Saxon hegemony of "Old Cambridge"— an austere and intellectual community fiercely proud of its role in the founding of the nation.

The "discovery" of the Washington Elm tradition, and the tree's subsequent transformation into a memorial of national significance, appears to have been largely driven by the metamorphosis of Cambridge from a quiet academic town into a booming manufacturing city. The Washington Elm tradition was invented, as it were, to provide continuity with a past under siege by the forces of modernity. Prior to the 1840s, the Washington Elm was not a feature in local histories; it is absent from Revolutionary-era accounts, and makes no appearance in traveler's descriptions—extraordinary omissions given the tree's subsequent importance. Few maps published before the middle of the nineteenth century refer to the tree, while those published afterward prominently indicate its location and name. Indeed, for more than half a century, the story seemed nonexistent.[54]

By this time, Americans were also beginning to develop a sense of their own national identity. The Jacksonian period launched the United States as an economic and military power and was marked by a flush of nationalism. A resurgent interest in America's own colonial past brought about a new piety for the founding generation (who were fast disappearing from the scene) and a burgeoning interest in what one critic called "relics of our national infancy."[55] In the 1830s, Ralph Waldo Emerson mused on the irony of this surge of filial worship in a land so fresh with possibility. "Our age is retrospective," he wrote in *Nature*; "It builds sepulchres to the fathers."[56]

Or it invented sepulchral elms. While the origins of the Washington Elm tradition are obscure, they lead back to an imaginative antiquarian named John Langdon Sibley. In an 1837 issue of *The American Magazine of Useful Knowledge*, Sibley related that under a "Glorious old tree," Washington "drew his sword as commander-in-chief of the American army, for the first time." The witness elm was thus worthy of reverence as a "sacred memorial of the past and the present."

The Washington Elm, c. 1908 (Courtesy of the Cambridge Historical Commission)

"Amidst the changes which have taken place in the world, and particularly in America and New England," Sibley reasoned, this tree "has stood out like a watchman" guarding the grave of memory. Sibley lamented the "spirit of modern improvement" that had defaced the tree with signboards, and called to save the elm from the ax of progress. "May no unkind hand," he willed, "mar [this] last tree of the native forest."[57]

Sibley was not alone, however. The great fabulist Washington Irving also labored on the elm tradition, invoking the tree and its glorious associations in his *Life of Washington* in 1855.[58] And during the Centennial in 1876, the Washington Elm gained further fame when the diary of a colonial woman named Dorothy Dudley was published. The document, whose author had purportedly witnessed Washington's doings on the Common, contained a breathless first-hand account of the day's events. The Dudley diary found its way into many a schoolbook and inspired numerous renderings of the scene before it was shown to be a complete fraud—the work of a creative soul drunk with patriotic sentiment.[59] Other writers contributed similarly fabulous embellishments. In one account from 1874, Washington had actually built a *platform* in his Elm, in which he was "accustomed to sit and survey with his glass the country round."[60]

Whatever its provenance (and however specious), the Washington Elm tradition gradually became part of the nation's mythological canon. In 1864, during a surge in patriotism brought on by the Civil War, a stone tablet was placed at the base of the tree. The marker carried a simple inscription, said to be from the pen of Henry Wadsworth Longfellow. "Under this tree," it claimed, "Washington first took command of the American Army, July 3rd, 1775."[61] By 1875, the centennial of Washington's arrival at Cambridge, the elm tradition was firmly ensconced as national myth. A spectacular celebration that July focused on the tree. The elm's lower limbs were adorned with bunting, and one intrepid soul managed to scramble to the top of the tree, affixing an American flag to a swaying limb.[62]

The Washington Elm's symbolic power remained well into the twentieth century. "In the heart of every American who loves the history of his country," wrote J. R. Simmons in 1919, "there dwells a degree of respect and gratitude for this living representative of olden time."[63] As late as 1936, a children's essay by Erle Kauffman could claim: "Of course every boy and girl knows that it was an elm tree at Cambridge, Massachusetts, that shaded General George Washington . . . when he took command of the Continental Army." For Kauffman, it was primarily for the Washington Elm that this tree species was known as "America's tree of glory."[64]

Felling Sacred Trees

Under more critical eyes, however, the Washington Elm legend began to unravel. In 1923 a short piece published in the *Cambridge Tribune* showed that the tree was no relic of the aboriginal forest, but in fact had been planted by long-forgotten husbandmen. Studying its position relative to nearby trees, J. Gardner Bartlett determined that the Washington Elm was one of six elms of nearly identical age located at equal intervals of five hundred feet along Garden Street—the old edge of the Common. The trees were apparently planted around 1700 as part of "a methodical plan" to provide shade for livestock—and perhaps amenity for the town's inhabitants.[65]

Then, in a meticulously crafted essay published in 1931, the historian Samuel F. Batchelder refuted once and for all the legend of the Washington Elm. He accused the "traditionalists" of overlooking a floodtide of evidence proving that the story as handed down for generations was largely myth. But beloved traditions are not put to sleep so easily, and Batchelder was well aware that he was wrecking a piece of sacred patriotica. To upset the Washington Elm tradition "would be as painful a shock to our historic equilibrium," he wrote, "as to declare the truth that the Declaration of Independence was not signed on the Fourth of July." Doing so would be looked upon as an act "not only unpatriotic but unfilial." Not surprisingly, Batchelder chose his words carefully.

Washington was said to have taken command of the troops on July 3, 1775, in the colorful ceremony recounted by Sibley and others. But Batchelder could produce no evidence to support either the date or the event. The general was indeed in town on July 3, but he evidently spent the entire day inspecting fortifications around Boston. As the troops themselves were busily constructing trenches from Malden to Roxbury, it is impossible that the entire army could have been summoned on the Common to hail their new general. The Provincial Congress had in fact specified, on June 26, 1775, that the reception for Washington at Cambridge be "without any expense of powder, and without taking the Troops off from the necessary attention to their duty at this crisis."[66] Indeed, bringing in the army at such a perilous moment would have been suicide. And as for Washington's wheeling about dramatically on a stallion, his own letters reveal a man in "poor health" and "a good deal fatigued."[67]

The role of the hallowed tree was equally suspect. As Batchelder reasoned, it is unlikely that Washington would have felt it prudent to seek shade in front of a lot of hardscrabble farmers whose respect he needed to earn. This was not the idolized *pater patria* of later decades. In 1775, Washington was still a Southern gentleman on Yankee turf, and one who had come to relieve a popular New England general—Artemus Ward—of his post. Retiring under an elm or any other tree would have been considered an act of self-indulgence and no way for a new commander to appear before men he was to send into battle. Indeed, the actual transfer of authority between the generals most likely took place across the Common at Artemus Ward's headquarters.[68]

But even Batchelder found himself attempting to reconcile the "persistent association" of the general and the elm, and he conceded that the story must contain some grain of truth. If Washington did not take actual command of the colonial troops in a ceremony under the wide-spreading elm, perhaps he did *something* near or under the tree—even if it was no more than stop by it briefly, perhaps as General Ward rode out to greet him on the morning of July 2, in the pouring rain.[69] Irrespective of the actual role (if any) played by the elm, it emerged as the principal vessel bearing memory of the event. The historical meaning drifted toward it, and away from the very artifacts (the Common itself, for example, or Ward's headquarters, later torn down by Harvard University) that would been more precise—if less poetic—monuments to the day.

Regardless of Batchelder's revisionism, the legend of the Washington Elm refused to die—though the tree itself was passing on. Road realignment, and the enclosing of the Common in 1830, marooned the elm in the middle of Garden Street; its only protection from carriages and horsecars was a diminutive fence that was put up in 1847. In 1872, a massive limb crashed to the earth, the wood of which was used to construct a pulpit for a nearby church.[70] By the end of the century the once-noble tree was surrounded by streetcar tracks and a sea of asphalt. Its great crown had been hideously pruned; iron rods and bands supported rotting limbs. Washington's monument had been reduced to a punk-filled stump on a traffic island.

The storied tree finally succumbed to gravity in October 1923. A Parks Department crew had been dispatched earlier that week to remove a projecting limb. As they did so, the entire tree—sodden from recent rains—toppled over.[71] Word spread rapidly that the icon had fallen, and soon a crowd gathered. A hysterical reporter from the *Cambridge Tribune*, claiming to represent several historical societies, attacked the superintendent of parks as he arrived: "I forbid you to put a saw on it!" he shouted.[72] The crowd swelled and became unruly as relic hunters scrambled for pieces of the tree. The sole patrolman on the scene was quickly overwhelmed by "nearby residents and Radcliffe girls" who "went to work with the saws and axes of the park employees to remove souvenirs."[73]

The fall of the Washington Elm made local headlines and national news. One newspaper even suggested that the tree's death was the work of Communists.[74] The *Cambridge Chronicle* waxed sentimental. "In the recent death of the Washington Elm," it lamented, "the city and the nation have suffered an irreparable loss from our historic memorials. No other tree in all the world was so dear to American hearts. Thousands of pilgrims annually wended their way to the Cambridge common to see uplifted its venerable form whose spreading branches served to kindle anew the fires of patriotism in their pent-up souls. Indeed the passing of this precious relic has inspired thousands of Americans with a sense of almost personal human loss such as one might feel with the passing of a great figure in our country's history." With the demise of the Washington Elm, "the last surviving eye-witness" of the Revolution had gone. Its loss rubbed out a monument "greater than sculptured marble and more lasting than any tablet of bronze or granite."[75]

A commission was appointed shortly afterward to determine the fate of the treasured remains—now placed under lock and key in a city warehouse—and to recommend an appropriate memorial to the Washington Elm. Once a vessel bearing the memory of a historical event, the Washington Elm now graduated into an object worthy of veneration itself (as the poet George Crabbe put it, "Monuments themselves Memorials need").[76] The Washington Elm came to

*Bas-relief by Leonard Craske, 1949,
showing George Washington under
the elm on Cambridge Common*

overshadow the very event it shaded—and to which it owed its original
significance. It even nearly caused the removal of another monument to Washington in Boston. Walter Gilman Page, chairman of the commonwealth's art commission, went as far as to suggest that the great equestrian statue of Washington
in the Boston Public Garden "be moved to the site of the elm."[77]

Concerned "that the traditional sentiment . . . not end with the death of the
original," James Michael Curley—Boston's legendary mayor—offered his
municipal neighbor a young scion of the Washington Elm that had been raised
from a cutting and was thriving on Charlestown Heights.[78] But efforts to properly commemorate the Washington Elm remained unresolved for decades and
produced little more than a medallion in the pavement marking the former location of the tree.[79] In 1949, Frank Boland, proprietor of the nearby Commander
Hotel (whose stationery and chinaware carried an image of the elm), initiated a
campaign to commemorate the commemorative tree. Doing so reopened debate
over the veracity of the Washington Elm tradition.

Leonard Craske—a popular classicist who also created the sculpture of the
fisherman at Gloucester, Massachusetts—had already been commissioned to
design a bas-relief of Washington and his elm. He depicted precisely the scene of

patriotic pomp that had made Batchelder wince. After consultation with the U.S. Army's historical division, some of the grosser inaccuracies were eliminated.[80] With Harvard historian Samuel Eliot Morison's input, Boland and Craske edited the caption to read "General George Washington, having taken command of the Continental Army, reviews the troops on Cambridge Common from under the elm that grew near this spot, July 3, 1775."[81] This too failed to pass muster, and by the final casting all references to the good elm had been purged from the text; the tree was now but a mute companion to an equestrian Washington. The unveiling of Craske's piece, on July 3, 1950, was itself a grand occasion, including a parade, a "Dress Retreat," fireworks, and a banquet featuring "elm soup." One of the honored speakers was a young congressman named John F. Kennedy.[82]

As for the tree itself, the Parks Department received hundreds of requests for fragments—from "people of all classes and conditions," from colleges, genealogical associations, historical societies, fraternal lodges, women's clubs, elementary schools, veterans' organizations, the Mount Vernon Ladies Association of the Union, and even the august Smithsonian Institution. One man—who claimed Washingtonian lineage—wished to craft a box for buttons said to be from the general's coat. A sculptor offered to "carve a likeness" of Washington from the wood of the tree. Another suggested that a pair of chairs be made for the president and the vice president of the United States.[83]

Hundreds of small cubes were cut from the limbs of the Washington Elm, each labeled with a brass plaque and sent to prominent individuals around the country. Fragments of the main trunk were sent to the governors of the various states and territories, and a polished cross-section was presented to the museum at Mount Vernon—Washington's former home in Virginia. At least one picture frame was made, to hold a likeness of the late tree itself. Gavels were fashioned, too, with a pair being presented to the senate and house of representatives of each state.[84] Smaller cuts of the historic wood were sent to the governments of thirty-two countries.[85] Freed from its post of two hundred years, the remains of the Washington Elm sped around the world.

4

A SURFEIT OF LEAVES

Although the elm was a presence in the New England landscape from the earliest settlement period, it was still largely an occasional element. The wholesale planting of elms—as an amenity on the streets and commons of villages, towns, and cities—did not begin until the middle decades of the nineteenth century. By that time, New Englanders had begun to look with rekindled interest at the landscape they had settled and brought into fruition. A new longing for spatial beauty stirred in the land and soon produced the first organized efforts to improve the character and appearance of the townscape. Central to this mission was the planting of trees. By the end of the century, the once barren and unkempt villages of New England were clothed in verdure, and a new American institution had been born—the elm-lined street.

The Village Barren

If colonial New England was no howling wilderness, it was still a land well occupied by trees, as William Tudor put it, blessed with "a redundancy of forest."[1] The first generation of colonists made use of old Indian clearings as much as possible, but in time new settlements had to be carved from heavily wooded land. These nascent villages were moments of spatial order wrested from the forest. Trees were the enemy, more or less, and the last thing pioneer villagers needed was streets and lanes decorated with the very forest giants they had labored to clear. Oliver Wolcott, Jr., one of the early advocates of tree planting in New England, was upbraided on this very score. In the 1790s he decided to plant elm trees along the main street of his native Litchfield, Connecticut. Rather than receiving accolades, Wolcott was reprimanded by an elderly gentleman who "remembered the early days of struggle against the forest." "We no sooner get the woods cleared," he complained, "than you start fetching them back."[2]

By the close of the eighteenth century, most New England villages were neither tree-tossed nor particularly beautiful. Even Lenox, Massachusetts—later famed for its beauty—was "a pretty barren village" before the 1840s, "with so few trees that you could . . . look far and wide from the Courthouse steps."[3] Everywhere roads were rutted and unkempt; sidewalks were nonexistent, and the margins of streets were neglected zones where public and private blurred together. What trees did adorn streets and lanes were mostly wayside volunteers, or those in adjacent gardens that threw unintended shade onto passersby. Town commons and greens were equally impoverished. Although trees were occasionally set out to provide shelter for animals, commons were generally overgrown and used for pasture or training local militia. Boston Common, mother of all Yankee greens, was an unshaded field well into the nineteenth century, its interior barren except for the Great Elm and a handful of scrubby trees.

There were exceptions, however, almost all of which appeared in the valley towns of the Connecticut and Housatonic rivers. Settled in the 1650s, these fertile valleys gave themselves readily to agriculture, and a century later their flourishing villages and farmsteads possessed an air of verdant maturity. There, elm trees, long a wayside presence in the intervals, made an early appearance in town. Villages like Northfield, Deerfield, Hadley, Northampton, Longmeadow, Stockbridge, and Litchfield began planting elms in town as early as the 1750s, typically along the main street or in front of public buildings. Pioneering urban designers simply introduced into the townscape a long-familiar tenant of the pastoral countryside all around. Theirs was the first use of the American elm as an agent of civic beautification and spatial design in the United States.

Protests notwithstanding, the efforts of Oliver Wolcott, Jr., in Litchfield, Connecticut, soon rendered it a model for village tree planting. One of his first projects was to plant thirteen buttonwood trees to commemorate the states of the new Republic. But the trees soon fell prey to disease and subsequently died (all but one—the "Connecticut" tree, perhaps not surprisingly). From then on, Wolcott, assisted by his brother, set about planting elms, which "grew in many of the outlaying swamps and could be brought into town on the shoulders." The Wolcotts planted a number of such trees along South Street and elsewhere. They were later joined by John C. Calhoun, who set out elms at each of his several residences beginning in 1805. During the War of 1812, soldiers stationed on Bantam Road contributed to the greening of the town by planting a double row of elms along their camp.[4]

*The verdant village: Longmeadow, Massachusetts, in an engraving
by John Warner Barber, c. 1840*

*Deerfield, Massachusetts, as seen in an engraving by
John Warner Barber, c. 1840*

At Stockbridge, William Edwards set out a handful of elms along the main
street in 1786 in celebration of the signing of the Constitution. The Williard
family initiated the planting of elms along the Deerfield Common in 1809.
Northampton's early stock of elms was due to the largess of John Hunt, a wealthy
merchant who planted a row of trees in the 1750s, from which Elm Street later
took its name. At Northfield, Massachusetts, several rows of elms and maples
were set out in 1812 by Thomas Powers, a Northfield lawyer and distinguished
citizen.[5] John Warner Barber's field engravings of Deerfield, Longmeadow,
Northfield, and other towns of the Connecticut River valley—drawn from life
in the 1830s—all verify well-established town trees.

The sylvan beauty of these older valley towns was well noted — particularly by foreign travelers. They were praiseworthy in comparison with the typically barren Yankee town, and paradisiacal compared with the ragged upstarts of New York's western frontier. Basil Hall, a captain in the Royal Navy who toured Massachusetts and New York in 1827, described the country along the Erie Canal as "spotted over with new villages, as raw and unpicturesque as if they had just stepped out of a saw pit." Hall found the townscapes of the New York frontier desperately wanting in spatial beauty. Those of western Massachusetts, on the other hand, struck him as gracious, mature, and beautiful.[6]

The best of them, he found, were "embellished with ornamental trees."[7] Hall was particularly moved by Stockbridge, Massachusetts. He arrived at twilight on a summer evening, when the town seemed otherworldly, nestled beneath a verdant bower of elms. "The street, or rather avenue, through which we passed," wrote Hall, "was lined with double rows of tall trees, somewhat in the fashion of an Italian corso, or the beautiful prado of Spanish cities, and I almost fancied that even in those picturesque countries I had never seen a prettier place." Architecture deferred to the elms overhead; the houses lining the street were "almost hid in the foliage or lost in the shadows of the trees." "My imagination," mused Hall, "was carried away to the region of the tropics, where alone I had seen such a picture before."[8]

Hall found the Connecticut Valley towns of Northampton and Hadley similarly "impossible to overpraise." Their beauty he attributed to the double row of trees planted on either side of the main streets, under which ran "broad and agreeably shaded walks."[9] Charles Joseph Latrobe agreed, concluding in *The Rambler in North America* that the towns along the Connecticut owed their splendor and charm principally to the elms that "not unfrequently line both sides of the streets, and cluster about the older mansions."[10]

Nathaniel Parker Willis, writing in 1839, found the Housatonic and Connecticut valleys "gemmed with beautiful rural towns, many of them among the first in our country for prosperity, neatness, and cultivated society."[11] Like Basil Hall, he too was particularly impressed with Stockbridge. "Most small towns in America have traces of *newness* about them," he claimed in *Life, Here and There* (1850). "The stumps of a clearing, or freshly-boarded barns — something that is the antipodes of romance — meets your eye from every aspect. Stockbridge, on the contrary, is an old town, . . . the fields look soft and genial, the grass is swardlike, the bridges, picturesque, the hedges old, and the elms, nowhere so many and so luxuriant, are full-grown and majestic." Indeed, Willis found the town "embowered in foliage."[12]

But it would be decades before other towns and villages in New England followed the precedent set by such precocious communities. Although the spatial beauty that distinguished Northampton, Deerfield, Stockbridge, and other towns was early appreciated by visitors from abroad, they inspired little or no emulation elsewhere in New England. In time, however, this began to change. A broad shift in values in the 1830s stimulated a new awareness of nature, environment, and the native landscape. This in turn brought about a new interest in native flora—particularly indigenous forest trees. It also led to America's first environmental movement—a grassroots effort to bring order and beauty to New England's towns and villages. For guidance, the early village "improvers" turned again and again to the elm-tossed valley towns of the Connecticut and the Housatonic. These became models of spatial beauty throughout the region, and eventually across the nation.

The Environmental Awakening

Until about 1820, most Americans looked upon the natural world as a bumper crop awaiting harvest. Forests were seen as little more than an obstacle to be cleared away. With the rare exception of men like Thomas Jefferson, Hector St. John de Crèvecoeur, or William Bartram—each of whom early understood that America possessed a remarkable natural legacy—the prevailing attitude was that of exploitation. In time, however, the adversarial stance of earlier generations gradually transformed, beginning in the 1830s, into one of appreciation. To be sure, wanton exploitation continued through the nineteenth century, but now it was accompanied—and often checked—by a countervailing set of attitudes that valued stewardship and conservation.

A number of factors led to this burgeoning interest in nature, landscape, and environment. In part it was a reaction against the pace at which the land was being developed, and the rapid advance of settlement across the western frontier. The American landscape, which had long appeared limitless in extent and wealth, was beginning to show signs of depletion. Nicolas Collin, a friend of Benjamin Franklin's, warned of a coming shortage of timber if the wholesale destruction of forests continued. In a paper delivered at Philadelphia in 1789— "An Essay on Natural Philosophy and Its Relationship to the Development of the New World"—Collin argued that "our stately forests are a national treasure, deserving the solicitous care of the patriotic philosopher and politician." "Hitherto," he pointed out, "they have been too much abandoned to the axes of rude and thoughtless wood-choppers."[13]

The new sensibility toward nature and environment was also influenced by European Romanticism. Following Rousseau, Chateaubriand, Goethe, Schiller, and others, this vision of the world flowered toward the end of the eighteenth century in the hands of the English poets Scott, Byron, Coleridge, and Words-worth.[14] Romanticism, as a reaction against the Enlightenment, sought to temper rationalism and scientific method with the emotive, the spontaneous, the irra-tional, and the creative. To the Enlightenment mind, nature was a specimen to measure and classify; to the Romantic, nature was "a live vessel of spirit, a translucent source of mystery and revelation."[15] The Romantics venerated nature, seeing in the natural world traces of the divine.

Romanticism came to America through such writers as James Fenimore Cooper, William Cullen Bryant, Ralph Waldo Emerson, and Henry David Thoreau. It also inspired the first generation of American landscape painters, among them Washington Allston, Thomas Cole, and Asher B. Durand. William Cullen Bryant's poems "Thanatopsis" (1817) and "A Forest Hymn" (1825) were among the earliest expressions of Romanticism on American soil. Emerson fol-lowed, and scaled even greater heights. He sought "an original relation to the universe," and he found it in the fields and woods of Concord. It was in nature and the native landscape, Emerson believed, that lay the true fountainhead of American identity. "To possess Nature in America *thoroughly*," wrote Alfred Kazin, "was to confirm in every detail of life and thought America's indepen-dence." What need had the young Republic for the crumbling remains of the past when it possessed a landscape of unimaginable beauty and richness? As Emerson reasoned in *Nature* (1833): "Embosomed for a season in nature, whose floods of life stream around and through us, and invite us by the powers they supply, to action proportioned to nature, why should we grope among the dry bones of the past, or put the living generation into masquerade out of its faded wardrobe? The sun shines today also. There is more wool and flax in the fields. There are new lands, new men, new thoughts. Let us demand our own works and laws and worship."[16]

Indeed, the Romantic embrace of nature found ample service in forging a fresh identity for the young Republic. Following the American victory in the War of 1812, a new spirit of nationalism swept the land, growing stronger as the nation gained in military and economic power during the Jacksonian period. Americans no longer felt hostage to the customs and fashions of the Old World, and they no longer believed themselves an inferior people. Europe might possess profound legacies in music, literature, art, and architecture; but, as Emerson sug-gested, America had Niagara, Lake George, the White Mountains, the Connecti-cut, and the Mississippi. The paintings of Cole, Durand, and other landscapists brought many of these scenes to life on canvas. Such a natural inheritance more than equaled the artificial grandeur of the Old World, in American eyes at least.

Central to the environmental awakening of the Jacksonian period was a belief that the contemplation of wild nature produced positive moral and spiritual effects upon the observer. Moreover, it was believed that a person could derive similar value by reproducing the essence of such scenes closer to home. In other words, by "improving" his grounds according to certain aesthetic principles, he could realize bountiful dividends both moral and spiritual. "Taste, the perception of the beautiful, and the knowledge of the principles on which nature works," wrote painter Thomas Cole, "can be applied, and our dwelling-places made fitting for refined and intellectual beings."[17]

And this application of "taste" could be just as effective in the civic realm as it was in the domestic; improvement could transform village space just as it transformed the home grounds, yielding spiritual uplift for all. As an advocate of village improvement put it decades later, by affording to nature "the assistance of Art, its appropriate handmaid," improvement could bring about "a most gratifying development of two kinds of beauty": one, "in the most outward aspect of the village itself," and the other, "in the interior life of the people."[18]

The environmental awakening thus brought about not only an appreciation for wild nature but a longing to impart some of its value to the domestic and—more important—the civic environment. It produced, as John R. Stilgoe put it, "a new craving for spatial beauty."[19] Americans were indeed ready for this new day. By the 1830s they had moved beyond what Susan Fenimore Cooper called "the first rude stage of progress."[20] They now wished more of life, and longed for the comforts of cultivation and civilization. The rawness of the American scene, once taken as an inevitable part of the settlement epic, was no longer acceptable. The dishevelment of farmsteads, village streets, and town commons was now examined through a moral lens, which revealed a plethora of hazards.

From the start, trees played a central role in this dawning era of environmental awareness. "Would it not be a regulation well deserving the attention of the General Court," urged a Connecticut newspaper in 1798, "to require every town to plant the sides of the public roads with forest trees?" Though the article's point was economic (fast-growing species would "pay for their planting by their growth"), the author clearly articulated a new sensibility toward environment.[21] The Reverend Lyman Beecher directed his pulpit toward similar aims. In a sermon on July 17, 1824, he exhorted his Litchfield congregation to engage in acts of public spiritedness, which had the result of inspiring a party of townsmen "to transplant forest trees wherever they are needed through our streets."[22]

In the 1820s the *New England Farmer* began publishing essays on the subject of improvement, and it soon became the major voice of sylvan improvement in the region.[23] In August 1825 a piece appeared noting that "the value attached to shade trees is by a great part of the community very improperly appreciated."

The writer appealed to the purse, arguing that "the value of most farms would be raised ten or fifteen per cent by the addition of shade trees about the buildings and along the public road." Moreover, trees "give the country an appearance of wealth, that nothing else can supply; . . . the most spacious and princely establishments without them appear covered with the most prison-like gloom."[24]

The following year the *New England Farmer* published a longer appeal: "In a young region, where all the disposable industry must be consumed in freeing the earth from those stately forests, whose leaves have alternately shaded and enriched the soil through the successive Springs and Autumns of many centuries, it is not surprising, that little attention should be paid to the preservation of those beautiful ornaments of a cultivated country, the green trees, which afford so luxurious a retreat from the Summer sun." But where the "warfare with the original settlers of the country has eased," the writer added (implicating New England), "it is remarkable that so little care should be bestowed on the comfort of the traveler, or convenience of the resident, by planting trees along the wayside." He implored readers to do so: "Would each individual bestow these in planting that portion of his land which borders on the public roads with trees, our highways, instead of being bleak, barren, and sultry, would seem like avenues of green, joining village to village, equally sheltered from the burning sun, and the driving storm."[25]

Not only roads but burial grounds and other spaces, too, would benefit from improvement. In an 1827 tract from the *National Aegis*, a writer criticized the decrepit condition of "those inclosures appropriated for the sepulchres of the departed." He thought most New England cemeteries were places "abandoned to every unsightly bramble that roots in soil," a condition he found to both "dishonor the dead" and "reproach the living." With modest intervention, however, these could be transformed: "How much more fit to cherish the recollection of lost friends, and to inspire appropriate reflections would they become if the remains of those we have loved and respected, were placed in their last repose beneath the shadow of noble trees; if instead of exciting emotions of disgust by their rudeness, they ornamented the landscape with objects of loveliness." The writer reproached the "wasteful neglect" that had turned New England's burial grounds and roadsides into eyesores, and suggested that a remedy "might probably be found by our Agricultural Societies," which, among other things, could "offer premiums to the individuals who would serve the public and themselves by planting their lands bordering on the highways, with suitable trees." This action, he believed, would bring about no less than the "improvement of the face of the earth."[26]

Other appeals were aimed squarely at patriotic sentiment. In 1831 the *New England Farmer* wrote: "No pains and no reasonable expense should be spared by the farmer in setting out useful and ornamental trees around his house and the public road." He should do so out of love for the homeland. "Our fathers made sacrifices for our country with sword in hand," the writer argued; "it belongs to their children to make them with the spade." Indeed, "the good of the country" required that a tree be planted "in every unoccupied corner."[27] By 1835, appeals for tree planting began addressing specifically the civic realm of town and village. That year, the *New England Farmer* published a tract whose author began by quoting one of the English Romantics: "'There is a pleasure in the pathless woods,' says Byron, but there is none in the woodless paths. It must be confessed that naked streets are particularly uninteresting, and be there never so many of them, as broad and straight soever as you may please, still they add nothing to the beauty and picturesqueness of a town." Indeed, the writer concluded, "a bald head is not comely, neither is a street seemly which is not well set with trees."[28]

The Romance of the Exotic

Until the environmental awakening, New England's native forest trees were considered rude and unsuitable for the purposes of art. With the exception of those Connecticut and Housatonic villages that had set out elms in the eighteenth century, most of the town trees planted before the 1830s were imported "exotic" species. In spite of gaining independence from the most powerful colonial overseer in the world, Americans nursed an inferiority complex vis-à-vis Europe. Even as Americans boasted of their liberation from the Old World and its "catalog of errors," they also longed for its rich cultural heritage and tended to favor things European.[29] Even into the Jacksonian period, an era of hale nationalism, a measure of such cultural inferiority still obtained. In 1830, the *New England Farmer* wrote scornfully: "It is a trait in our patriotism to favor foreign productions and neglect better that we have at home; . . . we dare not admire or praise a book till it has been praised in Europe."[30]

This self-deprecation extended to the landscape and the trees that grew upon it. Before the environmental awakening, American space was considered rough and unfinished, not yet graced with the rich layer of memory that made the Old World so fanciful to poets and painters. American trees were considered uncouth, too-virile rustics, inferior to the picturesque sylva decorating the canvases of Lorrain and Poussin or tufting the storied vales of Tuscany. When it came to decorative and ornamental planting, Americans often chose imported trees over native. Andrew Jackson Downing lamented this trend when he asked, "who plants an American tree—in America?"[31]

Native trees were shunned not only because they were "common" and lacked the gracious associations of antique lands, but because they carried the stigma of the forest, which in many parts of the United States remained a formidable obstacle well into the nineteenth century. Exotics, on the other hand, bore the stamp of cultural refinement, and even an air of sophistication. William Tudor observed in 1819—with some incredulity—that a farmer would often "cut down oaks that were near his house, and plant Lombardy poplars, as more ornamental." (The "example of better taste," he added optimistically, "will gradually prevent the repetition of similar absurdities.")[32] Foreign trees were indulged like exotic pets. In an age when few people had the opportunity to travel abroad, such sylvan imports were indeed emissaries from strange and distant lands.

Few exotics more thoroughly penetrated the American scene than the Lombardy poplar *(Populus nigra italica)*. A species of columnar form and extremely rapid growth, the tree was among the first to be planted extensively in town and urban settings in the United States—so extensively that Downing would later look back on its heyday as an "epidemic." The Lombardy rage was part of a general interest in classicism and the antique world that peaked around 1812. In this period, such architects as Thomas Jefferson, J. J. Ramée, and Benjamin H. Latrobe turned to the architecture of ancient Greece and Rome as an appropriate building style for the new Republic. American painters like Benjamin West and Washington Allston traveled to Italy to paint its archaic landscapes—the very scenes absent in upstart America. The tree, a fixture in the pastoral landscapes of northern Italy, became associated in the American mind with the timeless allure of the Old World.

Just how the Lombardy rage began in America is unclear. The earliest introduction of the tree in New England—and possibly in the United States—likely occurred at Cambridge, where Benjamin Waterhouse reared specimens he brought back from Italy around 1779. He later planted a row of Lombardy poplars in Harvard Yard, the first formal planting of trees in that hallowed space.[33] Other accounts point to William Bartram, the great Philadelphia botanist, who may have unpacked the first Lombardy specimens in 1783.[34] William Prince, a nurseryman in Flushing, New York, contributed greatly to the tree's popularity. By 1800 Prince had more than a hundred thousand poplar seedlings in cultivation, which were "disseminated far and wide" before propagation was attempted by others.[35]

The use of the Lombardy poplar in America may have had an even more distinguished pedigree. Samuel Eliot Morison claimed that the tree had been introduced by none other than the classicist Thomas Jefferson. In the early decades of the nineteenth century, he wrote, "it was a sign of unterrified democracy in New England" to plant Lombardy poplars, the "dendrological badge of Jeffersonian Republicanism." Of course, the Federalists turned the badge against its benefactor, pointing out that the Lombardy's "soft, pulpy wood and attraction for worms resembled the brain of the gentleman who introduced them."[36]

The Lombardy poplars on Salem Common, in George Ropes, Salem Common on Training Day, *1808 (Courtesy of the Peabody Essex Museum, Salem, Massachusetts)*

Regardless of its provenance, the Lombardy poplar took America by storm. Major port cities like New York, Boston, and Philadelphia—receivers of the first shipments of the trees—planted hundreds along their main streets. In 1803 Jefferson lined Pennsylvania Avenue in Washington with double rows from the White House to the Capitol. The Park Street Mall, along Boston Common, was similarly planted.[37] The perimeter of Salem Common bore a heavy burden of Lombardy poplars, a remarkable scene of sylvan excess captured by George Ropes in his *Salem Common on Training Day*, painted in 1808.

Portsmouth, New Hampshire, also indulged the Lombardy rage. Around 1792, John Langdon, U.S. senator and later governor of New Hampshire, placed a number of the trees in the front of his residence, an act that set off a planting binge that transformed the city in the next several years. At first the "thrifty and elegant" trees were confined to front yards, but soon the citizens were "stirred up to give them place," one chronicler reported, "in all of our most public streets." The Portsmouth Lombards had been purchased in Boston, "at a high price"; no weedy elms from local woods, these costly artifacts were set out with great care, "well boxed" against the predatory nibblings of horses.[38]

Another popular exotic in the early nineteenth century was ailanthus, or tree of heaven *(Ailanthus altissima)*. Seeds from the species, a native of Asia, were sent from Peking to the Royal Society of London in 1751 by Pierre Nicolas le Chéron d'Incarville, a Jesuit missionary whose chief effort had been to convert the Chinese emperor to Christianity.[39] Ailanthus first appeared in North America in Philadelphia, where William Hamilton cultivated the species in 1784. By 1804 it had made its way to New England, first in Portsmouth, Rhode Island.[40] William Prince of New York was again among the first to make the species available commercially, having had specimens sent him around 1820 by a London nurseryman. The plants were received under the homely name Sicilian tanner's sumac and distributed as such until their real identity was established. The revelation of the tree's exotic provenance propelled it into stardom. As W. R. Prince recounted in 1861, "after the error in the name was corrected, and 'Chinese Ailanthus' was substituted for Sumach, a potent charm came over the entire tree, and every one gazed on it with wonder and admiration, and for many years it was impossible to supply the demands at treble the former prices."[41]

By the summer of 1832 the Thorburn nursery in New York had several ailanthus trees growing at their Liberty Street premises. "All who behold must admire them for their luxuriant growth and graceful oriental foliage," wrote a correspondent to the *New England Farmer*. "We should admire much to see those trees freely introduced in our streets; a work which can very easily be done, since their growth is very rapid."[42] Many towns and cities followed his advice.

Rediscovery of the Native

But the groundswell of interest in the American landscape stoked by the environmental awakening, and the rise of a nature-centered nationalism, led to a new appreciation of native American plants—and a backlash against the very exotics that had earlier been so prized. Native forest trees, once considered déclassé, were soon to be hailed as objects of national pride. What the fathers felled, the sons set out with care. The hale spirit of "nature's nation" demanded allegiance not to the effete offspring of foreign lands but to America's own trees—the "hardy and glorious sons" of the native woods.[43]

"There are trees in every American forest," observed the *New England Farmer* in 1830, "that are seldom transplanted into cultivated ground, which, if they were exotics, would be cultivated with great expense and care." Sassafras was an example, a native tree "almost unknown in gardens," yet it possessed many aesthetic and formal qualities; its growth, too, was "nearly as rapid as the Lombardy poplar." But, asked the *Farmer*, "who can find a grove of Sassafras, while there are so many tasteless avenues of poplar?"[44] Otis Turner, a New York farmer, expressed well the new arbor-nationalism in an 1832 letter to the *New England Farmer*. "I would choose for my trees those of my own country," he announced, "and the elm should hold the first rank."[45] Planting indigenous trees was "a debt which civilization owes to our native soil," suggested another contributor, a means of restoring to the land "some of those ornaments of which it once boasted a profusion." Indeed, the "genius of improvement" must now "cherish some representatives of the magnificent wilderness which it has spirited away."[46]

Jacksonian America thus embraced native American trees, and purged the alien sylva an earlier generation had planted. Once loved, the exotics now fell by the score. The Lombardy poplar—now the "meanest of all trees"—was the target of especially brutal treatment.[47] Those of Portsmouth, New Hampshire, planted in the 1790s, lost their appeal within a generation. The poplar's short life, and its increasingly ratty appearance as it aged, only accelerated the purges. As a Portsmouth chronicler later wrote, "Their decapitated trunks, shorn of every vestige of beauty, sending out a seven fold number of new shoots, had more the appearance of the fabled hydra than a product of Eden." Everywhere the trees began to disappear—except in graveyards, "where they seemed left to show the downward progress of beauty."[48] The inhabitants of Hadley, Massachusetts, having set out poplars in 1800, later wiped the town clean of the foreigner—elms and sugar maples went up in their stead.[49] In Salem, too, the Common that bristled with poplars in 1808 was shaven clean and planted with elms by the 1830s.

In Boston, the change in arboreal allegiance was led by Mayor Josiah Quincy, Sr. According to legend, Quincy struck out for the Common one morning in 1826, ax in hand, and felled "the old poplar trees which used to disfigure the Park street mall"; that same day he planted American elms in their place.[50] For others, the pen was sharper than the ax. Oliver Wendell Holmes ridiculed the Lombards that stood by his boyhood home in Cambridge. He associated the tree not with bright-morning America, but with the tired Old World—and with death itself: "Whether, like the cypress, these trees suggest the idea of the funeral torch or the monumental spire, whether their tremulous leaves make us afraid by sympathy with their nervous thrills, whether the faint balsamic smell of their leaves and their closely swathed limbs have in them vague hints of dead Pharaohs stiffened in their cerements, I will not guess; but they always seemed to me to give an air of sepulchral sadness to the house before which they stood sentries."[51]

The ailanthus came in for even harsher treatment. This was partly due to characteristics that made the tree unpleasant and difficult to manage—it was wildly invasive, and some trees produced an offensive odor. But rejection of the ailanthus also revealed the racist underbelly of Jacksonian America, a nativism that became more and more virulent as foreign immigration escalated toward mid-century. If the Lombardy poplar was a foreigner, at least it was associated with

Europe and the familiar lands of Western antiquity. The ailanthus, on the other hand, was an Asian tree, evoking peoples and lands profoundly alien to Anglo-European America. If the Lombards lost their appeal because their symbolism was exhausted, the ailanthus was purged because it was the Other in sylvan form.

Leading this charge was none other than the good tastemaker Andrew Jackson Downing. Downing had himself once championed exotic sylva, though never to the exclusion of native trees. But he soon turned against the very imports he had recommended earlier. "Down with the Ailanthus!" he charged. Americans had been "seduced by the oriental beauty of its foliage," and now the tree threatened to overrun the land. The ailanthus was, he claimed, a "usurper in rather bad *odor* . . . which has come over to this land of liberty, under the garb of utility to make foul the air, with its pestilent breath, and devour the soil, with its intermeddling roots." The root suckers by which the tree propagated Downing compared to "little Tartars that will beget a new dynasty, and overrun our gardens . . . without mercy." For the ailanthus "has the fair outside and the treacherous heart of the Asiatics."[52]

Indeed, Downing rejected the tree for more than its invasiveness or offensive odor. "We confess openly," he wrote, "that our crowning objection to this petted Chinaman or Tartar, who has played us so falsely, is a patriotic objection."

> It is that he has drawn away our attention from our own more noble native American trees, to waste it on this miserable pigtail of an Indiaman. What should we think of the Italians, if they should forswear their own orange trees and figs, pomegranates and citrons, and plant their streets and gardens with the poison sumac tree of our swamps? And what must an European arboriculturalist think, who travels in America, delighted and astonished at the beauty of our varied and exhaustless forests—the richest in the temperate zone, to see that we neither value nor plant them, but fill our lawns and avenues with the cast off nuisances of the gardens of Asia and Europe.

"Oh!" he lamented, "that our tree planters . . . knew and could understand the surpassing beauty of our *native shade trees*."[53] For Downing, the righteous path was clearly marked, and it was shaded by American trees.

5

THE VERDANT VILLAGE

The new longing for spatial beauty, and its emphasis on native sylva, produced a period of elm planting in New England that transformed the townscapes of the region. Before the 1840s only a handful of New England towns had planted trees on their streets and commons—among them Deerfield, Litchfield, and Northampton (so, too, had certain cities, as will be discussed in the next chapter). But such efforts were sporadic, and largely the work of public-spirited individuals. As an organized collective action to improve the civic realm, elm planting—and village improvement in general—did not truly begin until the 1840s.

The Great Sheffield "Tree Bee"

It was at Sheffield, Massachusetts, that the village improvement movement began, and there that the American elm was established as the principal tool of spatial beautification. A small town along the Housatonic, Sheffield was already well known throughout the region for the great Sheffield Elm, a totem in the community since its founding in 1733. But except for this forest giant (and a short row of Lombardy poplars set out around 1820) Sheffield had planted few town trees. In 1846, however, things began to change. That spring two young men—Frank Ensign and Graham A. Root—rallied their fellow citizens and organized a "Tree Bee." The event, something of an arboreal barn raising, was met with great enthusiasm; it began in late May and lasted for two weeks. The entire community participated in the effort—men carrying saplings and working spades; women furnishing noonday meals ("and by other kind acts encouraging the men"); children steadied the small trees as they were set in the ground.[1]

Sheffield planted one thousand trees in all—every one an American elm. Starting from the Sheffield Elm, the column of verdure marched down the main street of town like progeny going forth from the old tree. Along with its totem elm, Sheffield's tree-lined avenue became a touchstone of local pride, a feature that would "excite the attention and admiration of visitors" and distinguish the town as one of the most beautiful in Massachusetts.[2] What had been a barren, unkempt thoroughfare "much overgrown with tangled grass and burdock and large patches of mayweed" now emerged as an essay in spatial beauty.[3]

The Tree Bee was a defining event in the evolution of Sheffield's collective identity. In 1896, the town staged an elaborate celebration to commemorate the fiftieth anniversary of the planting—a "red letter occasion," which drew long-departed daughters and sons "to revisit old scenes" and sing praises to the trees. The elms, "in whose honor the people congregated," reported the *Berkshire Courier*, "were decorated with flags, and beneath their green arcade a procession moved to the Old Elm." Sermons and speeches lauded the civic spirit that so richly endowed Sheffield. "No costly granite shaft or stately pile can compare," one orator proclaimed, "with the grandeur of this magnificent avenue of elms"; it was a monument to "the public spirit and enterprise of any and everyone that participated in the Tree Bee." Urging a renewal of that spirit, he remarked that "the old elms have in themselves a peaceful and suggestive force for every educated man and woman," which would inspire future efforts to "continue the good work started so auspiciously 50 years ago."[4]

Sheffield's Tree Bee was an event unprecedented in New England, and it clearly signaled the region's growing interest in environmental design and spatial beauty. The town may also have had access to some of the most influential intellectuals of the environmental awakening. The conduit was a local minister named Orville Dewey. Born in 1794, Dewey studied at Williams College and Andover Theological Seminary before joining Boston's Federal Street Church (where he befriended Ralph Waldo Emerson).[5] The young clergyman moved to New York in 1835, where he became pastor of the Second Unitarian Church on Mercer and Prince streets. The post put Dewey back in touch with an old boyhood friend who was now the editor of New York's *Evening Post*. His name was William Cullen Bryant.[6]

The men developed a fast friendship. Bryant, whom Dewey referred to as "our Magnus Apollo," saw to it that the minister was elected to the Sketch Club, becoming its first clergyman member.[7] Membership in this organization admitted Dewey into Bryant's inner circle of friends, a diverse group of "artists and gentlemen" that included Thomas Cole, Asher B. Durand, and Andrew Jackson Downing. Dewey discovered in this crowd kindred spirits, and he came to relish its intellectual milieu. He later wrote that the club "was a kind of heart's home to me while I lived in New York."[8] Even after returning to Sheffield permanently in the spring of 1848, he remained close to his New York friends. Bryant, who summered in nearby Great Barrington, was a frequent guest, and on one occasion Dewey invited the entire Sketch Club to his Sheffield home.[9]

Through his association with Bryant, Cole, and other Sketchers, Dewey would have been steeped in the new nature-centered philosophy. Bryant himself had a marked impact on at least one fellow Sketcher, Asher B. Durand, who created several canvases inspired by Bryant's poems (his painting *Kindred Spirits*, one of the masterpieces of the Hudson River school, portrayed Bryant and Cole in the Catskills).[10] Bryant used his editorship of the *Evening Post* to rally support for a public park in New York City, and in this way came to befriend Andrew Jackson Downing. Dewey almost certainly would have met Downing in this way. The combined influence of these men — the poet and the landscape gardener — may well have cultivated in Dewey a fresh appreciation for nature, one that perhaps encouraged him to augment the spatial beauty of his own hometown.

Dewey may well have been the formative figure behind the Tree Bee of 1846, although conclusive evidence is lacking. He was residing in New York at the time, but he returned to Sheffield frequently and was in close contact with family there. In fact, Graham Root, one of the Tree Bee organizers, was Dewey's nephew. In any case, by the time he returned to Sheffield in 1848, Dewey had cultivated more than a passing interest in village improvement. For in 1852 he founded an organization dedicated to improving the spatial beauty of his hometown — one that would carry on the legacy of the Tree Bee and, in effect, help institutionalize the planting of elm trees throughout New England. He named his group the Elm Tree Association; it was the first village improvement society in America.

The chief mission of the Elm Tree Association was to bring spatial beauty to Sheffield — by improving "the appearance of the fields and public places," by grading walkways, and, more than anything, by planting elms throughout the town.[11] But Dewey charged the Elm Tree Association with more than just an aesthetic mandate. For him, spatial beauty and social justice went hand in hand. Deeply committed to improving the human condition in the here and now, Dewey deplored the "anchorite's dreaming of heaven."[12] His improvement society would cultivate — along with elm trees — "a common interest and a common feeling" among its fellow citizens, and seek "to remove prejudices, and bring us nearer together."[13] It was at a meeting of the Elm Tree Association in 1856, beneath the Old Elm itself, that Dewey delivered a speech that gained him renown in the North (and infamy in the South) as a fiery opponent of slavery.[14]

The speech became known as the "Elm Tree Oration," and Dewey closed it by invoking the tree: "Long may its brave old arms stretch themselves over this humble spot, in a free and happy land! May the green sod beneath it, never be wet with fratricidal blood!"[15]

The Village Improvement Movement

The village improvement movement, born at Sheffield in 1852, received the support of the Massachusetts General Court a year later. On May 10, 1853, a statute was passed that authorized the formation of organizations dedicated to village improvement: a group of "ten or more persons" assembled "for the purpose of encouraging agriculture, horticulture, or improving and ornamenting the streets and public squares of any town or city by planting and cultivating ornamental trees therein, may become a corporation by such name as they assume." Such groups would enjoy the same "rights, powers and privileges" accorded libraries and lyceums.[16] Within months of the new statute, a second village improvement society was founded in nearby Stockbridge. It helped speed elm-planting fever across New England.

At the second annual meeting of the Elm Tree Association, in August 1853, Mary Hopkins of Stockbridge was elected an honorary member.[17] Hopkins had visited Sheffield earlier that year to learn more about the association's initiatives. Upon returning to her town, she posted a notice on an elm in front of the Stockbridge post office urging townfolk to attend an assembly at Laurel Hill. The purpose of the meeting was to discuss "measures for the regular improvement of the Burying Ground, the streets, the walks, the public grounds and Laurel Hill," a park on a small prominence in town.[18]

The meeting was fruitful. Stockbridge had once been praised for its beauty, but in recent years its charms had faded. Its citizens knew that action was needed, and at that first meeting "a determination was formed to organize a Society for the purpose of carrying out consistently and permanently the object of village improvement." That society was named the Laurel Hill Association, and it intended to labor away "till every street shall be graded, every sidewalk shaded, . . . in short, till art combined with nature shall have rendered our town the most beautiful and attractive in our ancient commonwealth." The Laurel Hill Association thrived under Mary Hopkins's leadership, and it became the model for village improvement societies around New England and elsewhere in the United States.[19]

The Laurel Hill Association set for itself a number of objectives, chief among which was planting elms. Following the guidelines of a townwide improvement plan drafted in 1853, the association embarked on an intensive three-year elm-

*Newly planted elms in Woburn, Massachusetts, engraving by
John Warner Barber, c. 1840*

planting campaign. It set out more than four hundred saplings along the streets, each "not less than ten feet in height."[20] The association enlisted the support of the whole community. Designated sites were made public, and townsfolk were encouraged to donate the actual tree and set it in the ground. There were incentives: a silver cup was awarded "to the planter of the best 15 trees," and membership in the association itself was promised "every person over 14 years of age, who shall plant and protect a tree . . . or pay the sum of one dollar annually in money or labor." Even children were recruited, as guards to protect the saplings against demons both real and imagined: "Any boy who would undertake to watch and care for a particular tree," for two years, was rewarded by having the tree "called by his name."[21]

The improving zeal of the Laurel Hill Association soon extended outward, as members planted trees "along every road leading out of town as far as our geographical boundaries." The minutes of an 1866 meeting reported: "It needs no prophets ken to portray the charm and beauty of drives in every direction beneath the shade and shelter of Nature's canopy of verdure." Economics urged the same: such splendor would bring about a "consequent enhancement of the reputation of our Town abroad." Moreover, "if our sister towns should . . . emulate us in this behalf, the next generation would be able to ride through the length and breadth of Old Berkshire during the heats of summer with all the comfort of pedestrians beneath the green and cool arcades of the forest, and dust and wheels alone distinguish the drive from the stroll."[22] Elm trees were not only beautiful, they could help drive regional development.

The labors of the Laurel Hill Association indeed transformed Stockbridge, placing it on the map as one of the gems of the Berkshires. "Not with the utmost stretch of your imagination," exclaimed one long-absent resident, "could you conceive what a remarkable change had been wrought by these forty years of well-directed effort. There was nothing particularly beautiful about the town when I moved away. Now it seemed to me like Paradise." The cemetery, once a disheveled browsing ground for cattle, was trimmed and enclosed by hedges. The streets were clean and level, the walks well groomed with neat grassy borders; the church green, "once a barren level," was a tree-tossed park. And everywhere there were "magnificent, over-arching elms."[23]

From the Berkshires, the village improvement movement sped across New England. In Amherst, the Ornamental Tree Association was formed in 1857 to improve the public common and public walks throughout the village "by grading, graveling, and lining with trees," and to do "anything which may render the public grounds and ways of our village more attractive and beautiful."[24] Scores of other communities followed suit, and by the 1880s some twenty-three village improvement organizations had been formed in Massachusetts alone, with another fifty in Connecticut.[25] Led by the Elm Tree and Laurel Hill associations, these improvement societies helped bring about a dramatic transformation of the New England village, one that set a lasting standard for environmental design in America.

Broker of Beautification

The muse of improvement spread far and wide with the help of the fickle tastemaker Andrew Jackson Downing. Although a New Yorker at heart, Downing was well acquainted with New England and had repeatedly praised the beauty of Deerfield, Northampton, and other Yankee towns. Although much of Downing's work focused on the domestic environment, instructing America's emergent bourgeoisie to create tasteful and educative home grounds, he was also interested in the design of civic space. By the time he died in 1852, Downing had written extensively on the improvement of towns and villages, urging with missionary zeal the planting of street trees.[26]

In addition to his probable influence on Orville Dewey, Downing may have helped shape the Laurel Hill Association. Its founder, Mary Hopkins, would have been familiar with Downing's work through her brother Albert, a professor at Williams College who founded a Landscape Gardening Society there several years earlier. It is impossible that such a group could have failed to know his work. The minutes of the Laurel Hill Association often refer explicitly to Downing.[27] Still, there is no conclusive evidence linking the early Berkshire efforts to him. Moreover, caution must be exercised in attributing every stirring of village beautification in this period to Downing. In light of his later fame, it is easy to project backward Downing's influence. Downing was as much a product of the new environmental sensibility as he was one of its most capable advocates. Ideas about improvement were in the air at a very early date in New England: the *New England Farmer* had published tracts on the improvement of home and village when Downing was still a boy.

Nevertheless, Downing's impact on his age—and on the village improvement movement in general—was profound. Few men in the first half of the nineteenth century had a better grasp of the emergent interest in spatial beauty, or were better equipped to give it direction. Downing was the first advocate of environmental design to reach a wide audience, and he did so at precisely a moment when members of the growing middle class in America began seeking guidance on the tasteful appointment of their grounds. Possessed of an evangelism and moral certitude all but absent in the design professions today, Downing was an "apostle of taste" who exerted an immense influence on the appearance of American space in the antebellum period.[28]

Downing was born in 1815 to a nurseryman in Newburgh, New York, and he took a keen interest in horticulture and landscape architecture at an early age. He studied the works of major British theoreticians and practitioners of landscape gardening, and was able to adapt their insights to the American scene. While still in his teens, Downing began writing for various agricultural and popular journals, including the *New England Farmer*. The essays led to a larger work titled *A Treatise on the Theory and Practice of Landscape Gardening Adapted to North America*. Published in 1841, the *Treatise* was an immediate success, establishing its twenty-six-year-old author as an authority on matters of landscape design in the United States.

Although the domestic realm was his first love, Downing also wrote on the subject of civic improvement. In a series of essays published between 1847 and his death in 1852, he implored his readers to look beyond the bounds of their own property and beautify the shared public environment. To Downing, the unimproved village was a blight on the national landscape, but one that could easily be transformed into a thing of beauty by planting trees. "The first duty of an inhabitant of forlorn neighborhoods," he wrote in the *Horticulturalist* in 1849, "is to use all possible influence to have the *streets planted with trees*." The naked aspect of so many towns in America was not due to "want of means" but "simply from a poverty of ideas, and a dormant sense of the enjoyment to be derived from orderly, tasteful and agreeable dwellings and streets."[29]

Downing believed that planting street trees improved not only towns but also the moral fiber of their people. "Indeed," he wrote, "a village whose streets are bare of trees, ought to be looked upon as in a condition not less pitiable than a community without a schoolmaster, or a teacher of religion; for certain it is, when the affections are so dull, and the domestic virtues so blunt, that men do not care how their own homes and villages look, they care very little for fulfilling any moral obligations not made compulsory by the strong arm of the law."[30]

In his evangelism for planting trees, Downing repeatedly invoked New England—particularly the older valley towns of the Housatonic and Connecticut valleys—as the standard bearer for spatial beauty. "Show us a Massachusetts village, adorned by its avenues of elms," he wrote, "and you also place before us the fact, that it is there where order, good character, and virtuous deportment most of all adorn the lives and daily conduct of its people."[31] Deerfield, Northampton, Stockbridge, and other towns were touchstones in Downing's evangelism of the verdant village. In these places, "the verdure of the loveliest elms waves like grand lines of giant and graceful plumes above the house-tops, giving an air of rural beauty, that speaks louder for the good habits of the inhabitants, than the pleasant sound of an hundred church bells."[32]

The sylvan richness of New England valley towns more than compensated for an architecture that was often "meagre and unworthy of notice." The glory of the main street was not its buildings but its "avenue of elms . . . positively delightful to behold." Alas, New York did not fare well in comparison: "When we contrast with these lovely resting places for the eye, embowered with avenues of elms, gracefully drooping like fountains of falling water . . . some of the uncared for towns and villages in our own State, we are almost forced to believe that the famous common schools of New England teach the aesthetics of art, and that the beauty of shade-trees is the care of especial professorships."[33]

Downing duly noted the New England partiality for the American elm. The prescient Yankees had "perhaps accidentally" followed one of the most important principles of improvement: they avoided novelty in selecting trees for their streets, and chose a species "such as the soil and climate of the place will bring to the highest perfection." In planting the American elm, New Englanders heeded the spirit of the land, the genius of the place. This was, in Downing's view, particularly the case in the Connecticut Valley: "The Elm is, we think, no where seen in more majesty, greater luxuriance, or richer beauty, than in the valley of the Connecticut; and it is because the soil is so truly congenial to it, that the elm-adorned streets of the villages there, elicit so much admiration. They are not only well planted with trees—but with a kind of tree which attains its greatest perfection there."[34]

Downing applauded (and thereby publicized) the activities of improvement associations, such as Northampton's Ornamental Tree Society, "whose business and pleasure it is to turn dusty lanes and bald highways into alleys and avenues of coolness and verdure."[35] He lauded the Rockingham Farmers' Club of Exeter, New Hampshire, and reprinted a passage from one of its reports: "If you would prevent a restless spirit, if you would save him from that lowest species of idolatry, 'the love of money,' and teach him to 'love what is lovely,' adorn your dwellings, your places of worship, your schoolhouses, your streets and public squares, with trees."[36] That a farmer's club in New Hampshire should eloquently express the essence of village improvement suggests that Downing was often preaching to the choir—at least in New England.

Downing urged those inhabitants of "graceless villages" to become "apostles of taste" who would labor to convert the aesthetic heathen. He understood that doing so would not be easy; the crusader would need to endure the "sneers and derision from the ignorant and prejudiced." But he remained confident that once "the first half dozen trees" had been set out, other townsfolk would join the effort—even if for no other reason than competitiveness ("the principle of imitation will never allow a Yankee to be outdone by his neighbor"). The trees, too, would evangelize; "it is quite extraordinary," related Downing, "what sermons they will preach."[37]

> Their luxuriant leafy arms, swaying and waving to and fro, will make more convincing gestures than any member of congress or stump speaker, and if there is any love of nature dormant in the dusty hearts of the villagers, we prophecy that in a very short time there will be such a general yearning after green trees, that the whole place will become a bower of freshness and verdure.[38]

Forming an organization like the Elm Tree or Laurel Hill associations was the most effective path to spatial beauty. Backed by "the great weight of numbers," such groups could convert (by peer pressure if need be) those unconvinced of the benefits of improvement. And if the "zeal of the society" could not shame the philistines into action, the "silent and irresistible influence of sylvan beauty" would, in time, do the job.[39]

"We heartily commend," wrote Downing in 1847, a "plan of *Social Planting Reform*, to every desolate, leafless, and repulsive town and village in the country."

> There can scarcely be one, where there are not *three* persons of taste and spirit enough to organize such a society; and once fairly in operation, its members will never cease to congratulate themselves on the beauty and comfort they have produced. Every tree which they plant, and which grows up in after years into a giant trunk and canopy of foliage, will be a better monument (though it may bear no lying inscription) than many an unmeaning obelisk of marble or granite.[40]

Although Andrew Jackson Downing did not conceive village improvement in New England, he was its most effective advocate. Downing helped marshal a series of isolated initiatives into a popular movement, spreading the message of improvement to a large and receptive audience throughout the region. By praising the earlier accomplishments of those verdant villages in the Connecticut River valley, he helped establish a vision of spatial beauty that placed the American elm at center stage. For Downing, no tree could match this one for the beautification of towns. He agreed heartily with the conclusion reached by the Rockingham Farmers' Club: "Above all others, for the street, the *Elm* is to be preferred. For beauty, gracefulness, *grandeur* even, it has no equal in New England."[41]

The Manufacture of Identity

After about 1850, other factors began influencing the spread of village improvement in New England—accelerating both the emulation of local "model villages" and the embrace of ideas about improvement preached by Downing. These had the effect of further spreading the ideal of the elm-tufted town throughout the region. Spatial beauty was once valued solely as an aesthetic and moral imperative; now economics joined the picture, for improvement might be an antidote to forces that had begun to weaken the economy of rural New England. By the 1850s, New England's agricultural economy was in decline. The depression first affected the remote hill towns of Vermont and New Hampshire, which were far from urban markets and cursed with thin and stony soil. These literally "went downhill," as inhabitants moved closer to valleys served by the rail lines.[42] But decline soon visited the venerable towns of southern New England too. The sources of this decline were manifold and complex.

During the Jacksonian period the United States expanded vigorously. By 1840, settlement had pushed far beyond New England and opened vast tracts of land in western New York, Pennsylvania, and Ohio. The new territory's fertile agricultural land was far superior to the meager soils of New England (even the once-rich soils of the Connecticut Valley had become depleted). With the completion of the Erie Canal in 1830 and the extension of the railroads, western farms began flooding eastern markets with cheap and plentiful produce. The Yankee cultivator was faced with withering competition. If he could not quickly retool and find a profitable niche market—such as dairy farming or fruit growing—he would be ruined.

His children often chose to forgo farming altogether. The glimmer of urban life in Boston, Springfield, New Haven, or New York lured many a Yankee youth away from the family farm. So did new economic opportunities made possible by industrialization. The burgeoning mills at Lowell and Lawrence in Massachusetts were employing hundreds of New England farmgirls by the 1840s. What ensued was a "brain drain," in which many of New England's best and brightest left the countryside. The outmigration, a trickle at first, increased steadily in the decade before the Civil War.

Decline baffled the rural elite. Like a parasite, distant forces seemed to be sapping New England of its very life—its prosperity as well as its children. In its wake, New England's verdant landscape, cultivated steadily for two hundred years, began to show signs of decline. It looked increasingly tattered and threadbare. In 1857, Orville Dewey was alarmed to detect evidence of this decline in the towns of the Housatonic: "What is it that is coming over our New England villages, that looks like deterioration and running down?" he asked. "Is our life going out of us to enrich the great West?"[43] Once considered simply a failure of "taste" on the part of the citizenry, an unkempt or disheveled townscape now evoked something more frightening, like sickness or even death.

In this light, environmental design became a tool with which to check the processes of decline. Perhaps young people would be less lured by the glamour and excitement of the city, reasoned many a town father, if their hometowns were more beautiful. Through improvement, a village might "instill in the youth that love of beauty and morality which would enable him to withstand the attraction of urban wealth and vice."[44] At the same time, it was understood that the verdant village might have something to offer the city dweller, too—many of whom had themselves hailed from New England farms and villages. Perhaps spatial beauty would attract affluent vacationers from the very cities that were draining the flower of rural youth.

City people did indeed wish to summer in the shade of Yankee elms. By the 1860s, tourism had come to rural New England. Successful middle-class inhabitants of Boston and New York, often impelled by a nostalgic longing for the places of their youth, began "summering" in Vermont, New Hampshire, and western Massachusetts. They sought respite from industrial urbanization, and an assurance that the lifestyle and landscape they once knew still survived. Rapid social transformation and the influx of immigrants during this period appeared to threaten the old hegemony of Anglo-Saxon New England. That culture was believed to persist in the countryside. And where it did not, it could be created.

As Dona Brown has written, a process of "sentimentalization" began to occur, out of which would emerge "a mythic region called Old New England—rural, preindustrial, and ethnically 'pure.'" City dwellers sought places that matched an "imagined world of pastoral beauty"—which nostalgia had constructed—the ideal New England village of yesterday.[45] And towns—desperate for income—struggled to meet these expectations. To do so, they would often manufacture an identity that never existed. This involved making certain that the church was gleaming white (regardless of what color it may have been), and that the common was a manicured showpiece. In Rutland, Vermont, providing such an ensemble required outright fabrication: its village improvement society "exploited the image of the New England village so literally," writes Richard Berenberg, "that they dug up a church yard cemetery to create a village green, which, through the caprice of history, they had never possessed."[46]

Even more central to the expected image of the archetypal Yankee town were elm trees. Those towns that had not planted elms for their own purposes earlier did so now—and with desperation. They were competing with places that had inherited a rich sylvan estate from earlier improvements. Villages embowered with elms, such as Stockbridge, Deerfield, Northfield, Longmeadow, Litchfield, and Northampton, were again emulated—this time not as paragons of aesthetic beauty but because such places were attracting a lion's share of the summer vacation trade. Elm trees were understood to be an essential feature in the commodified image of the rural Yankee town. Without an elm-shaded common and bosky streets, such a village would be bypassed and left to rot.

"Mistress of the Scene"

The verdant village, central to New England's identity and self-concept, attracted more than just summering merchants from the city. Village elms moved Yankee pens, and drew the attention of some of New England's most perceptive writers. Henry David Thoreau wrote eloquently of the elms of his native Concord, Massachusetts. He often found himself favoring tree over townsmen. "I have seen many a collection of stately elms," he confided to his *Journal* in January 1856, "which better deserved to be represented at the General Court than the manikins beneath—than the barroom and victualling cellar and groceries they overshadowed." Elms may have been set out by villagers, but they towered—literally and figuratively—above these mortal souls. "I find that into my idea of the village," he wrote, "has entered more of the elm than of the human being." Indeed, for Thoreau, the elms were "worth many a political borough"—and certainly more than most politicians. "The poor human representative of his party sent out from beneath their shade," he wrote, "will not suggest a tithe of the dignity, the true nobleness and comprehensivness of view, the sturdiness and independence, and the serene beneficence that [the elms] do. They look from township to township. A fragment of their bark is worth the backs of all the politicians in the union."[47]

The autumnal elm, with its "early and golden maturity," made a particularly strong impression on the Concord naturalist. "It would be worth the while," he wrote in *Excursions*, "to set out these trees, if only for their autumnal value."

"Think of these great yellow canopies or parasols held over our heads and houses by the mile together," urged Thoreau, "making the village all one and compact —and *ulmarium*, which is at the same time a nursery of men! And then how gently and unobserved they drop their burden and let in the sun when it is wanted, their leaves not heard when they fall on our roofs and in our streets; and thus the village parasol is shut up and put away!"[48]

The great fall of elm leaves in October transformed Concord into "a scene of a great harvest-home," with its paths and walks strewn with the summer's spent array. In their form and color, the great yellow masses reminded Thoreau of sheaves of wheat; it was "as if the harvest had indeed come to the village itself." Now, he suggested, "we might expect to find some maturity and *flavor* in the thoughts of the villagers at last." Would there be, he pondered, an "answering ripeness" in the lives of the men who lived beneath these glorious harvest domes? He found it untenable that such beauty could be paired with mean and illiberal thoughts. "Under those bright rustling yellow piles," wrote Thoreau, "how can any crudity or greeness of thought or act prevail?"[49]

As he watched a farmer disappear beneath the village elms, his wagon creaking with the burden of a bumper crop, Thoreau was tempted to follow the man to the granary, perchance to witness a "husking of thoughts, now dry and ripe, and ready to be separated from their integuments." But he turned away, knowing it would be "chiefly husks and little thought . . . for, as you sow, so shall you reap." For all his seriousness of purpose, however, Thoreau retained a playful, rhapsodic voice; the Concord "ulmarium" made him a child again. Standing beneath a cluster of October elms "warm from their September oven," Thoreau imagined that he stood "within a ripe pumpkin-rind"; "I feel as mellow as if I were the pulp," he quipped, "though I may be somewhat stringy and seedy withal."[50]

Henry Ward Beecher was another literate Yankee who labored to fathom the village elm. Beecher, whose father, Lyman, had long ago inspired tree planting in Litchfield, could not imagine the New England village without the elm. A leading clergymen of the nineteenth century, Beecher was also an amateur horticulturist who in 1859 wrote a small book titled *Plain and Pleasant Talk About Fruits, Flowers, and Farming*. In it he proposed that "the great main-street of every village should be lined with White [American] Elms, set at distances of fifty feet." Like most village improvers, Beecher concurred with the prevailing practice of planting exclusively one species along thoroughfares. "It is better for *effect*," he argued, "that each street . . . have *one kind* of forest tree, so that an avenue of similar trees be formed." And in Beecher's estimation, no tree matched the American elm for this purpose.[51]

It was for a later work of fiction that Beecher became truly famous—his 1867 novel *Norwood; or Village Life in New England*. So popular was the book that a town near Boston actually renamed itself "Norwood." In the book, Beecher described a mythic village perched on a hill overlooking the "fat bottom-lands" of the Connecticut. Peering out from under its shade trees, "you will say that no fairer village glistens in the sunlight, or nestles under arching elms!"[52] The "largeness of moral feeling" and "subtle sympathy with Nature" that characterized its people was manifest in its landscape, too, for the entire length of Norwood's main street was lined with the "peculiar glory" of New England—the American elm.

For Beecher, the elm was so central to his construction of this ideal town that he spent much of the novel's introduction discussing the tree. It remains one of the greatest soliloquies ever penned to an American tree. "No town can fail of beauty," Beecher proclaimed, "though its walks were gutters, and its houses hovels, if venerable trees make magnificent colonnades along its streets. Of all trees, no other unites, in the same degree, majesty and beauty, grace and grandeur, as the American Elm." While there may be "single spots" more beautiful in other lands, wrote Beecher, "such a series of villages over such a breadth of country, amidst so much beauty of scenery . . . cannot elsewhere be found upon the globe." It was a beauty largely borne of trees—and elms ruled the scene: "The Elms of New England! They are as much a part of her beauty as the columns of the Parthenon were the glory of its architecture."[53]

But not all observers were so seduced. Henry James, a far more discriminating critic writing a generation after Beecher, was not one to be swayed by coquettish towns, however lush. By the late nineteenth century, many New England towns had slipped quietly into decline, in spite of valiant efforts to attract tourism. The telltale signs of poverty and hardship were often obscured—by the very elms set out in a bid for beauty. So magnificent were these trees by the turn of the century—so superb a decoy—that they effectively concealed the squalor of their depleted communities. To James, the great columns were a seductive facade, a specious veil of verdure. Elms lend an air of Potemkin subterfuge to the New England scene. "Having spoke of them as 'elm-shaded,'" he wrote of New England's villages in *The American Scene*, "you have said so much about them that little else remains."

> It is but a question, throughout, of the quantity, the density, of their shade; often so thick and ample, from May to November, that their function, in the social, in the economic, order would seem on occasion to consist solely of their being passive to that effect. To note the latter, accordingly, to praise it, to respond to its appeal for admiration, practically represents, as you pass beneath the great feathery arches, the only comment that may be addressed to the scene.[54]

The American Scene was written when Henry James returned, in 1904, to the United States after a twenty-year European hiatus. It recorded his impressions of

Boys in "The Street" lined with elms, Deerfield, Massachusetts, before 1877 (Courtesy of the Society for the Preservation of New England Antiquities)

a national landscape profoundly transformed in the interim. The upstart cities he knew as a young man were now great metropolitan centers, teeming with immigrants whose tongues and customs baffled him. But the once prosperous towns and villages of rural New England seemed to be moving in the opposite direction, vanishing into the deep shade of forest trees. In town after town, James encountered a solemn march of elms. "The scene," he wrote, "is everywhere the same; whereby tribute is always ready and easy, and you are spared all shocks of surprise and saved any extravagance of discrimination."

> These communities stray so little from the type, that you often ask yourself by what sign or difference you know one from the other. The goodly elms, on either side of the large straight "street," rise from their grassy margin in double, ever and anon in triple, file; the white paint, on wooden walls, amid open dooryards, reaffirms itself eternally behind them—though hanging back, during the best of the season, with a sun-checkered, "amusing" vagueness; while the great verdurous vista, the high canopy of meeting branches, has the air of consciously playing the trick and carrying off the picture.[55]

Of course, it was during summer that the subterfuge was most effective, when the elms were richly draped with leaves. The veil of verdure was at its peak, conveniently, when the towns of New England received their city visitors. Return in winter, however, during "the months of the naked glare," and the facade was gone. Now the "white paint looks dead and dingy against the snow, the poor dear old white paint—immemorial, ubiquitous, save as venturing into brown or yellow."[56]

James allowed that some of the wealthier towns in Massachusetts and Connecticut did possess architectural distinction to match the splendor of the elms. He found Farmington, Connecticut, to have a certain aristocratic air, but he stopped short of asserting that it "might brave undismayed the absolute removal of the mantle of charity"—the verdant screen of elms. Even with its confident old homes, standing proudly along the street ("in the manner of mature and just slightly-reduced gentlewomen seated against a wall at an evening party"), the "great elm-gallery there struck me as not less than elsewhere essentially mistress of the scene." And the mistress betrayed few secrets, even to so perceptive an observer as Henry James. The New England village street, with its silent march of elms, remained inscrutable, and James found that, in the end, he had done no more than lift "the smallest corner of this particular veil."[57]

Most observers were, however, content to let the veil remain. In planting the American elm so extensively in their towns and villages (and regardless of motivation), New Englanders forged one of the archetypal and most enduring images of American place—town common resplendent with overarching elms, and "Elm Street" flanked with sylvan loggia. What had once been an occasional feature in the landscape had become one of the most essential elements of the Yankee scene. As poet Nathaniel Parker Willis put it, New England had become a realm of "ten thousand princely elms."[58] The tree—and its eponymous street—had become the quintessence of Yankee space.

6

CITY OF ELMS

The muse of improvement visited cities as well, and not far behind was its tree-planting handmaiden. At Cambridge, New Haven, Portland, and Springfield the pursuit of spatial beauty often antedated work in smaller communities. "Tree societies" in the larger towns and cities emerged in the 1830s and 1840s from the same longing for civic beauty that produced the village improvement movement. As early as 1844, Keene, New Hampshire, had a Forest Tree Society, organized to plant elms on its main commercial street. At Portsmouth, New Hampshire, a similar group was active before 1850; there, elms had been "extensively planted in all our principal streets, by the public spirit of individuals in some cases, but more generally by the Portsmouth Tree Society." In Massachusetts, citizens of Springfield organized in the 1840s to plant elms on Federal Street, reserving "special days in which to turn out and transplant them from the woods in the northeastern portion of the city."[1]

The Urbanity of Improvement

That cityfolk should be at the vanguard of spatial beautification is hardly surprising. After all, the "improving impulse" was largely cosmopolitan in origin. It flowed from the same fountainhead of urban reform that yielded efforts, in the 1830s and 1840s, to combat intemperance, make asylums more humane, secure women's suffrage, and abolish slavery.[2] Nearly all such initiatives first stirred to life among the progressive clerisy of northern cities such as Cambridge, Boston, Hartford, and New York.

The urban pedigree of tree culture and nature appreciation in general—a seeming paradox indeed—was expressed in an 1828 Portland *Yankee* editorial. In the essay, John Neal blasted those who would fell trees and clear the land of "its proud, and beautiful, and *protecting* growth." He took particular aim at those who lived closest to the soil, whom he expected to be stewards of nature's bounty. If "they who are bred up in the country" did not recognize the value of trees, asked Neal, "who should?" The answer was clear: "They who do *not* live in the country — they who do *not* live among them — they who are *not* always at war with nature; in other words, the people of towns and cities. To them, there is no luxury like green trees — no wealth like the wealth of the overshadowing oak, the enormous elm." Indeed, "If you could transplant a few of the forest trees of the neighborhood, into such a city as New-York, or Baltimore, or Philadelphia, or Boston," Neal suggested, "you would make it the most desirable place of residence on earth." "What a luxury" the trees would constitute. "What a guarantee for health; what a magnificent embellishment for the palaces, and houses, and shops of a large town!"[3]

The urbanity of improvement may be read at the village end as well. As we have seen, village improvement after 1850 was often a response to largely urban forces of social, political, and economic change. Small towns struggling to retain a sense of self-respect in the face of growing urban power used environmental design as a means of keeping their sons and daughters from wandering off to Boston, Lowell, or New York. Once the main task of tree planting was accomplished, improvement societies often sought to provide a range of urban amenities, from paved streets to streetlights, in the hope that such modern accessories might take the rustic edge off their town and diminish somewhat the allure of the metropolis.

In cities, improvement and elm planting carried a different set of implications. To the urbanite, the problem was one of lost contact with the natural world and a diminution of "rural values" considered vital to one's wellness and moral equilibrium. If the village saw in the elm essentially urban values of grace, beauty, and spatial sophistication, the city saw in it a keepsake of nature and the vanishing rural landscape. Elms evoked the pastoral New England countryside, and promised to transpose its grace and charms to the heart of the city.

The meaning of elms in the urban environment differed even in the context of a single community as it evolved over time. This was especially the case in the latter half of the nineteenth century. As cities endured industrialization and rapid urban growth, the act of planting a tree took on a whole new meaning. The fluid symbolism of the curbside elm was well expressed at Keene, New Hampshire. Keene's identity shifted as it evolved from village to city, a story that can be extracted from accounts of efforts to improve the town common and plant elms along the main commercial street. In each period of the community's development, elms represented different things to the people of Keene—from rural stultification to the quintessence of urbanity.

The first stirrings of organized improvement in Keene took place as early as 1788, when elms were set out along Main Street. The fruits of this early collective action did not last long, however. That May the *New Hampshire Recorder* lamented that "a number of the trees . . . were girdled by some unknown profligate"—an "outrage against good taste." Why exactly these sylvan innocents were slaughtered is not clear, but it seems to have had to do with the image the trees were projecting about the town to outsiders.[4]

Other improvement efforts followed, and by the 1840s a Forest Tree Society was founded "to fence in and ornament a small central portion of the Common," and to plant elms on the streets of the nascent city. At its annual meeting in September 1844, the society reported having planted 140 elms on streets the previous spring, and it had designs for the common and center of town.[5] Not all agreed that planting elms in the business district of the growing city was necessary or even wise. Merchants were bitterly opposed to the tree planting, fearing that the elms would conceal their signboards and shopfronts. Others opposed the greening of the common because the trees would limit its use as a training field by the militia, or as a marketplace by local farmers.[6]

But even more revealing of Keene's evolving self-image was the objection that the trees would "give the town a countrified look," causing outsiders to "cease to believe that we were metropolitan in fact, or in aspiration."[7] No longer village and not yet full-fledged city, Keene residents feared their city's march toward urbanity might be hobbled by elms. Faced with protest, the Forest Tree Society abandoned its work, and no further elm plantings took place. By 1850, however, Keene was rapidly on its way to becoming a city. Its self-image changed in turn, and so did its attitude toward elms.

The new day did not come about without some guerrilla action on the part of the Forest Tree Society. On a June morning in 1851, two men and a team of oxen appeared at daybreak on the common. Within several hours they had plowed a large circular area to ready it as lawn. At the center the Society men placed a single elm, "as a test of the question whether an enclosure with trees would be tolerated or not." Convinced that the sapling elm would soon be uprooted in protest, the planters made no effort to even water the transplant. Yet, in spite of some grousing, the vanguard tree stood unmolested. The elms had prevailed.[8]

By the fall, an "almost universal demand that the Park should be enlarged and enclosed" underscored a sea change in attitudes toward trees. More money was

Central Square, Keene, New Hampshire (Courtesy of the Historical Society of Cheshire County)

raised and more elms were set out on the common—later renamed Central Square—and the surrounding streets. Merchants discovered that trade did not evaporate "on account of the leafy concealment of the signboards."[9] The old fears of being considered rubes by the outside world vanished; the elms, no longer a threat to Keene's cosmopolitan aspirations, were left in peace. Now confidently urban, Keene could accommodate a keepsake of the countryside smack in its business district. Ironically, elm trees eventually became the city's mark of distinction. When Keene was named a municipality in 1874, it was already known throughout New England as New Hampshire's Elm City.

The Philanthropy of Elms

As the verdant village was largely the fruit of private initiative, so too was the city of elms—at least at the beginning. Antedating the emergence of tree societies and associations, it was the "public spirited individual" who pioneered the beautification of city streets in New England. Long before tree planting became a sustained municipal activity, philanthropy set out many a curbside elm. Property owners often planted short rows of trees in the ambiguous zone between private yard and public street. Before sidewalks became commonplace, the boundary between public and private was frequently unclear and street margins were commonly annexed de facto by abutting landowners. In most instances this "taking" of the commons was harmless; and, as it often led to the planting of trees, it generally met with public approval. Given that municipalities themselves did little or nothing to green the streets, such private-sector activity was a true benefit.

Examples of sylvan largesse abound in the local histories of nineteenth-century New England. Main Street in Concord, New Hampshire, accumulated its canopy of elms over the course of several decades, contributed by a number of community leaders (whose actions in turn inspired similar acts of generosity). The chain of giving began in 1764, when a short row of public elms was set out by the Reverend Timothy Walker, transplanted from a nearby swamp. Three of the eight original trees survived into the twentieth century, long enough to become part of the urban landscape of the state capital. Soon after the Walker trees, another "noble row of elms" got its start in 1774, the handiwork of Dr. Ebenezer H. Goss. A generation later, Charles Walker planted a row of elms on the west side of Main Street, in front of the mansion he erected in 1802. Hazen Kimball, scion of another leading Concord family, continued the elming of Main Street, as did Samuel A. Kimball, who set out elms in 1818.[10] The piecemeal philanthropy of Concord's "representative men" produced, by the 1860s, a Main Street embowered by more than two hundred elms.[11]

Main Street in Springfield, Massachusetts, owed its earliest elms to the generosity of Joseph Stebbins, a tavernkeeper and Revolutionary officer who "brought the trees from the West Springfield meadows on his back" and, with the help of his two sons, planted them down the center of the main street. As one chronicler later recounted, the Stebbins elms were for generations "the pride and admiration of people entering the city."[12] Boston Common gained most of its early trees through a series of private initiatives. The first formal plantings occurred as early as 1723, when English elms were set out in a row along today's Tremont Street.[13] Fifty years later, John Lucas and Oliver Smith raised money to improve the commons; with "liberty granted" by the selectmen, the two men planted another row of trees along Tremont Street. These eventually formed a grand promenade known as the Great Mall.[14]

An enterprising philanthropist would often enlist the support of his fellows. In 1829, Major Ingersoll of Springfield led an effort to plant elms in Court Square, at the very center of the city; he circulated "a subscription to meet this expense" among Springfield's men of record. The Ingersoll planting helped earn Springfield its title "City of Trees."[15] In a similar initiative at Concord, New Hampshire, a column of elms along the schoolhouse lot was set out by John Abbot in 1832, paid for by public subscription.[16] Such sylvan largesse on the part of the citizenry was often encouraged by community leaders and sometimes by the municipality itself.

In Portsmouth, New Hampshire, in the 1790s, the citizens were "stirred up" by the governor to plant trees "in all our most public streets." Though Lombardy poplars were planted at first, these were eventually replaced with elms.[17] In Portland, the *Eastern Argus*, one of the city's newspapers of record, urged its readers in 1831 to plant trees in "the front of their dwellings." "To us," offered the *Argus*, "there is no spectacle more cheering than to witness rows of trees, systematically arranged along the streets, throwing out their fragrance to the air. The expense which will enable the gratification of this commendable taste, is quite trifling; and, when we reflect upon the advantages which are known to be derived to the health, by trees taking up a portion of the deleterious gas with which the atmosphere is charged, we would think none, who can afford it, would deny themselves the luxury."[18]

Unfortunately, most Yankee elm benefactors have long been forgotten. Unlike buildings, trees often leave no paper trail, and the origins of most have eluded the pens of chroniclers and antiquarians. Springfield possessed a magnificent stock of mature elms as early as 1840, yet even its fastidious antiquarians were stumped as to who the original planters were. "It is to be sincerely regretted," opined one writer in 1891, "that the names of those benefactors . . . who have made their avenues and streets so beautiful by planting noble elms to cast grateful, luxuriant shade upon the coming generations, are unknown."[19] But not all were forgotten. Some philanthropist-planters planted so well that their actions were immortalized. No finer example exists than James Hillhouse, father of the City of Elms.

Hillhouse of New Haven

With the exception of its Puritan founder John Davenport, no man played a greater role in shaping the identity of New Haven than James Hillhouse. His extensive elm-planting campaign transformed the city into one of the most celebrated in nineteenth-century America. A boyhood friend of the patriot Nathan Hale and a commander of the Governor's Guard during the Revolution, Hillhouse became one of Connecticut's leading men in the early decades of independence. He represented Connecticut in the United States Senate and for fifty years was the treasurer of Yale College. But it was as a planter of trees that Hillhouse is best remembered.

American elms had been planted in New Haven as early as 1685, when William Cooper contributed a pair of elm saplings to the Reverend James Pierpont's new home. But it was not until 1759 that more coordinated efforts took place.

Portrait of James Hillhouse by John Vanderlyn (Courtesy of the Yale University Art Gallery)

That year, Jared Eliot observed that "in New Haven they have planted a range of trees all around the market place and secured them from the ravages of beasts"—an undertaking he commended as "truly generous and laudable."[20] And although its benefactors have long been forgotten, the 1759 planting set an early example for arboreal philanthropy in New Haven. The trees grew rapidly, and they may even have helped save the town during the Revolutionary War.

Elm-lined Temple Street in New Haven, Connecticut, c. 1865 (Courtesy of the New Haven Colony Historical Society)

According to legend, General George Garth, commander of the British forces invading New Haven, refrained from razing the town in July 1779 because he was so moved by its sylvan beauty; "it is too pretty to burn," he reportedly muttered, and led his men away.[21]

In the aftermath of the war, New Haven strove to become a center of commerce and culture, competing with Boston, New York, and Philadelphia. With incorporation as a city in 1784 a renewed enthusiasm for public improvement swept through New Haven, fueled by a "consciousness that the place had entered upon a new order." Lacking the resources to underwrite capital projects, the upstart city appealed instead to the largesse of its leading families. One of the new city's first official acts was to urge "any gentleman who might agree to defray the expense" to oversee the fencing of the Green.[22] James Hillhouse had himself urged the city to set aside money for improvements, but he soon realized it could not afford to do so. Hillhouse decided to raise the necessary funds himself by appealing for public subscription in the spring of 1786. The document, signed by seventeen of New Haven's leading men, raised money specifically for the planting of a "Row of Elms" on the lower part of the Green.[23]

Several years later, Hillhouse initiated an even more ambitious planting campaign, this time focusing on the newly built Temple Street. Construction of this thoroughfare, which passed through the Green itself, had been authorized by the Common Council in the spring of 1787, at Hillhouse's request. Following its completion in 1792, Hillhouse planted elms along the entire length of the thoroughfare, set out at forty-foot intervals.[24] The initiative was not entirely selfless, for the original northern extension of Temple Street (later renamed Hillhouse Avenue) ran through extensive lands owned and later developed by Hillhouse himself. The planter's philanthropy was not without a keen business edge. After Hillhouse returned from Washington around 1810, he did indeed develop much of this property, including one of the city's most exclusive residential districts.

All told, the plantings led by Hillhouse between 1786 and 1800 established the trees by which New Haven would eventually achieve world fame as the City of Elms. The era itself became known as the Great Planting.[25] Hillhouse "set the little town . . . agog by his labors," wrote antiquarian Henry Howe. Children who lent a hand in the Great Planting would, decades later, themselves be celebrated for their role in greening the city. The roster of young tree-planters included a future president of Yale College and justice of the United States Supreme Court—one Henry Baldwin, who often boasted of his youth, "I held many an elm while Hillhouse shoveled in the earth."[26]

In the decades following the Great Planting, Hillhouse continued to serve as nursemaid and steward of the city's elms, replacing saplings that had withered or failed to thrive.[27] As he got older, he often planted larger and larger trees—acknowledging, perhaps, his dwindling days. In 1810, Hillhouse supervised the planting of a series of immense elms on the west side of Temple Street. Each more than a foot in diameter and forty feet tall, shorn of branches, the trees reminded Henry Howe of "huge forking poles with attached roots." Remarkably, the ungainly transplants burst into verdure. By 1883 they had become "monarchs trees under whose grateful shades [we] are but too happy to walk."[28]

The planting of elms in New England cities must be situated historically and placed beside earlier efforts both here and abroad to vegetate the urban environment. In Europe, the practice of planting urban trees has a long, rich pedigree, though it was neither as ancient nor as universal a practice as one might expect. Moreover, *sponsorship* of the urban forest was radically different. Where town-and-city trees in the United States were the eclectic handiwork of private initiative, the tree-lined boulevards and avenues of Europe were more aristocratic in origin. The Yankee urban forest was a democratic project. The trees that adorned Europe's great cities were, on the other hand, public improvements bestowed by king, pope, or emperor—noblesse oblige with an arboreal twist.

Before the seventeenth century, few European streets or public squares were lined with trees. There was little need for urban trees because cities were compact and the countryside was readily accessible. Buildings were often tightly packed, providing the shelter and shade that trees would supply (the urban fabric was usually too dense to accommodate vegetation in any case). Renaissance principles of city planning celebrated the controlled forms of classical architecture and had little use for trees in the creation of well-proportioned urban space. What nature did exist in the city was generally confined to enclosed private gardens and interior courts.[29]

This began to change in France in the early seventeenth century. There, the allée of the Italian Renaissance garden became adapted for urban use. Allées first appeared in semipublic French royal parks such as the Tuileries, where they were used for promenade, strolling, and games. The Renaissance allée served as the immediate antecedent of the urban boulevards built in Paris in the seventeenth century. By 1615, Amsterdam's flourishing merchants enjoyed the shade of elm trees lining the city's new canals, a form that was widely emulated throughout the Netherlands. Other European cities placed trees along riverbanks, quays, and harbors.[30]

The emergence of new urban games among the aristocracy led to the development, in Italy, France, and England, of tree-lined malls and *cours*—"recreational variants of the garden allée." Known as *le jeu du mail* or *palmail* in France (pall mall in England), the new game involved hitting a ball with a wooden mallet across an open expanse of lawn, a playing field that was often adorned with rows of trees. At first, malls appeared within the confines of private estates, but in time they were built as quasi-public amenities. The first public mall in Paris was built alongside the city's walls by 1600. Berlin's Unter den Linden and London's Pall Mall, in place by the 1650s, both derive from this tradition.[31]

Another pastime among the European elite, pleasure riding in carriages, led to the creation of the Cours de la Reine along the Seine. Inspired by Italian precedent—the Corso of Florence—the Parisian carriageway was built by Marie de Medici in 1616, and featured a "new type of quadruple allée." The form was emulated elsewhere in France (the Cours de Vincennes, also in Paris, was open to anyone who could afford a carriage), as well as in other European cities, such as Madrid, which built its Prado in the 1650s. The cours hold particular significance for the evolution of the tree-lined street, for, as Henry W. Lawrence has argued, it "transformed the garden allée into a place for vehicles, albeit one not yet integrated into a city's street system."[32]

In the French countryside, the chief post roads were often lined with trees beginning in the sixteenth century, a practice that led to more formal planting of rural avenues on the peripheries of cities—often in association with large hunting estates or leading to rural chateaux. These "exterior avenues" served as a model for later large-scale urban design interventions by Baron Eugène Haussmann, Adolphe Alphand, and others, and they often became tree-lined urban thoroughfares themselves as they were engulfed by subsequent development.[33]

Trees adorned the medieval ramparts of a number of northern European cities, or they were planted in place of the ramparts as the cities expanded. The origin of the term *boulevard* can itself be traced to the demolition, ordered by Louis XIV in 1670, of the old Parisian city walls. In place of the ramparts, tree-lined promenades were constructed, radically altering the meaning of *boulevard* (in its medieval origins the word, related to *bulwark*, referred to the elevated section of a city's perimeter defenses). Because they were on the edge of town, the sylvan boulevards were little used at first, but by the late eighteenth century they had become among the most fashionable thoroughfares in Paris. Napoleonic conquest in the early nineteenth century distributed the promenade form; under the auspices of Napoléon I, promenades and boulevards were built in Brussels, Düsseldorf, Rome, and Turin.[34]

The systematic planting of roadside elms in the countryside became common in eighteenth-century England, derived from French practice.[35] Similar use of the tree on estates, in formal columns flanking avenues, was introduced by the French landscape designer Claude Mollet in the seventeenth century, although evidence suggests even earlier native efforts.[36] English landscape gardeners Henry Wise and Charles Bridgman favored the formal use of elms, and Bridgman designed the great elm-lined radiating avenues at Kensington Palace Gardens. Batty Langley in 1728 offered advice on preparing elms "to transplant out in Avenues, Walks, Parks, Hedge-rows, etc.," and he considered the "beautiful Verdure, and delightful Shade" of the English elm "Encouragement sufficient for us to propagate it as much as possible."[37]

Regardless of species, the apotheosis of the tree-lined street in Europe occurred in France in the mid–nineteenth century. In this period, such improvements as new paving materials, street lighting, drains and sewers, mailboxes, and sidewalks all contributed to a renewal of the street as both infrastructure and civic space. In Paris the Champs-Elysées and the Grandes Boulevards were rebuilt by the comte de Rambuteau in the 1830s, a prelude to the more extensive interventions two decades later under Napoléon III. Providing trees on thoroughfares in the heart of Paris was motivated only partly by aesthetics: they were primarily intended to improve health conditions by providing shade on the newly widened streets and by "removing harmful elements from the miasmas thought at the time to cause diseases," according to Lawrence.[38]

With the rebuilding of Paris by Haussmann and Alphand in the 1850s, the tree-lined street reached its apogee. Paris set a standard for urban renewal elsewhere in Europe and established the tree-lined boulevard as a major element of modern urban design. Even with the new emphasis on trees as a public amenity, the earlier autocratic element did not fully vanish. "The imperial rule of Napoleon III after 1852," writes Lawrence, "found the tree-lined boulevard a fitting expression of both aspects of civic power for a benevolent despot."[39]

The Street Tree in America

In America, benevolent autocracy had little role to play in the evolution of the urban landscape. But then again, neither did trees. Vegetation was largely absent from most American cities before 1850, though there were important exceptions. In 1807 a Territory of Michigan law specified that trees were to be planted on the streets and boulevards of Detroit. A commission charged with the selection of a state capital for Mississippi recommended that streets of the new city be filled every other block with native trees, in part as a means of reducing the threat of fire.[40] John Quincy Adams, sixth president of the United States and a Massachusetts native, planted scores of elms on Pennsylvania Avenue in Washington in the 1820s; earlier efforts to green the young nation's capital had relied on Lombardy poplars.

In Philadelphia and New York trees had been set out on streets from the earliest days of settlement. These were impressive enough to earn the praise of foreign visitors (though such attention may have derived in part from the novelty of these sights on American soil). Philadelphia, founded by William Penn in 1682, had an abundance of verdure from the start (the "green country town" was in fact founded beneath an elm later known as Penn's Treaty Elm). Penn had incorporated a series of public squares in the layout of his town, and the earliest extant plan clearly indicates trees bordering each of these spaces. Houses were provided with sufficient space to accommodate "gardens and orchards," while the main streets were embellished with trees.[41]

By 1818 street trees lined Philadelphia's principal thoroughfares.[42] In that year, John M. Duncan, an Englishman who visited the city on a tour of the United States, noted with irony how Philadelphia's streets were named after "the various kinds of timber with which the ground was formerly covered," including Chestnut, Walnut, Spruce, and Pine. He relished the "freshness and purity" of the city and its expansive walks, many of which were "skirted with Lombardy poplars."[43] A decade later, the Englishman William Newnham Blane described Chestnut Street as "shaded by rows of fine trees growing at the edge of the pavement."[44] James Silk Buckingham, writing in 1841, found that Philadelphia's trees brought "a verdure, freshness, coolness, and shade most agreeable to the eye, and most delicious to the feelings of the passenger. . . . Scarcely anything can be imagined more beautiful, in streets at least, than the sight of one of these long avenues, reaching from the Delaware to the Schuylkill, a length of two miles, lined with trees throughout the whole way, and the termination of the vista at each extremity reposing on the opposite banks of the respective streams."[45]

New York enjoyed a curbside forest even earlier in its history. "I found it extremely pleasant to walk in the town," wrote Swedish naturalist Peter Kalm in 1748, "for it seemed quite like a garden." "In the chief streets there are trees planted, which in summer give them a fine appearance, and . . . afford a cooling shade." The plantings displayed a certain degree of sophistication, for "one seldom met with trees of the same sort," noted Kalm; species alternated block by block for variety and to avoid a total loss in the event of disease (a lesson tragically ignored by later generations).[46] Andrew Burnaby, an Englishman who visited North America in 1760, was similarly impressed by New York's "spacious and airy" streets, in which rows of trees "form an agreeable shade, and produce a pretty effect."[47] By 1818, both Broadway and Wall Street were lined with trees "planted at the side of the pavement," another European visitor wrote.[48]

But most American cities—including those of New England—remained woefully barren of street trees well into the nineteenth century. In New England, local municipal governments did occasionally plant trees, but such instances were rare. Most tree planting efforts were, as at New Haven, initiated and financed by private individuals. Occasionally, tree planting was the result of a public-private partnership. In 1798, silversmith Joseph Holt Ingraham of Portland, Maine, purchased a large tract of land that he subdivided into house lots and sold. He presented a strip of land to the town for a new street, which the selectmen agreed to build. On Ingraham's petition, the selectmen "laid out for the use of the town of Portland a town or private way" to be called State Street.[49]

The street was in effect Ingraham's gift to the town, and the town in turn planted its new municipal thoroughfare with elm trees.

The process did not rest well with some Portland citizens, for reasons unknown. The State Street elms, like their peers at Keene, were hacked down furtively in the night. A notice published by Portland's selectmen in the *Gazette* on October 18, 1800 (titled "TWENTY DOLLARS REWARD"), called for the arrest of the "evil minded person or persons" who "wantonly injured most of the Trees that have been lately set out in, and as an ornament to, State Street, by cutting round them."[50] The girdled trees presumably were replaced shortly after, for in a few decades State Street was known as the pride of Portland, lined by "mighty monarchs . . . whose overhanging branches embower it in foliage."[51]

Combined public and private action similarly beautified Cambridge Common. An initial attempt in 1823, "to make certain improvements on the Common . . . by setting out trees," never got past a committee of selectmen appointed to weigh in on the matter. A second effort several years later proved more successful. On June 5, 1830, a panel of private citizens was "authorized and empowered, at their own expense" to secure a number of physical improvements to the Common, which included installing a fence to enclose it and planting its perimeter with elms.[52] Though sanctioned by the selectmen, the fiscal obligation for this civic embellishment was clearly "met by private contributions."[53]

Though rare, there were occasional instances of more purely municipal activity. Boston mayor Josiah Quincy, Sr., introduced an abundance of municipal verdure to Boston Common in the 1820s.[54] Tree planting there was pursued with such vigor that by 1838 some complained that the space had become overgrown ("We do not need the whole Common as a mere *parasol*," wrote one critic).[55] One of the first extensive municipal efforts to plant trees in New Haven occurred in 1839, carrying forward the work begun by James Hillhouse years before.[56] In 1840, the selectmen of Manchester, New Hampshire, laid out their city's principal thoroughfare, Elm Street. One hundred feet wide, the new boulevard was crowned with a center island planted with a great column of elms.[57]

Not until the late nineteenth century, however, did municipalities begin to accept full responsibility for the planting, care, and upkeep of the urban forest. After a promising start in 1839, New Haven's municipal leaders did little planting until late in the century.[58] In Cambridge, tree planting emerged as a focus of governmental stewardship only in the 1880s, as part of a general broadening of municipal responsibility for the streetscape. But before it could concern itself with planting street trees, the city of Cambridge had to take care of a crucial matter of business: it had to first wrestle back from private hands the margins of the streets themselves.

Cambridge became a city in 1846, and within twenty years it was among the forty largest in America.[59] Settled in the early seventeenth century, Cambridge was already well endowed with historic buildings, sites, and trees. These were an eclectic lot. Some, like the Washington Elm, had inadvertently become street trees long after being set out on the Common to shelter livestock. Other elms had been set out over the years by public-spirited men like Thomas Brattle. On returning from England after the Revolution, Brattle "planted a long walk of trees for the especial benefit of the students" along a street that would later bear his name; there, Harvard men "might take their exercise sheltered from the sun."[60]

As in other New England towns and cities, many of the elms in Cambridge were planted by real estate developers, beginning with the early in-town "residential suburbs," such as Cambridgeport and East Cambridge. Between 1811 and 1873, many old Cambridge estates were subdivided into house lots for occupation and sale, creating more than eighteen miles of new streets. Elms were often set out in front of the new homes by speculative developers seeking to attract buyers; the streets they created and adorned were later accepted by the city as part of the municipal infrastructure. Broad new avenues were developed around 1810 by Andrew Craigie and the Lechmere Point Corporation. Considered "a great public improvement," such arrow-straight thoroughfares as Cambridge Street provided quick access to the Charles River and Boston, and were likely also flanked by trees.[61]

But just who owned these trees in their eclectic array and the ground they were rooted in became a matter of dispute. The lack of accurate surveys or enforcement on the part of the town encouraged, over the years, "boundary creep" on many Cambridge streets. Battling encroachment became a central concern of the town selectmen, and it kept the city's stewards busy long after incorporation in 1846. Reclaiming the public rights-of-way remained an issue for almost every mayoral administration in the city's early years, particularly as Cambridge grew and traffic increased. The new city government literally waged a turf battle in its determination to prove itself an able keeper of the public realm.

In 1836 the town of Cambridge authorized its selectmen to conduct a comprehensive survey of its thoroughfares and prepare "a plan with the streets properly defined as now laid out."[62] They hired James Hayward, a surveyor, to record all encroachments, take the names of perpetrators, and measure their infractions. Needless to say, Hayward gained few friends, particularly since some of the most profligate encroachers turned out to be affluent and influential Cantabrigians. The truly public ways—streets laid out or adopted by the town and maintained for common use—posed little problem. Those streets that were actually private, but over which the public had been granted right of use, were another matter altogether.[63]

In certain cases, a company had been granted a temporary charter to develop a particular thoroughfare for public use, but then failed to restrict development from creeping into the public right-of-way. Causeway Street (now Main Street) in Cambridge had been laid out in the 1790s by the proprietors of the old West Boston Bridge. This corporation had been authorized to "take and hold this land for a road, and for no other purpose." The broad thoroughfare, originally a hundred feet wide, was to revert to public ownership at the expiration of the charter. "It would therefore seem the duty of this corporation to preserve this roadway entire," noted Hayward, and "to protect it from every encroachment." Instead, he discovered, the company's "infidelity or remissness" had resulted in a thoroughfare hemmed in by accretions throughout its length; "in some places . . . there is not room for a suitable side walk."[64]

Other streets were more fully in private hands, having been laid out by developers such as Andrew Craigie. Medford Street was one—a thoroughfare that, in the 1830s, had not yet been officially accepted by the town. While free use of such ways by the public had been assured by the original proprietors, individual property owners who purchased adjacent land often challenged the authority of the town. The lingering perception of the street as entirely private space made enforcement of the easement difficult. In response, Hayward reminded the owners that the street had in fact been "laid out and devoted to the public . . . in the early arrangement of the streets in the lower part of Cambridgeport parish." He stressed that "Lots were sold bordering upon it, and giving the grantees a special interest or property in it, besides the general devotion of the street to public use, and the record to that effect placed in the public registry. There is little doubt that the right to have this street preserved from encroachment may be legally vindicated." Such private streets were, in Hayward's view, "part of the public commons and the property of the town."[65] By the turn of the century, most were in fact accepted or adopted by the city and became part of the municipal street system—a move meant chiefly to eliminate the potential for municipal liability for accidents on private thoroughfares that were often in poor repair.[66]

Encroachment into the actual carriageways was a serious enough problem, but even more encumbered were the spaces flanking the main roadbed—the side paths or foot walks. This was contested soil. Many property owners simply assumed that they were free for the taking. "There seems to be an opinion prevailing," Hayward reported, "that the borderers on the public roads have an unlimited control over all that part of the highway which is not occupied by the carriage path."[67] Owners of adjacent properties exploited these marginal zones, quietly augmenting their domains by erecting fences, porches, small out-buildings, and other accretia.

They also planted trees there, embellishing the public way even if doing so diminished its actual extent. Again, Hayward found himself fighting for the public interest. "The truth is," he remarked, "that the public, rather than the borderers, are mainly interested in the width, regularity, and suitable construction of the side path. And as the public have the right as well as the interest, it is proper that the subject should be under their control." Not all agreed. "Many people," lamented Hayward, "seem to suppose that the side walk is the exclusive property of the owner of the bordering estate, and that if his neighbor is allowed to have a ten feet walk, he has certainly a right to a five feet walk, because, indeed, he takes but half as much of the highway." And "in pursuance of this notion," Hayward added, the rogue borderer often set a row of trees, "in the very centre of what ought to be a public walk; as though the *sole* or *principal* object of a public way were the accommodation of teams and carriages, while the comfort and safety of men and women are entirely overlooked."[68]

Hayward had no objection to the trees themselves; he only protested their use as minions of privatization. Indeed, he well understood the value of street trees and considered them essential to the good streetscape. Hayward had repeatedly emphasized the importance of wide streets to facilitate the smooth flow of traffic, check the spread of fire, and "afford a freer circulation and a purer state of the air in the warm season." But he also believed these provided abundant "opportunity for planting their borders with trees, which, being in themselves an ornament, and an additional security against the spread of conflagration, afford in summer a comfortable shade to the house which they adorn, and the passengers who walk the streets, and tend to the greater health of the community by their effects on the atmosphere."[69]

Hayward understood that tree planting as an official act would send a clear message as to who held authority over the streetscape. Elms planted in an orderly column not only would be "in themselves an ornament" but would scratch a sylvan line in the sand and clearly mark the limits of private encroachment. Toward this end he recommended that "an *agency* on the subject of the public roads" be appointed—the "special discretion" of which would be "the public commons, and the margins and side walks of the streets." Into the hands of this body—a "Board of Commissioners of Streets," as he called it—should be placed "the entire control of the roads generally, and all questions relating to their construction, and to the character and details of any improvements." The board should keep "informed of the precise boundaries of the streets, and should be instructed to resist, in the beginning, every encroachment upon, or any irregular or inconvenient interference with, the public highway." And finally, the board should be duty bound to "prescribe, in any street where improvements of the kind were to be made, the *precise line* upon which trees might be planted."[70]

The City of Cambridge inherited the town's earlier struggle for streets, carrying out many of Hayward's recommendations. In his inaugural address, the city's first mayor stressed that "the subject of public roads is one of great importance, and will require no small portion of your attention."[71] Prior to 1846, care of public thoroughfares rested in the hands of the warden of the almshouse, for no other reason than "much of the labor on the roads could be advantageously performed by paupers." In the city's second year of operation, it was decided that a superintendent of streets should be "annually elected by the City Council."[72] Even though for the first few years' appropriations for streets would still be shared with the almshouse, creation of this office was a step toward Hayward's vision of a discrete agency with broad responsibility for the city's thoroughfares.

The early annual *Reports* of the City of Cambridge reveal a gradual expansion of responsibility regarding street improvement. At first the city was concerned mainly with pragmatic issues of paving, drainage, and lighting, but eventually its scope of activity broadened to include aesthetic matters. This also reflected a growing interest on the part of the citizenry. "If I mistake not," observed the mayor in 1848, "there is one matter in which there is great unanimity in the wishes of the people; namely, a more thorough improvement in some of our streets, as well in the foot-ways, as in the carriage-ways." He urged "every good citizen" to remove whatever constructions had been built into the street, and thus "restore to the public what he has temporarily enjoyed by its forbearance."[73]

By midcentury, progress was being made. Residents proved cooperative, and many venerable encroachments were removed. Restoration of the flanks of Broadway and Hampshire Streets was complete by 1849. In his annual address to the City Council that year, the mayor reported that the majority of property owners bordering these thoroughfares were "fully reconciled to the change." In fact, "they have lost nothing in point of room about their buildings." For what had been taken back by the city had been improved in the form of "ample footwalks." And when these "shall be shaded by forest trees, the alterations made will be pronounced not only public improvements, but private benefits." In sum, the mayor emphasized that "every estate will be enhanced in value by the improvement of the whole."[74] The municipal elm, symbol of the city's burgeoning authority, was also an agent of reconciliation.

Over the decades, Cambridge appropriated increasing amounts of money for improvement of its streets. Carriageways were paved, drainage was improved,

Municipal elms, Cambridge, Massachusetts, c. 1865 (Courtesy of the Cambridge Historical Commission)

and street lamps were installed. Improvement focused on the street edges too. In 1851 it was reported that "a good beginning has been made in constructing sidewalks for the convenience and safety of foot-passengers." Indeed, "there is scarcely any class of expenditures where the same amount of money would benefit so many persons."[75] Older informal side paths, once contested space, were upgraded into sidewalks of gravel or wood plank. Emphasis on the improvement of the street edge also meant planting trees. An increasing portion of money earmarked for sidewalk improvement went toward purchasing, setting, watering, pruning, and trimming trees—line items that appear consistently in municipal budget reports after 1850.

After the Civil War, the pace of tree planting and beautification continued. In 1869 the mayor decreed that "a certain number of shade-trees be planted each year on the borders of such streets as are not so favored." "Our city is a magnificent park of itself," declared the mayor in 1871, "growing more beautiful every year by the embellishment secured by the combined and reciprocal influence of private wealth and public improvement." He urged all Cantabrigians to "spare our ancient and historic trees" and "plant new ones in our streets." In this way, "private enterprise will soon imitate our example, and make our goodly city, what it is fast becoming, the most desirable place for a residence in all our land."[76]

The management of street trees emerged as a legitimate area of municipal responsibility as part of a general modernization of the street that occurred toward the end of the nineteenth century. New England cities such as Cambridge, New Haven, Portland, and Springfield underwent rapid development in the wake of the Civil War, and their populations burgeoned with immigration from Europe and elsewhere. With the growth stimulated by industrial urbanization came increased traffic and a demand for urban thoroughfares that could withstand heavy use by new forms of transportation. The horsecar and electric trolley combined with other urban technological innovations to dramatically change the appearance and complexity of the city street.

The meandering path of the village and the dusty town lane were replaced by the modern street, an increasingly complex piece of infrastructure that carried the lifelines of the modern metropolis. The antebellum street, with its vague boundary between public and private, its grassy margin and unpaved surface, had become by the 1870s a machine in its own right, a conduit for buried wires, gas lines, sewer pipes, and rail trackage, with telegraph wires, power lines, and street lamps overhead. Elms and oxcarts no longer ruled the scene.

The complexity of the modern street demanded intensive management. As the various parts of urban infrastructure were owned and operated by numerous private companies (often in competition with one another), responsibility for overall coordination of the streetscape fell to the municipalities. The increasingly complex matrix of pipes and wires in ground and overhead—as well as new concerns over municipal liability—transformed the act of planting a street tree. What once required only faith and a spade now called upon the coordination of multiple urban systems. The earliest trees on town streets were simply placed on the margins of the unpaved thoroughfares. Images of city streets from midcentury often show mature elms planted decades earlier growing in the carriageway itself, often several feet out from the sidewalk (these were *literally* street trees). In time, trees came to be incorporated directly into sidewalks, which were themselves rapidly becoming paved. By 1833 in Portland, elms were already being "planted in breaks of the curbstone of the side walks—or in small openings left in the bricks."[77] A photograph of Cambridge Street in Cambridge from 1865 shows newly constructed sidewalk with grassy berm and robust young elms; the once-contested street edge had evolved into a carefully managed strip of urban space.

By the turn of the century, stewardship of the urban forest had become fully a municipal responsibility. In the view of William F. Fox, author of an early manual on municipal forestry, "the planting and care of street trees belongs to the city government as much as street paving." In Massachusetts, municipal control over the urban forest was codified by legislation passed in 1890 stipulating that "the mayor and aldermen of cities . . . are authorized to designate and preserve trees in highways for ornament and shade, not less than one tree in every thirty-three feet and of one inch or more" in diameter.[78]

In Cambridge, custody of the urban forest remained the jurisdiction of the Street Department until 1894, after which responsibility was transferred to the park commissioners. The *Report of the General Superintendent of Parks* that year provided a retrospective on the city's street trees, the first extended discussion in the municipal record of the Cambridge urban forest. It was a celebration, but also a call to arms. "How much our city is indebted to its trees," the author wrote, "not merely in the matter of adornment but for utilitarian reasons as well, it would be difficult to state." Cambridge, the report pointed out, "has few natural opportunities for fine landscape effects; but in the extent and beauty of its foliage and in its magnificent specimens of native trees, our city, in the past, has offered an attraction to homebuilders which has been no small factor in the city's growth." And, "While we would search in vain upon the assessors' lists of public property for an inventory of the shade trees," the writer continued, "it would not be a difficult task to show that, collectively, these trees are among the most valuable of the municipal properties."[79]

But the urban forest inherited by the city park commission in 1894 was in sorry shape. The report criticized past wardens for having neglected so valuable a municipal resource. That urban forestry "should have been made an adjunct of the strictly mechanical business of road building, shows that the governing powers in the past have been largely indifferent in the matter of shade tree cultivation. Indeed, the city corporation has done but little to foster our shade trees." The report acknowledged that the canopied streets of Cambridge owed no small debt to public-spirited individuals. It praised the "valuable services rendered in the past by the numberless citizens who, although without 'the power to charm a listening world,' have given individual effort to tree culture upon our public streets, and have never failed in voice or act, to come to the defence of our leafy inheritance."[80]

But rapid urbanization made it evident that "individual efforts, however manfully maintained" were no longer adequate to meet the needs of stewardship. "However valuable individual effort has been in the past," the report argued, "it is evident that the time has come when the matter of tree culture upon our public streets . . . must be a municipal enterprise." Care of this arboreal inheritance, and its perpetuation, required the "systematic effort of an organized department of the city works," lest Cambridge, "noted for her abundance and beauty of foliage . . . descend to the list of nearly barren cities."[81]

Moreover, while philanthropy created a priceless inheritance, it did not necessarily meet the standards of modern urban design. In the past, uncoordinated private action led to a haphazard collection of street trees; however beautiful, the urban forest did not conform to new principles of order, symmetry, and "good taste." Systematic official effort was needed "to raise the standard of shade tree culture to the requirements of the more cultivated taste which now prevails in the art of urban forestry." Indeed, "the rules of city street decoration no longer permit each individual property owner to plant trees how and where he pleases." Rather, street planting must now be directed "with reference to the street as a whole."

> Already it has been suggested that all architectural work upon a street should be in harmony with a general plan, and that individual tastes would not be permitted to spoil the general landscape effects, by incongruous or eccentric efforts. But the public taste is not yet educated to this standard, and no doubt private rights will be urged long and vigorously before such a standard is reached. In the matter of shade tree culture, upon the public streets, however, the question of individual rights, cannot reasonably be insisted upon.[82]

In Cambridge and other cities in the late nineteenth century, tree planting became institutionalized as part of the modern urban management enterprise. Urban forestry emerged as part of a larger movement toward scientific management and expertise in the nineteenth-century city, which produced reform movements in education, sanitation, and recreation. Like the sanitary engineer and the playground supervisor, the unlikely hybrid known as the urban forester was a product of the modern industrial metropolis. Urban forestry was a new area of municipal expertise, "an art requiring special knowledge, cultivated taste and a natural sympathy with plant life," but also a scientific enterprise.[83]

This new rational approach to the urban forest sought to impose uniformity of species in streetscape plantings. In the past, the ad hoc efforts of private individuals had favored elms but often mixed these with maples, catalpas, horse chestnuts, and other species. The rational eye of scientific urban forestry judged such admixtures undesirable. It sought to impose a new standard of formality and order on the streetscape. "Good taste," Cambridge insisted in 1894, "demands the observance of two rules as essential in street tree planting. First, that but one variety of tree be planted upon a street, and, second, that the trees shall be planted at uniform distances." Craigie Street was praised for its "noble line of elms," but others were rebuked for having allowed a motley assortment of species to detract from an overall design.[84]

When it came to what single species should be used, the American elm had little competition. In the 1894 report, the superintendent of parks recounted the long history of the tree in Cambridge, suggesting that the tree "has claims upon Cambridge above that of any other tree," and pointing out that the city still possessed "not a few specimens of native growth . . . whose roots have never been handled." It recommended that "some of the main highways of the city, such, for example, as Harvard and Magazine Streets, should be devoted entirely to elms, and all the tree work done upon these streets from this time forth should be with the purpose of finally establishing well-matured specimens of Ulmus Americana at regular distances throughout their entire length."[85]

A Perfect Urban Tree

The American elm possessed a set of physical properties that, combined, made the tree extraordinarily well suited for urban planting. Many of these qualities were not immediately evident. Planting an elm is an act of faith: the sapling tree shows little promise of grace or formal beauty. As one advocate of improvement observed, "no other tree, when young, throws out its arms so free and wild," a gangle of leaf and limb.[86] But, in a short time, an elm assumes loft and posture. Its formal and architectural qualities, combined with rapid growth and relative resistance to the strains of the pre-automobile urban environment, rendered it the perfect urban tree.

Elms are tenacious and will grow in a wide range of soil types. In spite of its preference for the moist soil of bottomlands, the tree tolerates drought and can withstand even prolonged deprivations of water. Elms are hardy. The trees were subjected to an increasing barrage of predators and parasites through the nineteenth century (elm-wilt, the tussock moth, and the elm-leaf beetle were just a few of the tormentors), but they rarely were killed outright. Like the weeds they once were, elms grew with astounding speed, particularly given fertile soil and abundant water. And elms gained aesthetic distinction in a comparatively short time, something of no little value to a nation in a hurry. A healthy elm could easily attain impressive height within the lifetime of its human benefactor, a fact that made elm philanthropy particularly rewarding. In as little as fifteen years a sapling elm could attain sufficient height to provide shade and transform the spatial envelope of a street. In 1847 Downing's *Horticulturalist* noted "a gentleman near Albany" who had planted elms from seed and "had them twenty-one inches in circumference when only eleven years old."[87] A later study confirmed that, with the sole exception of silver maple, the American elm was the fastest growing of some twenty native trees recommended for street use. A young elm three inches in diameter could attain a diameter of twenty inches in as little as twenty years. Of course, the tree was also relatively short lived, but this was the cost of early maturity.[88]

The Queen Elm, Springfield, Massachusetts, c. 1860 (Courtesy of the Connecticut Valley Historical Museum, Springfield, Massachusetts)

The elm also possessed architectural qualities that complemented the streetscape. The trunk of an elm is erect and typically does not ramify, or branch out, until it is high above the street. The principal limbs and the crown itself are thus lifted well above the street corridor. Air is allowed to circulate beneath, and traffic and building facades remain unobstructed by the tree's mass. Even large elms on a busy thoroughfare are relatively unobtrusive, as the bulk of the tree rides high above the streetscape. Moreover, the canopy of elms produces a dappled, broken light—not the dense, lawn-killing shade of a maple or an oak. The crown is lifted high enough to allow ambient light to penetrate the space beneath, and the small leaves allow plentiful sunlight to reach the ground. Elms provide shelter from the sun but are rarely claustrophobic. As Charles Sprague Sargent noted in *Garden and Forest*, "An avenue of Elms is never sombre, however cool and shadowy it may be. It does not shut out the light and air, but merely tempers them."[89]

In the New England city, elms afforded a great range of benefits. The trees helped purify the air and were thought to combat "miasmas"; they shielded pedestrians and horses from the summer sun, and to some extent from rain and wind; they were thought to play a role in checking the spread of fire; and they were seen as a visual amenity that raised residential property values. Municipalities later recognized that well-kept streets served as an indicator of a city's economic vitality; as in the case of Cambridge, a clean and orderly streetscape also signaled authority on the part of the city, symbolizing a strong and activist government. Indeed, few improvements contributed as dramatically or as quickly to a sense of municipal wellness as did lofty columns of elms.

But like most cultural artifacts, elms were multivalanced in their meaning; they signified on a number of planes simultaneously. Even as city elms served eminently pedestrian functions, they also possessed deeper value. A column of elms, thrusting its fury of limbs high above the shops and carriages, represented an interlude of almost sublime beauty in the nineteenth-century city—a sight that moved many a pen to praise. Elms in the city transcended the quotidian; they came to symbolize something far greater than the sum of their shade.

7

YANKEE ELYSIUM

The act of planting a tree in the city held special significance in the American context, due to a particular set of attitudes toward cities that had evolved from the country's earliest settlement period and persisted throughout the nation's history. In spite of having built some of the world's great urban environments, many Americans have long regarded cities as something impure or morally deficient, and antiurban attitudes have thrived among both the intelligentsia and the populace at large.

Wholesale urbanization in the second half of the nineteenth century did little to change this, and it even seemed to encourage more vehement reactions against the city. As New York and Chicago swelled in size and began to dominate the economic, social, and political life of the nation, Americans looked ever more wistfully toward nature and the vanishing pastoral heritage. They mourned the passing of an age in which life was governed by the rhythms of the natural world, for a lusty engagement with earth and trees was thought to produce better citizens and more moral men.

The Quest for Synthesis

To the founding generation of Americans, cities were associated with the threadbare regimes of the Old World; they were considered a source of tyranny and despotism, prone to mob rule. To be sure, cities were emerging in America in the colonial age; but Philadelphia, New York, and even Boston were only mushrooms in the night compared with Paris, London, and Vienna. The great cities of Europe were indeed appreciated by educated Americans, who knew these to be the fountainheads of Western culture. Jefferson and Franklin were among the many American intellectuals who reveled in the literary and cultural life of Paris, even as they railed against emulation. American artists and writers, from Washington Allston and James Fenimore Cooper to Nathaniel Hawthorne and Thomas Cole, made similarly appreciative journeys to the great metropolitan centers of Europe, where they were tutored by masters and toured landscapes encrusted with the relics of antiquity that America lacked.

But if Jefferson appreciated the Old World metropolis, he also believed that it should remain in Europe. America, with its unspoiled natural splendors and magnificent landscapes, possessed, in the minds of the Virginian and many of his contemporaries, an inheritance far greater than any city. Americans would do well to steer clear of Paris or London, they felt, and build instead an agrarian republic thinly spread across a vast and virgin land. Jefferson believed that democracy in America would flourish best if the nation remained a republic of yeoman farmers. He believed deeply in the moral superiority of agricultural life. In this new land, cities could only yield conformity and suffocate virtue. Cities added "just so much to the support of pure government," Jefferson famously claimed in *Notes on Virginia,* "as sores do to the strength of the human body."[1]

It would have pleased Jefferson to know that the United States remained a mostly rural nation well into the nineteenth century (as late as 1860 more than 75 percent of the population lived outside cities). Not surprisingly, the prejudice of most Americans was, in this period, strongly antiurban. After all, cities occupied a relatively minor position in the larger scheme of things, and most Americans had never even been to one. Rural America was the seat of political power. The decision to place most states' capitals at their geographic center rather than in their largest city was a manifestation of a distrust of urban areas and their unruly mobs. Locating the nation's capital on the tidal flats of the Potomac rather than in urban Philadelphia or New York was, likewise, motivated by a desire to keep the reins of government out of the hands of the urban elite.[2]

The skepticism about cities that was born of Jeffersonian agrarianism gradually devolved into a "dichotomy in American thought" that positioned country and city as irreconcilable opposites.[3] As Perry Miller has written, "The health, the very personality of Americans" became identified with nature, and "therefore set it in opposition to . . . the city."[4] Rapid urban growth beginning around 1840 exacerbated this tension. Boston, New York, and Philadelphia were receiving a vast influx of new immigrants from both Europe and elsewhere in the United States. Immigration caused congestion and severely crowded living conditions. By the time of the Civil War, the much-feared Dickensian city of the Old World had indeed arrrived in America.

The prospect of a densely urbanized United States disturbed many Americans, and triggered an "antiurban roar in the national literary pantheon."[5] In the process, the old Jeffersonian antipathy toward cities—which was largely a sociopolitical objection—gained a new facet. As cities became increasingly crowded and overbuilt, they in turn lost whatever connection they once had to nature and the countryside. This parting was especially symbolic because nature was now seen as a source of great moral, spiritual, and psychological value. If nature was so important for body and soul, then surely its absence in the urban environment was a monstrous liability—the source, perhaps, of madness and criminality. But there was hope: with calculated intervention, perhaps the moral deficiencies of urban life might be reversed. If villages could be improved with trees, then so could cities. A marriage of nature and the city could be arranged.

Thomas Bender, James Machor, and others have argued that America's burgeoning faith in rural-urban reconciliation has been masked by an overemphasis on the bipolarity of the dynamic. The traditional focus on country and city as oppositional entities "has obscured the fact," writes Machor, "that an equally significant strain of thought has conceived of the American scene as a place where that dialectic finally could be synthesized." Indeed, antagonism toward the city on the part of American intellectuals "formed only part of the artistic response to urbanization" in the nineteenth century.[6] Even Ralph Waldo Emerson, whose writings are often antiurbanist in tone, himself "tended to accept a dichotomy of city and nature not as a conclusion, but as a point of departure" for "the development of an artistic strategy of reconciliation."[7]

To the urbanist in Romantic America, it appeared entirely plausible that an *urban pastoral* could be realized, that a city of artifice could be built in concert with nature—with both city and country gaining from the union. The emphasis on synthesis and reconciliation is to be distinguished from a more purely pastoral impulse, which regarded the city as morally inferior to the countryside. Urban pastoralism looked upon city and country as equally necessary and important, and sought simply to strike a balance between the two. This was a fundamentally progressive stance, combining a respect for rural life and its traditions "with an energetic commitment to future development of the city."[8]

Faith in reconciliation, in an "ideal of an urban-rural society," expressed itself throughout both popular and high culture.[9] In New England, vanguard in so many things, urban pastoralism arrived early. Nehemiah Adams, a Boston clergyman with a penchant for purple prose, was one of its first champions. In 1838 he published a modest volume titled *The Boston Common, or Rural Walks in Cities*. The author's name in the book was given only as "A Friend of Improvement," and

Adams included an apologia for the slimness of his volume and his unworthiness as a scribe. He then urged his readers "to accompany us, at least in the imagination, to the Common, and engage with us in a little agreeable conversation as we wander along its noble avenues of trees."[10]

"Let us forsake, for a while, the noisy streets, and the ceaseless hurry of business, for a more quiet sphere of thought; and as we are ourselves children of nature, let us here learn from her the pleasures and the advantages of yielding to her dictates." On this imagined stroll, Adams held forth on the spiritual delights of nature, particularly as an ameliorative to the growing density and congestion of the city. "The larger a city is," Adams reasoned, "the more it ought to be interspersed with gardens and rural scenery"—for "a treeless city is too much like a desert. We feel oppressed, by the monotonous dominion of brick and mortar."[11]

> Man cannot bear to be always shut up from the inspiration of God's works. He must gaze on green trees, and breathe the breath of fresh flowers; his brow must be fanned by gales that have sped over green forests and fields—or his spirit will be faint within him. Ay, he must bring away garden and grove, and plant them in the very midst of the marts of trade.[12]

Indeed, the "marts of trade" would themselves be greatly embellished by the union. "Nowhere is the magnificence of art more imposing than when surrounded by that of nature," wrote Adams. "It is not degraded by the contrast; it is ennobled." Boston Common, a "sacred inheritance," was the gem at the center of his city. Its trees and still-open fields struck an almost exquisite counterpoint to the built city. The object, then, was to forge a reconciliation, a synthesis of urban and rural. "Who would not rear temples amid groves, and palaces in gardens? Art is naked; but Nature clothes her with the richest drapery. Proud as she may be, she must needs be a borrower of beauty; and her grandest designs must be sculpted with imagery of Nature's more perfect workmanship."[13]

Adams would have applauded the actions of Yankee elm planters like James Hillhouse. Indeed, what Hillhouse and others effectively achieved (for the most part unintentionally) was an urban pastoral in which elm trees functioned as the chief mechanisms of urban-rural concord. In an era preceding the rural cemeteries, the Olmsted park, the romantic suburbs, and other celebrated nineteenth-century efforts to achieve such synthesis, the simple planting of forest trees on city streets was perceived—if not specifically intended—as "a means of bringing the country into the city."[14] Elm trees were a fragment of the native woodland, a keepsake of *rus* set "in the very midst of the marts of trade."[15] The city of elms seemed to offer hope that the old dichotomy of city and country could be overcome, and that here on Yankee soil a new kind of city—a pastoral city—could be built.

As we have seen, in few places was elm planting a coordinated or sustained activity until relatively late in the nineteenth century, and in few instances was it clearly motivated by a quest for synthesis between nature and artifice. Intentions are often difficult to unpack. In the original subscription James Hillhouse circulated in 1786, inaugurating the elm-planting campaign that would transform New Haven, he proposed that it would "be Very Ornamental as well as Very Beautiful" to set "a row of Elms . . . in Front of the Public Buildings."[16] Similarly, in his later efforts to establish the Grove Street Cemetery—one of the first rural cemeteries in America—he sought to create a place of burial "better calculated to impress the mind with a solemnity becoming the repository of the dead."[17] From such evidence it can be inferred that Hillhouse was indeed guided by an aesthetic and perhaps even a metaphysical impulse that would have appreciated a union of nature and artifice.

Hillhouse's own life certainly encompassed both *rus* and *urbe*. A lawyer and politician, Hillhouse was part of the urban elite, but he also owned a farm on the outskirts of New Haven. If he was a skilled political figure in Philadelphia and Washington, Hillhouse also found time to maintain a nursery and stay abreast of developments in horticulture. He even translated parts of François André Michaux's *Sylva of North America*. He was also keenly interested in agriculture and could match Jefferson in his rhapsodic evocations of agrarian virtue. Agriculture, he wrote in 1793, "is most certainly an honorable and useful employment, and in my Opinion more congenial with human happiness than any other in life." "I have often lamented," wrote Hillhouse, "that my circumstances and situation in life did not enable me to devote myself wholly to agricultural pursuits."[18] With feet planted in both city and country, the elming of New Haven may well have symbolized for Hillhouse a synthesis of realms.

Yet even where elm planting had nothing to do with such lofty metaphysics, the apparent union of city and country that resulted was a common *perception* of New England's curbside elms—in New Haven and elsewhere. Even if the planter was guided by pragmatism alone, exalted values could be assigned the trees post facto. Literate observers read in the elm leaves at Cambridge, New Haven, Portland, and Springfield a felicitous union of worlds. Men like Charles Dickens and Anthony Trollope reveled in the delightful incongruence of "forest giants" on city streets, and understood that this juxtaposition yielded a new—and distinctly American—kind of urbanism.

At Concord, New Hampshire, curbside elms gave "a fine rural aspect to the whole" of the city, according to visitor James Silk Buckingham.[19] Edward T. Coke, visiting Northampton in 1833, described it as "the most delightful and enviable place I had ever seen; it is the very realization of a 'rus in urbe,' the streets being so thickly planted with trees of a primeval growth that their boughs are almost interwoven across the road, and the neat private dwellings and shops beneath them appear like a series of cottages and gardens.[20]

Not far off, the burgeoning city of Springfield impressed A. M. Maxwell in 1840 as a "perfect paradise," an appearance he attributed largely to streets planted with "rows of majestic and graceful elm-trees on each side."[21] Springfield's elms won it the title City of Trees. The view of the city from the Springfield Arsenal provided so fine a prospect of urban-rural felicity that it was reputed to be among the loveliest sights in nineteenth-century New England.[22] As a child in the late nineteenth century, Flora Graves Phelps recalled her astonishment at the scene spread below the arsenal's tower; it seemed incredible "that sometime a bustling city might be located down there in the valley," for "all that seemed visible . . . was a veritable woodland or forest."[23]

Portland's prodigious stock of elms—"the boast of our city and the admiration of strangers"—earned it the title of Forest City.[24] "In looking down . . . upon the central parts of the city," wrote William Wills in the 1860s, "a stranger is surprised by the embowered aspect which is presented to his view—a city in the woods." To Wills, the "tall and numerous trees" dwarfed the buildings, which seemed "to be nestling in the midst of a forest, through which the lofty spires, the dome of the new City Hall, and some other lofty edifices penetrate and give bold relief to the scene."[25]

To David T. Pottinger, Cambridge, Massachusetts, "seemed much more like the country than the city." Recalling his nineteenth-century boyhood in an essay titled "I, Too, in Arcadia," Pottinger described an idyllic pastoral in the midst of the city, the essence of an urban-rural synthesis: "One could walk among the aged elms . . . to the junction of Garden Street and Concord Avenue and look up in either direction through a green tunnel of magnificent elms toward the observatory. One autumn afternoon when the late sun shed a golden haze through the heavy trees, I came through the 1886–87 [class] gate and looked down the grassy sidewalks and along the dusty roadway. The only person to be seen in all this glory was a boy leisurely driving a cow ahead of him up Broadway."[26]

The apotheosis of urban pastoralism in antebellum New England, and the pinnacle of elm culture in America, was New Haven. It was a city of no mean stature: for most of the nineteenth century, New Haven was second only to Boston as a cultural and economic hub of New England, and no other city in America had a comparable stock of trees. By midcentury, the elms that Hillhouse had set out decades earlier were monuments of scale and grandeur. New Haven became world famous for its trees and was known as the City of Elms. Its remarkable fusion of *rus* and *urbe* attracted the pens of literate travelers.[27] None praised the New Haven elms more effusively than Nathaniel Parker Willis.

An 1827 graduate of Yale College who became one of America's most beloved literary figures of the nineteenth century, Willis was clearly smitten with New Haven. He attributed the city's profound beauty chiefly to its elms, "grown at this day," he wrote in 1839, "to remarkable size and luxuriance."[28] "If you were to set a poet to make a town," Willis speculated, "he would probably turn out very much such a place as New Haven." Even the houses, built modestly of wood, were "as fair to the eye as marble" in the preternatural light of elm shade.[29] Willis spent enraptured hours beneath the Hillhouse elms, and his descriptions of New Haven in *American Scenery* (1837) are a paean to urban pastoralism. "It has the appearance of a town roofed in with leaves," wrote Willis, "and it is commonly said, that, but for the spires, a bird flying over would scarce be aware of its existence. Nothing could be more beautiful than the effect of this in the streets; for, standing where any of the principal avenues cross at right angles, four embowered aisles extend away as far as the eye can follow, formed of the straight stems and graceful branches of the drooping elm, the most elegant and noble of the trees of the country." Indeed, Willis concluded, "the whole scene, though in the midst of a city, breathes of nature."[30]

With each passing year, New Haven's elms gained in beauty and stature. "No one can have failed to hear of the beauties of our forest city," rhapsodized Ezekiel Porter Belden in *Sketches of Yale College* (1843); well-stocked with elms whose "beautiful green arches" embraced the streets, New Haven could be "truly described as 'a city in a wood, or a wood in a city.'"[31] In the view of Emmeline Stuart Wortely, an Englishwoman who toured America in 1849, the "exceeding profusion of its stately elms" made New Haven "not only one of the most charming, but one of the most 'unique' cities I ever beheld."[32] Charles Dickens, visiting in 1842, understood that New Haven's elms forged a union of *rus* and *urbe*. Of the city, he said that "many of its streets (as its *alias* sufficiently imports) are planted with rows of grand old elm-trees." Dickens observed, astutely, "Even in winter-time, these groups of well-grown trees, clustering among the busy streets and houses of a thriving city, have a very quaint appearance: seeming to bring about a kind of compromise between town and country; as if each had met the other half-way, and shaken hands upon it."[33]

Decades later, another Englishman, William Smith of Yorkshire, added that New Haven's "grand foliage-arched streets, squares, and avenues, are a striking feature in the city, and make a lasting impression on the casual visitor." The "noble elms, which rise grandly in stately rows in every direction," he remarked,

The "elm arcade" on Temple Street, New Haven, c. 1870, detail from
Appleton's Journal

"give a charming rural aspect to the academic city, and are its pride."[34] For the City of Elms, hand of *rus* firmly in its grip, the reconciliation of urban and rural was more than a matter of idle metaphysics; it had become part and parcel of the city's identity around the world. According to the popular midcentury *Dinsmore's Guide*, the famed elm-forest-in-town distinguished New Haven as no less than "the handsomest city in the United States."[35]

So important to New Haven's identity were its elms that a regular column was dedicated to the subject in the *New Haven Daily Morning Journal and Courier.* Titled "New Haven's Elms and Green," the column ran for most of 1883 and 1884, written by a local antiquarian named Henry Howe. Howe's worshipful essays addressed a wide range of subjects within the ambit of the elms and Green. "Many of those who were born here do not fully appreciate their heritage in our elms and Green," he began; "Let them live away from them for thirty years, as has the writer . . . and their indifference may vanish."[36]

"The Gothic Thrust of Elms"

If elms were symbolic of a union between country and city, they also contributed to a profound spatial transformation of the streetscape. *Ulmus americana* possessed architectural properties that had long distinguished it among North American trees, as Luigi Castiglioni had observed as early as the 1780s when he noted that the elm's "wide-spreading and pendant" branches suited it particularly well "for making avenues and other ornamental plantings."[37] Many later writers affirmed this. Walter Prichard Eaton understood well the splendid architectonics of the elm; in his view, the tree possessed a "formal structure, and a consequent dignity," which rendered "remarkable fitness to comport with architectural lines, with geometrically designed vistas."

"We all know the type," Eaton wrote; "the noble trunk of massive girth, tapering very gradually upward to the first spring of branches, and then dissolving in those branches as a water jet might dissolve in many upward and out-curving streams, till the whole is lost in the spray of the foliage. Like many trees which grow alone, it develops an exquisite symmetry, but with the elm this symmetry is not only one of general contour but of individual limbs. Not only is the silhouette symmetrical, but the skeleton, branch balancing branch."[38]

These effects were multiplied magnificently when the tree was planted in long, parallel rows. Street elms produced "an architectural effect of permanent beauty," wrote Charles Sprague Sargent, "by the arched interlacings of the great bending boughs."[39] Forming a sylvan-architectural structure complete with columns and high ceiling, the trees brought about a remarkable spatial transformation of the streetscape. Good urban design, like good architecture, is measured by its successful definition of volumetric space; for, as Bruno Zevi has written, space is the protagonist of architecture, and of urbanism, too.[40] The young cities of America possessed little of the urban architectural fabric that so distinguished their European peers and created such memorable spaces in places like Venice and London.

But the elms made up for the paucity of loggias and colonnades. The trees created positive urban space out of the street. In situations where the carriageway was excessively wide, or the flanking buildings were too far apart or too meager and insubstantial to create a satisfying sense of enclosure, elms rescaled the street's spatial envelope into proportions that were more human. Henry Ward Beecher exaggerated little when he compared New England's elms to the columns of the Parthenon. The trees were indeed essential elements of Yankee urbanism.

The spatial delight imparted by the elm-lined street—with its rhythmic procession of trunks and lofty canopy—may well have drawn from the collective unconscious. Referring to the work of ecologist Eugene P. Odum, Robert Geddes has argued that it was the boundary between grassland and deep forest, rather than either one alone, that provided the ideal habitat for early humans; this zone, the "forest edge," enabled both *prospect* and *refuge*. Recollection of the forest edge may explain why architectural and urbanistic elements evocative of this space—colonnades, loggias, arcades, verandas, even porches—are so appealing and comfortable. The forest edge, Geddes writes, evolved into "an elementary source of . . . ideas and images of landscape and architecture." If the loggia or porch replicated the spatial conditions of the forest edge at the architectural scale, the colonnade of elms on city streets did so on a larger, urbanistic scale. As with the former, elms offered both outlook and shelter. Elm Street's appeal may well have been linked to a subconscious recollection of trees from the deep evolutionary past.[41]

The psychological appeal of the elm-lined street was joined by even more potent cultural symbolism. The plume-like shape of a pair of single elms formed something of a green Gothic arch; the mingling tangle of limbs evoked a kind of tracery against the sky. In number, the effect was amplified. A parallel column of elms was a Gothic cathedral in sylvan form. Again, this was less a matter of intention than it was of signification after the fact. Elms had been planted in urban situations long before Gothic revivalism stirred on American soil. With the flowering of this architectural style around midcentury, elms that had been planted earlier—for whatever quotidian reasons—gained a compelling ecclesiastical dimension. In time, evocations of Gothicism and Gothic religious architecture were among the most common tropes used to describe—and impart meaning to—New England's elm-lined streets.

To Nathaniel Hawthorne it was this Gothicism that so distinguished the American elm from its English cousins. On a visit to Greenwich Park, London, in 1856, the writer concluded that the English elms were "scarcely so beautiful . . . nor so stately, as an avenue of American elms, because these English trees have not such tall, columnar trunks, but are John Bullish in their structure—mighty of girth, but short between the ground and the branches, and round-headed. Our trees, 'high over-arched, with echoing walks between,' have the greater resemblance to the Gothic aisle of a cathedral."[42]

Given the origins of Gothicism, Hawthorne's judgment is somewhat ironic. The Gothic mode, which evolved in the Middle Ages, was revived as a historical style in England around the middle of the eighteenth century, the result of a burgeoning "scholarly interest in archeology, followed by a sentimental delight in decay."[43] Although there were expressions of the style in America during the colonial and Federal periods—most notably by Benjamin Henry Latrobe—it was not until the 1830s that Gothic architecture became a popular building style in the United States. Its acceptance was driven by a number of factors, including the popularity of the Gothic novels of Sir Walter Scott, a growing interest in Romanticism and its emphasis on the melancholic and sublime, as well as the perennial desire to emulate English fashions.[44]

But it also appealed to the emerging emphasis on nature and landscape that came with the environmental awakening. For Americans in the 1830s and 1840s, the Gothic mode seemed to articulate well the new role of nature as a fountainhead of moral and spiritual value, and national identity. Indeed, Gothic architecture possessed an inherent sylvan dimension, as its primitive origins were thought to have derived from forest vegetation. None expressed this more colorfully than William Cullen Bryant in his "Forest Hymn" (1825):

> The groves were God's first temples. Ere man learned
> To hew the shaft, and lay the architrave,
> And spread the roof above them,—ere he framed
> The lofty vault, to gather and roll back
> The sound of anthems; in the darkling wood,
> Amidst the cool and silence, he knelt down,
> And offered to the Mightiest solemn thanks
> And supplication.[45]

If the ill-fated Lombardy poplar was the sylvan expression of classicism, the elm was Gothicism in arboreal form. "When their limbs are bare," wrote Nehemiah Adams of the elms on Boston Common, "a perspective view of them gives as good a representation of Gothic architecture as man ever copied. A traveller might almost fancy himself again in York cathedral."[46] Henry Wadsworth Longfellow made a note in his journal of a predawn December walk "under the leafless arches of the elms, . . . the trees themselves more than ever like columns and ribbed ceilings of churches."[47] His poetic renditions of elms were equally evocative of the

Gothic: "And the great elms o'erhead / Dark shadows wove on their aerial looms / Shot through with golden thread."[48] At New Haven and elsewhere, Gothicism was arborealized, and the arboreal was made Gothic.

The elm-lined street was thus transformed into something far greater than the sum of its trees; the value of the elm as a moral tonic was now underscored by its architectural and ecclesiastical symbolism. Elms transformed the quotidian street into a sylvan cathedral, which in turn might render the city more sacrosanct. This was something Henry Ward Beecher understood well; for him city elms were "tabernacles of the air," which transformed the lowliest street into a verdant house of worship. "We had rather walk beneath an avenue of elms," he wrote, speaking broadly for his fellow citizens, "than inspect the noblest cathedral that art ever accomplished."[49] If the cathedrals of the Old World were carved of stone, those of "Nature's nation" would be borne on the limbs of elms.

"We cannot ever hope to have in this country a gothic cathedral," offered an anonymous writer from Northampton in an 1864 issue of the *Hampshire Gazette*, "but he who would understand the strength, beauty, variety and comprehensiveness of this flower of man's genius, need only to study one of our grandest elms. . . . The thing, in short, most like a gothic cathedral, is a grand old elm with its forest of branches, its population of birds, its mighty uplifted arches, and its depth of solemn shade."[50] A generation later, in the opening chapter of his novel *Elsie Venner*, Oliver Wendell Holmes claimed that no Gothic arch "compares, for a moment, with that formed by two American elms, where their lofty jets of foliage shoot across each other's ascending curves, to intermingle their showery flakes of green. When one looks through a long double row of these . . . he beholds a temple not built with hands, fairer than any minister, with all its clustered stems and flowering capitals, that ever grew in stone."[51]

Montgomery Clement Meigs took this metaphor literally, and he proposed building (or, more accurately, planting) just such a cathedral of elms on the banks of the Schuylkill River in Philadelphia. Meigs was no amateur when it came to building in bricks and mortar; the West Point graduate constructed Washington's water supply system, served as Lincoln's quartermaster general during the Civil War, and later designed the great Pension Building (now the National Building Museum).[52] But in a letter to *Architectural Review and American Builder's Journal* in 1870, the architect suggested exchanging trowel for spade, arguing that a "noble sylvan temple could be constructed in less time than the great cathedrals of Europe have taken to build, by planting the graceful New England elm in positions of the piers or pillars of a Gothic cathedral." Meigs included with the letter a plan for a "structure" of 200 by 260 feet, complete with transept, nave, and choir. "The plan of Notre Dame at Paris, or the cathedral of

*Montgomery C. Meigs, proposal for a "sylvan temple," 1870 (*Architectural Review and American Builder's Journal, *August 1870)*

Ulm could thus be planted," Meigs reasoned, "and in a few years, a temple of unequaled gothic tracery would rise into the air like Solomon's, without sound of hammer or tool of iron."[53]

But the epitome of sylvan Gothicism—and possibly the source of Meigs's inspiration—was New Haven, whose elms matured in almost perfect synchrony with the arrival and flowering of the Gothic in America. Founded as the New Jerusalem, its nine-square plan inspired by the biblical city of Ezekiel, New Haven was renewed in its allusions to providence by its great columns of elms. "I call it New Heaven," remarked the Reverend Swormstedt of Ohio. "Nowhere in the States did I see a more beautiful arrangement of trees," wrote William Smith at century's end, "for in many of the avenues the branches had united, forming Gothic aisles of rich green and sunlit interlacing bows." If the City of Elms was a sylvan cathedral—a "leafy temple," as Richard Upton Piper put it in 1855—Temple Street was its central transept. Surveyed and planted by Hillhouse in 1792, the thoroughfare passed through the Green, adjacent to the principal houses of worship. By the 1860s, Temple Street was described as "the grandest arch of trees on the globe," and it literally and figuratively overshadowed the nearby churches.[54] It was the city's most popularly reproduced feature; etchings and photographs of its great mantle of elms, the pièce de résistance of the City of Elms, were distributed around the world.

Nathaniel Parker Willis well understood the religious symbolism of New Haven's high Gothic canopy of elms, particularly those of Temple Street. To him, New Haven was "a vast cathedral with aisles for streets."[55] His *Elms of New Haven* is a melancholic appeal to lost youth, itself a Gothic paean to the "unhewn cathedral."

From every Gothic isle my heart fled home,
From every groined roof, and pointed arch,
To find its type in emerald beauty here.
The moon we worshipp'd through this trembling veil,
In other heavens seem'd garish and unclad.
The stars that burn'd to us through whispering leaves,
Stood cold and silently in other skies.
Stiller seem'd alway here the holy dawn
Hush'd by the breathless silence of the trees;
And who, that ever, on a Sabbath morn,
Sent through this leafy roof a prayer to Heaven,
And when the sweet bells burst upon the air,
Saw the leaves quiver, and the flecks of light
Leap like caressing angels to the feet
Of the church-going multitude, but felt
That here, God's day was holier—that the trees,
Pierced by these shining spires, and echoing ever
"To prayer!" "To prayer!" were but the lofty roof
Of an unhewn cathedral, in whose choirs
Breezes and storm-winds, and the many birds
Join'd in the varied anthem; and that so,
Resting their breasts upon these bending limbs,
Closer, and readier to our need they lay—
The spirits who keep watch 'twixt us and Heaven.[56]

Age of Elms

The Gothic elm cathedral represented the tree's symbolic apogee in nineteenth-century New England. The elm had, over the course of more than a century, accumulated a great range of associations. As an icon of the pastoral landscape, a harbinger of domesticity, a civic totem, a relic of pre-European settlement, or an arboreal monument marking great events and persons, elms bore extraordinary cultural freight. With the village improvement movement and the later extensive planting of elms in cities, the tree came to play a defining role in shaping the *civitas* of New England's towns and cities. Elm-lined streets were understood to be a mechanism of urban-rural synthesis, a means of bringing the country into the city. The metaphor of the Gothic cathedral added an ecclesiastical dimension to the varied symbolism of the tree, which, in the Romantic eye, was already divine.

By the end of the nineteenth century the tree was a ubiquitous element in the New England landscape, a commonplace of wayside, village, town, and city street. It is a rare portrayal of the region—whether in words or paint—that fails to include elm trees. The elm emerged as one of the definitive icons of Yankee regional identity, a sylvan symbol of land and people. This was something Sargent well understood in 1890, when he wrote: "In no other part of the country is there a tree which occupies the same position in the affection of the people as the Elm does in that of the inhabitants of New England."[57] Indeed, nowhere in America would a tree acquire such deep cultural resonance as the elm in New England. So powerful was this mingling of man and tree that elm culture eventually was exported to nearly every region of the United States, until the elm was not only a Yankee icon but an American one.

BOULEVARD OF BROKEN TREES

The streetscape of antebellum New England was an ideal environment for the growth of trees—particularly elms. In the absence of storm-water drainage systems and impervious pavement, water was plentiful. Oxygen and nutrients could pass easily to the roots, which were unmolested by excavation; sewer mains, gas pipes, and electrical conduits were still years away. Streetcar catenary was yet to appear, and there were no electrical power lines or telephone wires to make way for. Traffic was light, and there was little demand to widen thoroughfares. Vehicles were drawn by horses and oxen, and while street elms occasionally suffered the predations of these animals, in exchange they provided a steady supply of fertilizer.

Streetscape Modernization

But beginning in the 1860s, a series of modernizations transformed the semi-rural New England streetscape into an intensively managed corridor accommodating a variety of transit and urban services. In many instances, these changes required the outright removal of trees. The spirit of improvement, once the champion of elm planting, now often spelled the doom of the very trees planted by New England's pioneer environmentalists. More than anything, it was the widening of streets to accommodate increasing traffic that brought about the downfall of countless Yankee elms. The trees were, in the eyes of the municipal engineer, little more than traffic obstructions.

Outrage over the felling of town elms to expedite traffic erupted early. In 1864, the *Hampshire Gazette* published a lengthy tract protesting "a few of the devastations made by this monster, 'Improvement.'" Its writer descried the "defacing and despoiling" of Northampton, Massachusetts, "under the guise of straightening

Street elms in Portland, Maine, c. 1880 (Edward H. Elwell,
Portland and Vicinity, *1881)*

a street, and widening a thoroughfare," and took special aim at "those who would make haste to cut down the old elms" (trees that "once fully compensated for any shortcomings of brick and mortar"). In one instance, thirteen elms were destroyed "in order to have a straight street and a corner perfectly at right angles." The essay is a remarkably modern appeal for environmental stewardship: "We who live to-day must not forget that we are only life tenants, and we have no right to cut down the wood and despoil the estate; the generations who come after us have a vested interest in these century-old forest trees, the legacies of our thoughtful ancestors. Can we not, at least, by a little pains, harmonize our own need for increased business facilities, with the preservation of these priceless ornaments of our town?"[1]

Other, more subtle changes steadily altered the ecology of the street—making life increasingly difficult for its trees. Water mains were built or expanded and sewer mains installed. Both frequently required the regrading of streets, a process that often smothered the roots of adjacent trees or required outright removal.

Gas illumination technology was perfected in the 1850s, and during the following decade many New England towns placed mains in their streets. Competing gas companies would often each install their own mains, causing repeated excavation of the street.[2] This almost always resulted in severe damage to the root systems of adjacent elms, and commonly killed them outright. Leaking gas was also blamed for poisoning roots and hastening the decline of many a Yankee curbside elm.

With the electrification of the horsecar lines in the 1890s, catenary was installed along hundreds of New England thoroughfares. In many cases, flanking elms were tall enough to allow the wires to pass unimpeded; elsewhere, trees had to be removed or pruned dramatically to make way for the new infrastructure. Streetcar companies naturally had little love for the ponderous trees, for their wires were under a constant threat of being snapped by falling limbs. The trees, however, bore the brunt of this meeting of technology and urban nature. Tree trunks and limbs were often burned where they made contact with the wires, and sometimes entire trees were electrocuted (particularly during periods of extreme wetness). The plant essentially caused a short-circuit in the streetcar system, and it was found that the polarity of the current played a role in the severity of damage to the plant. A 1914 *Scientific American* article described "An Unusual Case of Electrical Injury to Street Trees" in which elms along New Haven's Street Railway Company lines began dying when the company switched the polarity of the overhead wires from positive to negative. The surge of current that once ran harmlessly down the bark was now passing through the living sapwood of the tree.[3]

Urban electrification also brought wires, and so did the arrival of telephone lines in the 1880s. In many communities, the earliest electrical lines were strung from the trunks of street trees themselves, but the living poles were soon replaced by leafless ones. By the end of the century, New England streets had erupted with utility poles and wires. Not everyone cheered the forward march of progress. In 1886, the *Hampshire Gazette* complained about "the recent raid" upon Northampton's Main Street by "electric light companies," whose "unsightly poles" meant the removal of many an elm.[4] Elms and utility companies began competing for space along the street—a struggle that would worsen as the trees aged and the power grid expanded. More affluent municipalities placed much of this wire underground by 1900, but on the typical New England street elm trees and wires became entangled—usually to the detriment of the trees.[5]

As society became more dependent on electricity, the conflict between elm trees and the utility companies grew intense. The trees were accused of causing hundreds of power outages, and very often it was a falling limb that snapped a wire and shut down a portion of the grid—particularly during storms. In the wake of a severe ice storm in 1953, even the tree-loving *Connecticut Woodlands* admitted that "95 to 98 per cent of storm damage to the electrical distribution system can be laid to falling branches or branches sagging into the lines."[6] The *New York Times* that year ran a story in which a leading Connecticut tree warden claimed that trees, particularly elms, were a threat to the welfare of public utilities. As he put it, most American cities were in urgent need of a pruning. Larger, "weedy" species should be removed at once, he argued, and replaced with smaller trees "of a character that can be trained around the wires."[7] Elms, very big and very weedy, must be sacrificed to appease the goddess of electricity.[8]

Change came from below as well as overhead. Most town and city streets in antebellum New England were unpaved, and often more resembled rural roads than urban thoroughfares. Even as late as 1890, 50 percent of the street mileage in major American cities remained unpaved. Those that had been surfaced were usually paved with brick or granite cobbles or wood blocks, or were simply bedded with gravel. None of these surfaces restricted the passage of water, nutrients, or oxygen to the roots of adjacent trees. Macadam, consisting of alternating layers of crushed stone, was first used in the United States during the turnpike boom of the 1820s, gaining popularity for streets after Frederick Law Olmsted and Calvert Vaux used it in Central Park in 1858. Macadam, too, was highly permeable.[9]

But as the function and purpose of the street began to change in the years following the Civil War, more durable—and less permeable—materials came into use. Cobbles and blocks offered horses a good foothold, but with the arrival of more sophisticated vehicles, smoother pavements were needed. Concrete was used both alone and as a base for asphalt, and the first paved asphalt street in America appeared in 1871, at Newark, New Jersey. Able to withstand heavy traffic and vehicle loads, the material quickly gained in popularity, particularly after manufacturing innovations reduced its cost. By 1925 asphalt and concrete were being used to pave approximately 40 percent of the streets in major American cities.[10]

Asphalt and concrete virtually sealed the surface of the street, depriving trees of water, nutrients, and oxygen. And along with the new paved surfaces came highly engineered drainage systems. These were meant to leave no standing water that could breed mosquitoes and pose other public health threats. But as the new infrastructure whisked away all rainfall, the thirsty roots of nearby elms were further starved. Water that once percolated into the soil and water table below was now moved swiftly off site. Finally, with the arrival of the motor vehicle, a toxic cocktail of pollutants was introduced to the streetscape ecosystem, including exhaust gases, crankcase oil, and fossil fuels.

The new environmental stresses that accompanied streetscape modernization had, by the early twentieth century, begun to weaken New England's curbside elms. The trees faced conditions radically less favorable to growth than those

Felling of the Cooke Elm in Keene, New Hampshire, to make way for a wider street
(Courtesy of the Historical Society of Cheshire County)

during the premodern era. Many older specimens simply perished, and young ones often grew stunted and deformed. The once tenacious and hardy elm was under siege. "The hard conditions of 'congested' urban life are coming upon us," lamented the city fathers of Cambridge.

> Gradually the surface of Cambridge is being encrusted with macadam and bricks; the lawns which separated the buildings from the sidewalks are disappearing in the yawning cellars of modern structures; apartment houses rise above the tree-tops; electric-light wires wither and kill the foliage above, while escaping gases suffocate the roots beneath. In the earth, on the surface, and above, the enemies of shade trees increase at an alarming rate, with the increase of city conditions.
>
> . . . The axe of the road builder becomes more terrible than ever the 'woodman's axe,' because directed by official hands; the change in the grades of streets, so often and so mysteriously decreed, is a sentence of death to many a mighty monarch of the ancient Cambridge forest. Ungainly telephone poles are substituted for living trees, and are planted with all the ceremony which city orders and ordinances can command.[11]

Environmental stress also made the elms more susceptible to diseases and insect pests that had posed only minor threats in the past. By the end of the nineteenth century, New England's elms were being increasingly victimized by a variety of pathogens. The elm leaf beetle *(Galeruca xanthomelaena)*, which arrived in the United States in 1834, often stripped elms of all foliage. At New Haven, the first invasion of elm leaf beetles took place in the 1890s, and was met by a citywide campaign to spray the trees with an insecticide. A second, larger invasion took place in 1908.

Frederick Law Olmsted, Jr., who had been in New Haven that year consulting on its new city plan, was "disturbed to find that the trees on the old Green were being ravaged by elm leaf beetles." This time the beetles had their way with the municipal trees. Although Yale University took quick action to protect its elms against the predator, the city was slower to respond, resulting in the loss of scores of mature elms. Grassroots action, however noble, was often misguided: in one instance, a local newspaper urged citizens to "bring out their teakettles and pour hot water on the pupae" of the beetles at the base of each elm. The effort, which was met with little enthusiasm, was dubbed the Teakettle Brigade.[12]

The increasing susceptibility of the elm to insect pests convinced some skeptics that the tree was no longer worth keeping. An 1890 article in the *New York Tribune*—prophetically titled "The Passing of the Elm"—claimed that the tree was becoming more and more vulnerable and a burden to maintain. ("The elms," the writer concluded in no uncertain terms, "must go.")[13] Subsequent writers also noted the elm's increasing frailty. Clarence M. Weed, writing in a 1913 issue of *The Craftsman*, pointed out that the elm was New England's favorite street tree partly because it "had until recent years practically no serious insect or fungus enemies." But now, he warned, both native pests and "insect enemies . . . introduced from foreign lands" threatened the beloved species. "One may travel for miles in New England," Weed related, "and see everywhere evidence of the decay of these noble trees."[14] In truth, the dying of the elms had only just begun.

Interloper

A truly formidable enemy from foreign lands arrived on American soil soon enough, a fungal interloper spread by the tiny elm bark beetle. The new disease was not unknown, for it had already laid waste to the great elms of England and northern Europe. The plague first appeared in war-ravaged areas of northern Europe in 1918, where it was known simply as the "elm death" and was believed to be caused by nerve gas and artillery fire during the war.[15] It was not until 1922 that the real causal agent of the "elm death" was isolated, by Maria Beatrice Schwarz of the Scholten Phytopathologisch Laboratorium in Baarn, Netherlands. Schwarz, a graduate student at the time, named the fungal agent *Graphium ulmi*, although the pathogen was later reassigned many binomial names (it was first known as *Ceratocystis ulmi* in the United States, and today as *Ophiostoma ulmi*).[16] Ironically, the pioneering work on the part of the Netherlands forever branded the disease with Dutch provenance; it was henceforth known as the Dutch elm disease.[17]

It had already devastated the European landscape. In 1920 the disease appeared in epidemic form near Rotterdam, and it was discovered soon after in Belgium and parts of northern France. By 1924 Dutch elm disease had entered the Rhine Valley, and it made its way to England two years later.[18] By the 1930s it was endemic across Europe, from Scandinavia to southern Italy and east to the Balkans. And then it hopped the Atlantic. Curtis May, a technician with the United States Department of Agriculture, was the first to discover Dutch elm disease in North America—detected in 1931 on three trees near Cleveland and one in Cincinnati. His discovery prompted an immediate search of the surrounding Ohio River valley countryside for a possible source. Elm wood at lumber mills throughout Ohio was inspected, and all elms presenting symptoms were sampled and sent to labs for testing. Forest pathologists in surrounding states conducted similar searches. Only two additional infected trees were discovered, both in Cleveland.[19]

It appeared that the outbreaks were isolated events. Scientists were baffled as to how the disease had been transported to North America, or how it could have leapfrogged the coast to appear hundreds of miles from any seaport. Logic suggested entry at a major port, but as late as August 1930 not a single infected elm had been identified in New York or southern Connecticut.[20] But then the picture began to change. In June 1933, several trees infected with Dutch elm disease were identified in northern New Jersey, followed by a handful in southern New York, including Westchester County, Staten Island, and western Long Island. A single dying elm in Glenville, Connecticut, was the first infected tree in New England. A total of six hundred diseased elms were identified that season, all within a thirty-mile radius of New York City.[21] Clearly, the pathogen had been introduced at port; the interloper had simply evaded detection.

As no European elm nursery stock had been allowed into North America since 1919, federal investigators turned to a new suspect: Carpathian elm burl logs imported from France and elsewhere in Europe for the manufacture of decorative furniture veneer. In July 1933, offending wood was intercepted at New York, Baltimore, Norfolk, and New Orleans. The logs were infested with the *Ceratocystis* fungus. It was also discovered that shipments of burl logs had been made to various cities in the Midwest as early as 1926, explaining the appearance of the pathogen identified by Curtis May in Ohio.[22] A quarantine on further imports of elm logs was ordered, but the following year another source of entry was discovered: dish crates from the United Kingdom made of elm wood had reintroduced the fungus at the port of New York.[23]

Not only were the intercepted logs infected with the Dutch elm disease, they were found to harbor whole colonies of European elm bark beetles—both *Scolytus scolytus* and the smaller *Scolytus multistriatus*. Unlike the fungus that had earlier wiped out the American chestnut, *Ceratocystis* spores are sticky and resist being windborne. They can be transported over long distances only by adhering to the body of an insect carrier—known as a vector. The larger beetle had been the principal vector in Europe; in the United States the smaller insect, *Scolytus multistriatus*, was the prime mover.[24] The beetle passed along the fungal spores when feeding on sapwood in twig crotches; the fungus then gained access to the tree's vascular system, where it produced tyloses, or protrusions, that eventually impeded the upward flow of water and nutrients and strangled the tree. So lethal was this process that a century-old elm could wither and die within a matter of months.

Although little more than two millimeters in length, the tiny beetle proved to be an able transporter, flying as far as three miles from its place of hatching. Moreover, the insect was small enough to be whisked aloft by winds, hitching a ride to places far beyond its natural range. The relationship between wind patterns and the spread of the disease, misunderstood at first, was established by way of an innovative experiment conducted by Ephraim Porter Felt in 1936. Nearly ten thousand toy balloons, filled with hydrogen and bearing tags, were released

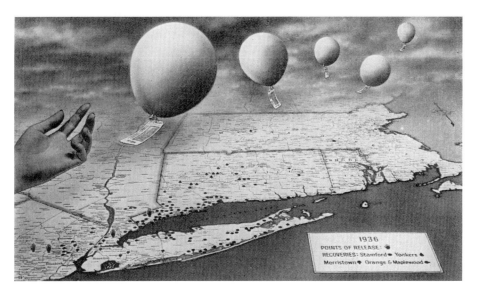

Illustration of E. P. Felt's 1936 balloon-drift experiment (E. P. Felt, "Factors Affecting Dutch Elm Disease Spread," Scientific Tree Topics *1:3, 1940)*
© American Map Corporation, NY Lic. No: 19702

from numerous points within a fifty-mile radius of Manhattan. Balloons retrieved later indicated travel speeds of thirty to forty-five miles per hour, with a pronounced easterly drift. A large number of balloons were picked up along Connecticut's southern shore, correlating closely with the known infestation zone of Dutch elm disease. Others were distributed across a wide area stretching northeast to Hartford.[25] The balloons indicated the likely path of the wind-and-beetle borne disease, a path cutting across the heartland of the Yankee elm.

Equally ominous was the fact that there were already large resident populations of *Scolytus multistriatus* farther north. The beetle had been discovered in Cambridge, Massachusetts, in 1909, where it had infested the elms in Harvard Yard. The insect was common in the areas of New York and southern Connecticut where Dutch elm disease was already present, but it was even more prevalent in Massachusetts. Should the contagion make it that far north, billions of insect transporters lay waiting there to carry it far and wide.

Yet the disease spread slowly in the 1930s, misleading many municipal officials who underestimated its virulence. Although the contagion reached epidemic proportions early in parts of southern New York and New Jersey, the zone of infestation appeared to be contained. Even Connecticut, infected since 1933, seemed to have things under control. "If the disease is spreading eastward," observed Walter O. Filley in the fall of 1936, "it is doing so very slowly, and there seems good reason to believe that its spread in that direction has been checked."[26] Massachusetts seemed safely distant from the killer; by the end of the decade there was still not a single infected elm in the Commonwealth.

"To Arms for the American Elm"

But if city officials were slow to recognize the severity of the new disease, foresters, plant pathologists, and landscape architects well understood that an environmental catastrophe was in the making. Throughout the 1930s, professional journals of forestry, city planning, and landscape architecture published scores of articles and editorials urging action against the plague. "It may be a flash in the pan," wrote F. A. Bartlett in *American Landscape Architect* in 1930, but "inasmuch as the American elm represents as high as 75 percent of the tree growth in many eastern cities and holds an important feature position in landscape design, the question of probable disease attack is one of the greatest scientific, economic, and aesthetic importance."[27]

Action to eradicate Dutch elm disease began early, but these efforts were often hobbled by limited knowledge about the disease and the mobility of its insect vectors. Some control activity actually aided the contagion's advance. It was believed, for example, that the elm bark beetle could not travel more than five hundred feet from an infected tree. One common control strategy involved creating a "barrier" of dead elms. Infected trees in this zone were killed off with copper sulfate but left to stand. Rather than stop the progress of the disease, the pileup of dead wood only hastened its advance by creating breeding places for the beetles.[28] As research revealed the true role of the vector in spreading the disease, control efforts focused on destroying the beetle itself. As with malaria or yellow fever, "controlling the carrier," wrote E. P. Felt, "controls the disease."[29]

By September 1934, some 6,500 infected elms had been discovered in New Jersey, New York, and southern Connecticut—a tenfold increase from the previous season. "Unless the Dutch elm disease can be wiped out within the next twelve months," warned Walter O. Filley of the USDA's Connecticut Agricultural Experiment Station, "America must lose her splendid elms." He continued, "An emergency exists that demands the use of emergency methods."[30] Lee A. Strong, chief of the USDA's bureau of entomology and plant quarantine, underscored Filley's conclusion: unless "a vigorous, consistent program is carried out to remove and burn every infected tree," he stated, "the elms of America may follow the American chestnut to almost complete destruction by disease."[31]

Americans were well aware of the chestnut's demise and how rapidly an alien pathogen could wipe out a native tree species. The American chestnut *(Castanea dentata)*, one of the largest and most valuable hardwoods of the eastern forest, was virtually extirpated in the early twentieth century by the chestnut blight, a lethal disease caused by the fungus *Endothia parasitica*. Because the *Endothia* spores were easily borne by wind, rain, and a variety of insects, the blight spread with astonishing speed, moving westward at a pace of twenty-four miles a year. The disease ultimately killed the equivalent of nine million acres of chestnut forest —the area of Massachusetts, Connecticut, and Rhode Island combined.[32] But as economically valuable as the chestnut was, it was principally a forest tree and played only a minor role in the daily lives of New Englanders. The elm, on the other hand, was ubiquitous.

The federal government took a lead in fighting the disease from the start, but red tape and bureaucracy stymied its best efforts. The Department of Agriculture's bureau of entomology and plant quarantine established a Dutch elm disease laboratory in Morristown, New Jersey, in the summer of 1934, and the Works Progress Administration supplied funds to hire men to combat the invader. The Civilian Conservation Corps was then at its greatest strength, with 365,000 men enrolled nationwide, promising a deep reserve of labor. The American Forestry Association implored President Franklin D. Roosevelt to draw upon the corps as "shock troops" to help cut and burn all dead and dying elms within the infected areas of Connecticut, New York, and New Jersey. "This tree army has already proved its worth and its adaptability to meet the emergency in the event other and better methods of combat are not readily possible," the association urged. "There can be no finer, more appropriate or more important service it could render the American people than that of saving the American elm."[33]

In December 1934 the WPA allotted $527,000 toward eradication work, enabling 1,200 workers and several hundred CCC troops to be employed that winter and spring removing and destroying "infected and suspected" elms in Connecticut, New York, and New Jersey.[34] By early February nearly 23,000 diseased, dead, or dying trees had already been removed; another 140,000 had been tagged for removal.[35] But work was not moving fast enough. More men were needed if all the dead and dying wood was to be cut and burned before the spring, when the millions of spore-bearing *Scolytus* beetles would begin emerging from their pupae. Scouting would have to be increased to identify new areas of infestation, including along rail corridors where the infected burl logs had been transported.

More money was needed, and fast. A crisis was looming, the American Forestry Association warned, and failure to deal with it would bring down the wrath of a tree-loving citizenry: "The American people are in no temper to stand by and see the elm disappear from the American landscape." The association accused the government of moving too slowly to combat the invader, and setting aside too

The "Dutch elm boys." Company 2102 of the First Corps Area of the Civilian Conservation Corps, Connecticut, 1937 (Courtesy of Marilyn Aarrestad, Shenipsit State Forest, Connecticut)

few resources. "The war on the Dutch elm disease must be a war to the finish. . . . Like any war, it calls for money." The association requested that $1.5 million be released from emergency relief funds to ramp up the eradication campaign; yet only $261,156 showed up in the budget for the following fiscal year.[36]

The situation improved somewhat in July 1935, when President Roosevelt authorized a large sum of relief funds—more than $2.5 million—to continue the fight. By that summer the contagion had already spread to an area of 4,500 square miles, and more than 600,000 elms in New York, Connecticut, and New Jersey had been destroyed in an effort to halt the disease. But irregular delivery of relief funds caused scouting and removal work to be halted several times in 1933 and 1934. Well-trained men were fired when the money ran out, and regulations governing relief fund dispersal prohibited their reemployment when money became available again. A new lot of men had to be brought in and trained from the bottom up in scouting, detection, and sampling work. Valuable time was lost. In the meanwhile, Dutch elm disease quickly regained whatever ground it had been purged from.[37]

By the spring of 1936 the Department of Agriculture seemed ready to throw in the towel. During hearings before the House subcommittee on agricultural appropriations, expert witnesses representing the Department of Agriculture suggested that it might be impossible to eradicate Dutch elm disease. Conservation groups were outraged. "If the American elm is to be saved," wrote Ovid Butler of the American Forestry Association, "now is the time for the American people to scotch any show of defeatism on the part of the Federal Government. Such an attitude will inevitably mean the doom of the American elm and an incalculable loss to communities and individuals throughout the country"; to abandon the American elm without a real fight, he stated, "will be a national calamity."[38]

Nevertheless, the Department of Agriculture continued to fund eradication efforts, and the campaign launched in the spring of 1936 resembled a military operation. The bureau of entomology and plant quarantine had more than 1,400 scouts in the field by June, scouring streets, roadsides, and woodlands for the telltale "flagging" (withered, dried-out leaves at the top of the crown) of an infected elm. Many young men were recruited from the CCC and trained at several camps in New Jersey. An autogiro—a kind of airplane-helicopter hybrid—was acquired to conduct aerial detection surveys. Observers in the slow-flying craft would spot unhealthy trees and mark their location on a map for ground crews to sample. At the lab in Morristown, a force of pathologists produced cultures from every suspect tree—as many as a thousand a day. By August 1936, a total of 1,286,912 elms had been removed and destroyed.[39]

But in 1937 the House subcommittee on agricultural appropriations slashed funding for Dutch elm disease eradication work. "The battle to save America's most cherished tree," *American Forests* wrote in protest, "is in grave danger of being abandoned at the very moment when victory is in sight."

> Unless the American people speedily wake up to the fact that the elm is the nation's greatest tree asset and that its protection warrants the expenditure of a few million dollars, the American elm will speedily make its rendezvous with death. When that happens millions of people, grief stricken by the loss of dearly beloved trees and burdened by the cost of removing their dead forms from yards, streets and towns everywhere, and of replacing them with inadequate substitutes, will cry out in angry rage. But it will be too late.[40]

In truth, it was already too late.

Panic began to set in. Full-page broadsides in *American Forests* cried "Remember the Chestnut and Save the Elm!" A "deadly enemy" had broken through the lines of defense, wrote Joseph Edgar Chamberlain. "Imagine the wiping out of the beautiful avenues of elms that shade and decorate our streets and parks and roads," he wrote, "which stand in monumental grandeur at the doors of millions of homes, which constitute one of the greatest charms of our life!" The destruction of our elms, Chamberlain concluded, "would be a bitter and calamitous loss."[41]

And then the fates dealt New England a second crippling blow. In the fall of 1938, Dutch elm disease gained a potent ally. It, too, was an interloper from abroad, this time from the humid west coast of Africa.

"A Wind to Shake the World"

The Great Hurricane of 1938 began innocently enough, as little more than a ridge of low pressure over the south-central Sahara. But the storm rapidly developed a "cyclonic whirl" as it moved over the former French West Africa. On the morning of September 16, it attained full hurricane force and began moving swiftly across the Atlantic. After the cyclone reached the Bahamas on the nineteenth, it turned northward along the eastern seaboard, following a trough of low pressure that aimed it straight for New England. At 3:30 on the afternoon of September 21, the cyclone slammed into the south shore of Long Island. The eye alone of the behemoth storm spanned forty miles.[42]

Sweeping over Long Island Sound, the hurricane crashed into the Connecticut shore near New Haven and then moved rapidly across the state just west of the Connecticut River valley. It was the most potent and destructive natural event ever to strike New England, and it wreaked havoc on the region's forests and trees. The wind alone was bad enough, gusting to more than 180 miles per hour in some places. But two other factors doomed the trees. First, there had been four days of torrential rains before the storm arrived, thoroughly saturating the soil and robbing roots of their purchase; second, the deciduous trees across the southern parts of New England were still in full leaf. Big elms were waterlogged and top-heavy, and their leafy crowns caught the full force of the coming storm. They didn't have a chance. Century-old trees were tossed about like matchsticks.

The elm-embowered towns of western Connecticut and the Connecticut River valley were the hardest hit. New Haven lay right in the path of the hurricane, and it was beaten mercilessly. In a matter of hours the City of Elms lost 13,500 of its trees, and another 7,000 were severely damaged. "It was at New Haven," wrote Everett S. Allen, "that New Englanders began to realize the magnitude of the storm's impact upon their natural heritage."[43] Hartford, too, was directly in the storm's path. The capital was inundated by the swollen Connecticut River, while 10,000 trees were blown down in its parks. Farther upriver, at Springfield, 17,000 trees were seriously damaged. Amherst lost 2,500 trees, and nearly all of the elms at Amherst College were destroyed. Nearly 8,000 street trees in Boston were blown down or severely damaged. Keene, New Hampshire, New England's other Elm City, lost hundreds of trees, as did Concord, Franklin, and Barre, Vermont. All across southern New England, the storm's tree toll was staggering.[44]

The Great Hurricane gave New Englanders a first, frightening glimpse of what their landscape would look like shorn of its elms. "Here, where the lordliest of trees stood," wrote H. I. Phillips of New Haven, "all is waste and desolation, a scant company left to stand out gaunt and broken, like the remnants of a lost battalion. . . . The glory of the years is gone, the beauty so long in the building is vanished in the twinkling of an eye."[45] The storm was selective in its destruction of trees. The majority of the elms knocked down were more than fifty years old—the loftiest and most valuable of the region's trees. Scores of communities were transformed overnight. David Morton fathomed the loss in a poem about the shattered elms of Amherst.

> It is not only that the trees are gone,
> Whose roots were in our breasts, as now we know,
> When the earth yielded and the breast held on,
> Not knowing any way to let them go . . .
> Not merely that the lost and wandering eye,
> Ranging horizons to the east . . . to west . . .
> Finds unfamiliar angles of the sky,
> And wanders on and finds no certain rest.
> Not this alone . . . Our minds had somehow been
> (For very long and happily in this place)
> Another sky that elms were branching in
> With such cool benisons of special grace,
> That we shall know, I think, a nameless lack
> Of something gone, of something wanted back.[46]

The winds blew down many elms, but this was only part of the storm's impact on the Republic of Shade.

The Great Hurricane left in its path an immense swath of detritus. All told, more than a million large shade trees were destroyed by the hurricane, many of them American elms.[47] The Northeastern Timber Salvage Administration estimated that wind-thrown timber—including downed trees in woodlands and forests—totaled 3.25 billion board feet—enough wood to cover 120 square miles with one-inch plank flooring.[48] Although much of the "hurricane timber" was salvaged, much more was simply left to rot. Thousands of fallen street elms were bucked up and piled in municipal lots and junkyards across the region, or stacked to cure as firewood.

For the elm bark beetle, this was heaven. *Scolytus multistriatus* breeds in the bark of dead or dying elms, and no finer rookery can be had than a pile of elm wood. The female insect bores under the inner bark of the dead wood, breeds, and lays eggs along the walls of tunnels known as "egg galleries." If the fungus is present in the wood, huge amounts of spores are reproduced in the egg galleries. The beetle larvae later hatch and bore a fan-shaped array of feeding tunnels through the cambium, each of which terminates in a pupae chamber. From these, a new generation of adult beetles later emerges, covered with the fungal spores, to fly off and feed on—and infect—healthy elms in the vicinity.[49]

Dutch elm disease and the Great Hurricane converged with remarkable precision, as if an unseen hand had guided each to a fateful rendezvous. In the summer of 1938, Dutch elm disease was known to have reached the Bridgeport area,

A storm-toppled tree and crushed car following the Great Hurricane of September 1938, Amherst, Massachusetts (Courtesy of the Jones Library)

Wind-blown elms in the wake of the Great Hurricane, Amherst (Courtesy of the Jones Library)

A hurricane-felled elm in Amherst (Courtesy of the Jones Library)

Stump removal in the aftermath of the hurricane, Amherst (Courtesy of the Jones Library)

and an infected tree had been recently discovered northeast of New Haven.[50] The storm made landfall at New Haven, close to the outer limit of the Dutch elm disease infestation. The hurricane met the plague to roll out a mighty red carpet of dead wood from Connecticut to Vermont. The presence of all this detritus likely helped fuel an explosion in the beetle population and assure the northward advance of both the insect and its lethal passenger. "Any situation that results in a large amount of recently killed, cut, or damaged elm wood," the Department of Agriculture later advised, "will cause tremendous increases in the population of this elm bark beetle."[51] Not since the European settlement of New England had there been a situation resulting in so much downed elm wood. And all around, remaining elms, both in town and in the surrounding woodlands, sustained the growing beetle population.

William P. Wharton, chairman of the National Conference on Dutch Elm Disease Eradication, well understood the high-risk conditions left in the storm's wake: "These innumerable elm windfalls will form breeding places for the bark beetle carriers of the disease," he warned. "Even though these wind-blown elms can all be removed, which seems impossible because of the extensive areas of forest land involved, the wood piles created will be a serious problem since they also are excellent breeding places for the beetles."[52] The disease did indeed spread in the wake of the hurricane, but it did so largely unobserved because of cutbacks in the number of field scouts searching for affected trees. As a result, relatively few diseased specimens were reported in the years following the storm. In the summer of 1938, 535 diseased elms were identified in Connecticut, with 18,152 total specimens in the major infestation area centered on New York City. In 1939, only 412 diseased elms were confirmed in Connecticut, with 10,786 in the metropolitan area. The following year the numbers were down to 378 and 4,444.[53]

The incomplete scouting reports were unfortunate indeed, for they created a false sense of security that the disease was under control. In reality, geographic expansion of Dutch elm disease in the wake of the hurricane was rapid, suggesting a correlation between the storm's path across Connecticut and the spread of the pandemic. In the four years preceding the storm (1935 to 1938), the area of Connecticut infected by the disease increased approximately 47 percent; in the four years following the storm (1938 to 1941), the infected zone exploded to almost 1,500 square miles—an increase of 258 percent.[54] The elm killer had spread across most of western Connecticut and as far north as Hartford, and was closing in on Massachusetts.

And the worst was yet to come. Events unfolding far from New England were soon to darken the elm's prospects further still. With the outbreak of World War II, manpower and resources being used to fight Dutch elm disease were diverted to combat the rise of fascism in Europe and Asia. In 1941, the Department of Agriculture stopped all work on controlling and combating the disease.[55] The burden of eradication fell to state and local governments, most of which could ill afford the expense of saving their elms. "War," wrote E. G. Brewer in 1943, "has made heavy inroads in America's . . . campaign to conquer the Dutch elm disease." The editors of *American Forests* appealed to the public to support the continued fight. "It is true that in the light of national defense needs, there are many federal activities that can and should be set aside . . . but stopping the elm disease is not one of them. The disease brooks neither temporizing nor delay. Abandon the battle for even one season and most certainly all will be lost."[56]

But the nation's priorities had changed. The American elm was fated to become one of the casualties of World War II. Now virtually unchecked, Dutch elm disease spread rapidly through New England. By the time the GIs returned home, the elms were dying by the millions. The disease had moved across western Connecticut and into Massachusetts by 1941. By 1945 it had advanced to Vermont, and was discovered in Rhode Island in 1946. Not long after, elms in New Hampshire and Maine began dying. By 1952 all of New England was under siege.

Toxic Mist

The number of elms killed during the war years was so large that sanitation alone (the scouting, removal, and burning of infected trees) was impossible. A new strategy was needed. Now, instead of removing every dead or dying elm in an attempt to eliminate the beetle's breeding places, work was concentrated on protecting healthy elms from initial attack. *Scolytus* had won the first round, but it might still be possible to save valued street elms by armoring each one against infection. And if World War II presented a major setback in the effort to save the elm, it also yielded a product that would become the chief weapon in the renewed fight against Dutch elm disease. This new tool was an insecticide—a contact poison "of prolonged residual effect"—that was soon known to the world as dichloro-diphenyl-trichloroethane, or DDT.[57]

DDT was first synthesized in 1874, but its usefulness as a pesticide was not understood until 1939. A Swiss scientist, Paul Hermann Müller, was the first to describe DDT's effectiveness as a contact poison, and he later received the Nobel Prize in medicine for his work. DDT was soon hailed as a miracle product that could eliminate the insect-borne plagues of humankind. The United States Army sprayed DDT extensively on New Guinea, Guadalcanal, the New Hebrides, and other Pacific islands to destroy malarial mosquito populations.[58] It was used in Europe to control the spread of typhus and to delouse refugees and prisoners liberated from concentration camps.[59] DDT was credited with saving millions of lives during World War II, helping make it the first conflict in which more people died of battle casualties than of disease.

A number of civilian applications were developed for DDT in the postwar period, and sales skyrocketed. Between 1945 and 1955 DDT production increased from 125 million pounds to 600 million pounds.[60] Suburban homeowners found it useful to control pests of the lawn and garden. Farmers discovered that a single application to crops would keep insect predators at bay for years. Millions of tons of DDT were applied on cotton fields in the South and cranberry bogs in New England. Apple orchards, cornfields, and potato crops were liberally dusted against a panoply of insect pests. And it was soon recognized that DDT could be used to eliminate the elm bark beetle.

Right after the war, the Department of Agriculture's bureau of entomology and plant quarantine began experimental spray applications of DDT to healthy elms. One of the earliest experiments took place in Englewood, New Jersey, in October 1946. City foresters employed a truck-mounted mobile unit equipped with an aircraft engine to spray a mist of DDT far into the treetops. "If the scolytus beetle knew what was good for him," declared the Englewood shade-tree commissioner, "he would surrender now unconditionally."[61] That spring most of the community's thirty-five hundred elms were sprayed "with various combinations and concentrations of DDT."[62]

Scientists at the University of Massachusetts later noted with approval similar experiments that demonstrated "fairly good protection" obtained by spraying "with *extra high concentrations* of DDT emulsion sprays applied by hydraulic sprayers and *extra large amounts* of 6 and 12 per cent DDT emulsions applied by mist blower or helicopter." While mist blowers worked well for smaller trees, it was the development of the hydraulic sprayer in 1947 that greatly facilitated the application of DDT to loftier elms.[63]

DDT indeed proved effective in killing the beetles, although researchers were skeptical from the start about its effectiveness against Dutch elm disease. "To what extent spraying for bark beetles will reduce the actual incidence of Dutch elm disease," offered the director of the Shade Tree Laboratories, "is not yet known but is being studied."[64] Regardless, spraying elms with DDT became the chief means of combating the killer contagion.

A survey by the Massachusetts Forest and Park Association showed that by January 1948 nearly two hundred Massachusetts cities and towns were spraying elms with DDT. In Connecticut, more than sixty communities had spraying programs in operation by 1951. The antibeetle campaign in Hartford resembled warfare itself. "In the spring of 1951," recalled Victor Jarm, Hartford's city forester, "our

BOULEVARD OF BROKEN TREES

160

anti-aircraft units sped into action. Our mist blowers roared through the city and sent up a thick smoke screen almost as if to hide the targets from the enemy. This was the start of our new offensive." "The war," he added, "was on."[65]

The elm bark beetle was not the only thing that DDT destroyed. It was understood that many beneficial insects caught in the toxic mist—spiders, honey bees, and a variety of beetles—were also killed. But although the potential danger of DDT was recognized as early as the mid-1940s, its impact on wildlife was not fully understood until much later. Neither was the persistence of DDT in the ecosystem. By 1950, just as elm-spraying programs were being launched all over New England, the Food and Drug Administration warned ominously that it was "extremely likely the potential hazard of DDT has been underestimated."[66]

Yet the public remained largely unaware of the poisonous cocktail being sprayed on their street trees. The first sign of trouble was a mysterious decline in songbird populations in several communities in New England and the Midwest that had been sprayed heavily with DDT. In 1956, researchers at the Cranbrook Institute of Science in Michigan began collecting birds suspected of having been inadvertently poisoned by DDT from the nearby suburban communities of Bloomfield Hills and Birmingham. Many of the birds were found to have toxic levels of the chemical in their brains, heart, liver, and other organs. Subsequent surveys on the Cranbrook campus, and at Michigan State University in East Lansing, revealed appalling mortality rates among resident robin populations. A clear link was emerging between DDT spraying and a sudden decline in the breeding robin population. Researchers at the Michigan State University zoology department found that the 250 pairs of birds on the Cranbrook campus before spraying began had been reduced to a mere 25 pairs by 1960, after several years of DDT spraying.[67]

Foresters and arborists, along with many tree lovers, questioned the veracity of the findings, and lobbyists for the chemical industry immediately sought to defuse what they considered a public-relations time bomb. Arnold Michlin, chief chemist at the Michlin Chemical Corporation—a major distributor of elm sprays—suggested that if application of DDT was confined to the dormant season, the birds would be saved and so would the trees. But what Michlin and most others underestimated was the persistence of DDT in the ecosystem. In particular, he failed to realize that the robins were being poisoned not only by the toxin at the time of spraying but by DDT concentrated in the bodies of other creatures upon which they fed.[68] DDT, it was later revealed, becomes rapidly concentrated upward through the food chain.

In spite of such reports, the public at large remained ignorant of the dangers of DDT until Rachel Carson began serializing *Silent Spring* in the *New Yorker* in

June 1962. Carson exposed the dangers of pesticides generally in the environment, but she took special aim at the widespread use of DDT to fight Dutch elm disease. When *Silent Spring* was published later that year, its impact was immediate and profound. Like Harriet Beecher Stowe's *Uncle Tom's Cabin*, it helped launch a major social movement. Carson's exposé became one of the formative texts of the 1960s environmental movement, and it swiftly turned the tide against the use of DDT for elm-disease control. The book unveiled a specter of ecological devastation that was silently stalking Elm Street, USA. Citing a 1958 study in Illinois that had demonstrated a link from DDT-sprayed elms to earthworms to dead robins, Carson wrote:

> The poison forms a tenacious film over the leaves and bark. Rains do not wash it away. In the autumn the leaves fall to the ground, accumulate in sodden layers, and begin the slow process of becoming one with the soil. In this they are aided by the toil of earthworms, who feed in the leaf litter, for elm leaves are among their favorite foods. In feeding on the leaves the worms also swallow the insecticide, accumulating and concentrating it in their bodies.

A study by a pair of researchers at Dartmouth College in 1965 verified the findings. After Hanover's 2,300 elms were sprayed in 1963, "151 dead or dying birds were found, many with signs of DDT poisoning, compared to 10 dead birds in a nearby community that had not been sprayed."[69] The birds were being killed by earthworms made toxic from feeding on DDT-laden elm leaves; they had become "biological magnifiers" of the toxin, passing lethal doses of the DDT on to their predators. Those birds that were not killed outright were often unable to reproduce. The toxin became highly concentrated in the reproductive organs of both males and females, affecting fertility rates and the viability of eggs. The result was a sharp decline in the number of offspring produced and, in some communities, the near extirpation of certain bird species.[70]

The power of *Silent Spring* came from Rachel Carson's ability to combine the discipline of a scientist with the sensitivity of a poet. She was appreciative of the beauty and cultural significance of the elm, "a tree," she wrote, "that is part of the history of thousands of towns, . . . gracing their streets and their village squares and college campuses with majestic archways of green." But the risks of attempting to save it with so potent a poison were far too great. "It would be tragic to lose the elms," wrote Carson, "but it would be doubly tragic if, in vain efforts to save them, we plunge vast segments of our bird population into the night of extinction."[71]

In a new round of grassroots activism, people around New England rose up in protest against elm-spraying operations. The activism could be strident at times, particularly in and around progressive college towns. Williamstown, Massachusetts, had developed an extensive spraying program to save the town's magnificent legacy elms, using DDT at first and then a related compound known as Methoxychlor. But shortly after *Silent Spring* hit the bookstores, students from nearby Williams College demanded that the town cease spraying operations. Because there was less traffic, less wind, and lower evaporation rates at night, spraying was often scheduled for the evening hours. But to the students this was Machiavelli in action; they were convinced the town chose the cover of night to conceal its evildoing. Night after night students—sometimes as many as two dozen—would descend on the tree warden's spray truck, rocking it violently or laying down in front to impede its progress. In an attempt to dissuade the protesters, the dean of students began riding in the truck's cab. But the tactic did little except get the college administrator dusted with pesticide. The Williamstown spraying program ended shortly after.[72]

Rachel Carson's book not only triggered a backlash against pesticides, it raised questions about the fundamental effectiveness of DDT in controlling Dutch elm disease. There was little or no evidence, she argued, to suggest that the substance was measurably reducing the number of elms that succumbed to the contagion. Disciplined sanitation efforts, such as one being carried out in Syracuse, New York, were proving just as effective as spraying—if not more so. But sanitation was costly and time-consuming. Spraying was fast, cheap, and had the added appeal of being a modern, "scientific" solution to the problem.

But however scientific it appeared, field evidence suggested that Carson was right: DDT was doing little to stop Dutch elm disease. The contagion reached epidemic proportions throughout much of southern New England by the late 1950s, taking a tremendous toll of trees. In January 1964, the Audubon Society charged that "millions of dollars have been wasted" in a effort to protect American elms by soaking them with the toxic substance. "It is nearly certain," stated Roland C. Clement, accurately, "that most elms will eventually succumb to this fungus disease." Subjecting the entire ecosystem to the unknown impacts of DDT was too great a risk to run. "The DDT program," he concluded, "has not worked."[73]

The formal end of the DDT era did not come until June 14, 1972, when William D. Ruckelshaus of the Environmental Protection Agency ordered that domestic usage of DDT be stopped. The agency had been studying the ecological impacts of DDT ever since *Silent Spring* was published, and its use had been restricted since 1969. Finally, the EPA concluded that "continued massive use of DDT posed unacceptable risks to the environment and potential harm to human health." Nearly all Federal registrations of DDT products were canceled, with certain exceptions related to public health. In the three decades before DDT was banned, some 1.35 billion pounds of the toxic substance had been applied domestically, much of it to combat Dutch elm disease and its tiny beetle vector.[74]

With or without DDT, prospects for the elm looked grim. In August 1968, the *New York Times* published an essay titled "The Vanishing American Elm." Its tone was elegiac. The essay's author, Walter Sullivan, wrote, "It now appears possible that, within a few years, this majestic tree, with its vase-shaped tower of branches, will have almost vanished from the New England scene." As if to confirm that observation, scientists at the Connecticut Agricultural Experiment Station that summer concluded that the situation confronting the American elm throughout New England "borders on the catastrophic."[75] There was little hope that the region's once rich heritage of elms could be salvaged. A tree that had been described as "the glory of New England" was being quickly reduced to bleaching hulks marked for removal.

A number of other methods for controlling the disease and its insect vector were proposed, but none proved very successful. Scientists in Ohio identified two chemicals present in elm bark responsible for stimulating the bark beetle's feeding instinct, and they searched for a way to a "switch" these off.[76] In 1970 a tiny wasplike insect *(Dendrosoter protuberans)* was introduced from France in an effort to combat the elm bark beetle by using a natural predator. The parasite deposits its eggs in the larvae of the beetle; once hatched, the insect larvae feed on the beetle larvae, killing them. But the bark of the American elm proved too thick for the insect's ovipositor to penetrate, and North American winters were too cold for the insect to survive.[77] Experimenters also tried injecting systemic pesticides and fungicides into the sapwood of trees, as well as vaccinations to inoculate the tree against the disease. But none of these strategies proved cost effective or practical.

By the 1970s, Dutch elm disease had ravaged New England and was moving rapidly across the Midwest, killing some four hundred thousand elms a year throughout the United States. The dying of the elms became part of daily life in New England, and in time it began to fade from the front pages. The pathogen had prevailed. Dutch elm disease gradually became accepted as an act of God not unlike the Great Hurricane of 1938. But the loss of a famous tree always drew forth a fresh round of elegies to the American elm's vanished glory and esteemed place in the Yankee landscape.

One such tree was the Great Elm of Wethersfield, Connecticut. Although most of New England's great nineteenth-century totem elms had long vanished, Wethersfield's sylvan elder persisted. Reputed to be the oldest and largest American elm in the United States, the tree had survived innumerable ice storms and hur-

The end of an era: the Wethersfield Elm being laid to rest, as portrayed in the Hartford Times *on May 29, 1953*

ricanes—including the big blow in 1938. But in the summer of 1945, the tree met its match; it was found to be infected with Dutch elm disease.

For the next eight years, town officials labored to save the landmark by trimming infected limbs (many of which were themselves the size of century-old trees). But Wethersfield was in the middle of one of the most heavily infested areas of New England, and the fate of the tree was sealed. Progressively cropped limb by limb over the course of several months, all that remained of the sylvan giant by the spring of 1953 was a massive stump. Removing it required digging a sixty-foot trench before the trunk could be lifted out of the ground, a task that took a team of workers three days to complete. The stump, weighing thirty-five tons, was finally removed and carted off on a flatbed truck on May 29, 1953.[78] A crowd of schoolchildren watched in silence as the truck drove off. The age of the Yankee elm was over.

Requiem for a Landscape

The introduction of Dutch elm disease to the United States was an ecological catastrophe unparalleled in American history. The decimation of the elms in its wake altered the ecology and the environmental quality of countless city streets. It was a natural organism, set loose in an alien environment, that destroyed New England's elms. But it was human design that stacked nature's deck against the tree. Elm Street was, in spite of its natural appearance, a highly artificial creation.

*Street furniture carved from the stump of a fallen elm, Oxford Street,
Cambridge, Massachusetts, 1998*

Ulmus americana is a solitary tree, and it almost never occurs naturally in pure
stands. Planting these trees in such great numbers, and in such close proximity, left
them in a profoundly unsustainable condition. It was only a matter of time before
a pandemic of some kind swept through this manmade forest and set things right.
Nature has an uncanny tendency to maintain its own equilibrium, irrespective of
human wishes. America's affection for the elm created the most extensive urban
forest in history; but it also set the stage for a plague of unprecedented proportions.
The ubiquity of the elm was its downfall; the tree was loved to death.

Would Dutch elm disease have attained epidemic proportions had the elm
not been such a universal feature in the New England landscape? Probably not,
for it is unlikely that populations of the elm bark beetle would ever have grown
so large without a superabundance of its favorite host. Moreover, the spread of the
fungus via intergrafted roots played a major role in the mobility of the disease—
one that was grossly underestimated for years. Not until 1968 did scientists realize that up to 60 percent of Dutch elm disease infections occurred below the soil,
far beyond the reach of DDT or any other prophylactic aimed at controlling the
elm bark beetle. Elm roots are promiscuous, and "sap transfusion" via roots can
occur between trees as far as fifty feet away.[79]

That planting such an unbroken overstory of elm trees might one day lead to
an uncontrollable contagion was indeed something farsighted arborists had warned
about long ago. "Cities should altogether beware of taking to *one* tree," wrote *The
Gardener's Monthly* as early as 1863. It was good advice, but it would take a hundred
years and the loss of the American elm for the lesson to sink in. Had the American

elm been planted more sparingly—interspersed with a variety of other forest trees—it is likely the tree would still be a presence in the New England landscape.

If the ecological and environmental impacts of the elm's passing could be measured, it would reveal a staggering toll. The removal of the shady overstory provided by the trees resulted in a dramatic increase in temperature—as much as twenty degrees in midsummer. This rapid warming occasionally had its own impacts. Some communities lost their street maples not long after the elms disappeared because of the jump in temperature on the denuded streets.[80] The urban elm forest also produced vast quantities of oxygen, and its leafy mantle functioned as a great filter that trapped airborne particulates—benefits that were lost when the trees began to die. In addition, the elm forest provided habitat for a range of bird and insect life. The Baltimore oriole, a species of songbird that favored the American elm as a nesting site, was perhaps the most visible of these creatures. Once common in New England, the bird followed the elms and gradually vanished from the scene.

But the greatest impact of Dutch elm disease was to rob New England of its quintessential urban feature, a tree that played a paramount role in defining the character and identity of towns, villages, and cities, and that endowed the region with grace and beauty in every season. Dutch elm disease destroyed the green mantle under which New England had matured; two hundred years of trees disappeared within a generation. The effect was staggering. Towns once recumbent in the deep shade of trees now shrank in the blinding sunlight, every crack and pore newly visible in the harsh light. The Jamesian veil of elm shade was not gently drawn aside, it was ripped away. "When you came into any town in New England the landscape changed," recalls Bill Chittick of Rhode Island; "you entered this kind of forest with 100-foot arches. The shadows changed. Everything seemed very reverent, there was a certain serenity, a certain calmness . . . a sweetness in the air. It was an otherworldly experience, you knew you were entering an almost sacred place." Now the sanctuary had been violated. Without the elms "you started to notice the severity of things—the utility wires and poles, the cracks in the hot pavement, which no longer were bathed in shadows."[81]

The contrast is a difficult one to capture in words, and even photographs taken before and after the elms can convey only a fraction of the impact of such a profound spatial transformation. That such convulsive change occurred when it did—in the late 1950s and 1960s—only added to its impact. The loss of Elm Street coincided with some of the most difficult urban and social transformations of the twentieth century. This was an era of racial discord and urban rebellion, ill-conceived urban renewal projects and highway-building schemes that gutted stable older neighborhoods across the region—many of which had been rich in elm shade. The passing of the elm also coincided with the great postwar

A more profound spatial transformation can hardly be imagined than the one seen on Gillet Avenue in Waukegan, Illinois, between 1962 (top) and 1972, after the pandemic had forced the removal of the trees. Although these photographs were taken in Illinois, they could represent any of thousands of similar elm-lined streets in New England. (Courtesy of John P. Hansel, Elm Research Institute, Westmoreland, New Hampshire)

exodus of the white middle class to suburbia, a migration that brought about the precipitous decline of many New England cities, from New Haven and Hartford to Springfield, Worcester, and even Boston. And through all this the elms came crashing down, laying waste, it seemed, the glory and essence of Yankee urbanism.

Henry Ward Beecher had long ago feared that such a fearful day might come. "What if they were sheered away from village and farm house?" he asked with chilling prescience in 1867; "Who would know the land? Farm-houses that now stop the tourist and the artist, would stand forth bare and homely; and villages that coquette with beauty through green leaves, would shine white and ghastly as sepulchres. Let anyone imagine Conway or Lancaster without elms! Or Hadley, Hatfield, Northampton, or Springfield! New Haven shorn of its elms would be like Jupiter without a beard, or a lion shaved of his mane!"[82]

A century later, we are still mourning the loss.

EPILOGUE: RETURN OF A NATIVE

Several years ago, one of the big savings banks in Boston launched an advertising campaign for a new suite of banking services. To catch the public's attention, the bank designed a poster featuring a mock newspaper front page on which all sorts of extraordinary stories were reported. One of these told of the discovery of an antidote for the common cold; another described intelligent life on Mars. Still another headline reported that a cure for Dutch elm disease had been found. That a commercial savings bank could assume the currency—and interest—of the tree's welfare among its customers speaks volumes of the lingering power of the American elm in New England. Of course, the imagined news story has yet to have any basis in fact. No cure for Dutch elm disease has been discovered, and every summer more of the surviving but embattled elms are lost to the disease. If the contagion itself remains unconquered, however, so does the will of people to restore this great native tree to its rightful place in the landscape. Even as hopes for an antidote have faded, efforts to develop disease-resistant cultivars of *Ulmus americana* have borne promising fruit.

Although the American elm has been functionally extirpated from the common landscapes of New England, it is by no means extinct. Specimen elms remain here and there across the region—in neglected back lots, on city streets, and in urban parks and playgrounds. It is not well understood why some elms survive while others succumb to Dutch elm disease. In some cases, local prevailing wind patterns may shield trees from bark beetle colonization. This could explain why several towns on the Maine coast, freshened by ocean winds, have been spared the worst of the pandemic. Blue Hill, Maine, is still shaded by magnificent century-old elms—living relics of a vanished era. So is Castine, Maine, an idyllic town located on a peninsula in East Penobscot Bay. It is possible that both have been spared Dutch elm disease because the airborne beetles have found it difficult to hitch a ride into town.

Studies suggest that a smaller percentage of elms in general are being infected by Dutch elm disease today. But this is more likely a result of the elm population itself having been so devastated already than of any budding resistance in the trees. As Peter Del Tredici, a botanist at Harvard University's Arnold Arboretum, has argued, more elms are surviving today simply "because the reduced elm population has resulted in lower elm bark beetle populations."[1] Yet, mysteriously, some elms remain uninfected even as their neighbors alongside succumb to the disease. Such trees survive most likely because they possess a kind of natural immunity to the disease. In their survival we are witnessing a Darwinian work-in-progress: specimens with a built-in defense against Dutch elm disease prevail to become the ones whose genetic blueprint is passed on to the future. But natural selection is not for the impatient. It could take millennia for a tree species to develop a natural immunity to a disease, particularly one newly introduced into an ecosystem. Many Asian elms are highly resistant to Dutch elm disease, but this is because they have coexisted with the pathogen for many thousands of years. In evolutionary time, Dutch elm disease arrived in North America only this morning. If any of us alive today are to see the American elm restored, evolution is going to need all the help it can get.

This is precisely what a number of crusaders—both in New England and elsewhere—have been working toward for decades now. Few have been at it longer than an iconoclastic New Hampshire businessman by the name of John P. Hansel. Born in New Jersey and a graduate of Princeton, Hansel was frustrated by the federal government's seeming capitulation in the battle to save the elm. He was also outraged at public apathy in the face of the elm's demise. New Haven had been "reduced to a row of stumps," he recalls, and yet few seemed moved by the loss. "I found it hard to believe," he explained, "that millions of us were concerned over the fate of a whooping crane or a stand of redwoods— which many of us will never see in our lives—while practically nothing new was being done about the fatal disease in the trees over our heads."[2] Between 1964 and 1967, Hansel sent out some ten thousand letters to drum up support for a renewed battle for the elm. He struck a chord. "The responses were poetic, they were passionate; there was no question that people wanted to save this tree." In 1967, bolstered by this groundswell of interest, Hansel founded the Elm Research Institute.

Hansel correctly understood that the real front line was not on Elm Street but in the laboratory. Almost immediately, the institute began funding a range of university-based research projects. To Hansel, cooperation among researchers was essential; this was no time for territorial bickering and secretiveness. In funding labs, he sought to eliminate repetitive research and encouraged scientists to pool their knowledge.[3] Annual meetings were organized in which work was reviewed and new ideas were discussed. In this time of crisis, no approach was too absurd. Pheromonal lures that might divert the beetles away from potential mates were considered; so was an extract from a tree in India meant to mask an elm's olfactory signature from even the most tenacious beetles. One earnest fellow even proposed injecting elms with Coca-Cola to ward off infection; another was convinced that driving scores of galvanized nails into the tree's trunk would do the trick.[4]

The Elm Research Institute was soon underwriting some of the most innovative elm research in North America, including laboratories at Cornell, Iowa State, the University of Wisconsin, the University of Maine, and the State University of New York's College of Environmental Science and Forestry in Syracuse—a city mercilessly battered by Dutch elm disease. Research concentrated at first on the development of a systemic fungicide that would help still-healthy elms survive an onslaught of Dutch elm disease. One promising agent, developed by the DuPont corporation but not available in North America, was known as Lignasan. DuPont acknowledged the potential of this compound for combating the pandemic, but it apparently feared a public-relations disaster should it fail. In 1983 Hansel finally persuaded the chemical giant to donate Lignasan to the institute and, moreover, to grant it exclusive rights to sell the product in the United States.[5]

However potent, Lignasan was useless without an effective delivery system. Hansel had explored a number of sophisticated devices meant to pass a fungicide into the tree's vascular network, including one that applied so much pressure that it blew off the bark of a test tree six feet up the trunk. Another required fifty drill points, used specialized injectors, and took hours to set up. The solution, elegant and simple, came one autumn afternoon while Hansel was horseback riding in the New Hampshire woods. He spied a syrup bucket hanging from a maple tree on what is known as a "spile." Why not simply tap the elm and deliver the fungicide by gravity or under very low pressure?

This insight was soon combined with the work of institute researcher Edward Condo, who determined that a systemic fungicide injected at the base of a tree would spread upward throughout the entire canopy by a "manifolding effect." Previous experiments concentrated on injections higher up the trunk, which often resulted in only selected limbs receiving the agent.[6] Condo memorably demonstrated his theory by injecting a vegetable dye into the base of an elm, turning all the tree's leaves bright red within hours. In 1975 the institute began selling an affordable, easy to operate low-pressure fungicide injection system. Hansel followed this by organizing a volunteer corps known as the Conscientious

Injectors, members of which went about treating elms on local streets and parks throughout New England. The effort was a huge success. By the mid-1990s more than a hundred thousand elms had been treated. According to the institute, the survival rate of these trees has exceeded 95 percent, compared with less than 50 percent among untreated elms over the same time period.[7]

But systemic fungicides were only part of Hansel's war chest. The institute also funded research to develop a disease-resistant variety of *Ulmus americana*. Such efforts carried forward the work on disease-resistant elms that had begun in the 1930s at Cornell University and the Department of Agriculture, which World War II had interrupted. Two scientists at the University of Wisconsin's Department of Forest Ecology and Management, Eugene Smalley and Dale Norris, led the institute's charge. Their search for a disease-resistant American elm began with controlled pollinations between parents exhibiting superior resistance to Dutch elm disease (some of which were survivors of screening programs conducted at Cornell in 1933). Between 1969 and 1971 they produced seedlings that were raised for a year in outdoor seedbeds, and later transplanted to field locations and injected with a potent cocktail of *Ophiostoma ulmi*, the fungus that causes Dutch elm disease. Selected survivors—those which developed less than 10 percent crown damage—were then "increased vegetatively" and subjected to another round of *O. ulmi* inoculations in 1978.[8]

The labor bore fruit. By the 1980s Hansel's researchers had produced a resistant variety of *Ulmus americana*. The mechanics of the defense system itself are not fully understood, but they appear to be associated with the tree's ability to temporarily "localize the pathogen." Some evidence suggests that trees with smaller, shorter vessels are more resistant to the fungus, and that such trees may release a chemical barrier that neutralizes the pathogen. Alternatively, the resistant elm may be able to shut down parts of its vascular system in order to "compartmentalize" the infection.[9] In any case, the new elms were by no means *immune* to Dutch elm disease. The pathogen could in fact thrive in the new tree, but its lethal effect would be minimized.

Smalley and his colleagues designed a certain degree of genetic diversity into their new elms. Rather than simply clone the survivor seedlings ad infinitum, they instead raised these to maturity and cross-pollinated them with other resistant elms. The outcome was an even more genetically diverse generation of elms from which a "multiclone" *grex* (Latin for flock) of five disease-resistant varieties was selected.[10] Originally tagged the "500 series," the trees were eventually given the more memorable name of American Liberty. After years of breeding involving some forty-three families and three thousand individuals, the Liberty elms had an enviable pedigree. As Smalley described it, the parents of the new tree were "survivors of over 60,000 inoculated American elm seedlings selected from many locations over the northern range of American elm." The "genotypically diverse, multi-clone variety with similar phenotypes" was not only resistant to Dutch elm disease, it also exhibited the vigorous growth and classic form that distinguished the species.[11]

Like a litter of puppies, the five clones were not all identical. One of the grex—clone W-510—showed particular promise. Technically, it was no more resistant than were its siblings, but W-510 had a substantially shorter period of susceptibility to the disease—the critical window in early summer when *O. ulmi* enters the tree's vascular system. It also propagated easily and established itself quickly in field plantings.[12] Knowing they had a winner on their hands, Smalley and his colleague Donald T. Lester filed for a patent on the new elm in October 1985. The researchers were well acquainted with the process, having filed at least two earlier patents for disease-resistant non-American elm hybrids.[13] Now they had pinned their hopes—and those of the Elm Research Institute—on a native son named "Independence."

It is not entirely clear why, after seeking a patent on an admittedly superior individual of the grex, the Elm Research Institute then continued to promote and distribute the entire original group of Liberty elms without distinguishing among the clones. Ostensibly it was done to maintain the inherent diversity of the multiclone. A "monoculture" of Liberty elms, in other words—say a boulevard lined with several hundred trees—would in fact be a medley of a half-dozen pedigrees. As Smalley put it, "The multi-clone approach to release of American elms for urban planting may counter the problem inherent in wide-scale planting of identical genotypes with limited genes for resistance to DED."[14]

But this remains conjectural. After all, the Elm Street of yesterday was—genetically speaking—a total mutt, and that did little to stop the disease once its weakest link became infected. Critics have further claimed that certain individuals of the Liberty multiclone may vary considerably in their resistance to Dutch elm disease. Smalley's own research has shown that when exposed to a particularly aggressive strain of the Dutch elm disease pathogen, several of the clones exhibited intense foliar discoloration, while Independence and a yet-unnamed clone known as W-502 "remained virtually symptomless."[15] Moreover, masking the true parentage of each of the five has made accurate assessment of the individual Liberty clones difficult, if not impossible.

This was made all too clear in research carried out in the 1990s by geneticist Dr. Alden Townsend of the U.S. National Arboretum's Agricultural Research Service. Townsend inoculated rooted stem cuttings of eight American elm cultivars with a "mixed spore suspension" of the causal fungi for Dutch elm disease.

Comparing the effects over the course of seven years, Townsend found "significant differences in disease severity among all clones tested." Specifically he determined that, of the eight cultivars tested, "crown dieback and mortality over time" was greatest for American Liberty. This was not welcome news for the tree's proponents, but because Townsend had no way of knowing which of the Liberty multiclone he was testing, the outcome remains inconclusive. In this case, the multiclone strategy appears to have backfired, as the whole lot was dragged down by what may have been only one of the less resistant clones.

Field reports from as far away as Cincinnati have affirmed possible problems with the Liberty elm, although—again—it is not clear which of the clones may be the culprit. In a joint effort with nearby Williams College several years ago, Williamstown, Massachusetts, planted about one hundred Liberty elms on its streets. The trees had been nurtured by tree warden Bob McCarthy for several years before being set out in the mid-1990s. Every one of the elms was vigorous and healthy until the summer of 2001, when nearly all succumbed to a new surge of Dutch elm disease in the area. "It was like someone hit them with a blow-torch," he recalls. By the end of the summer Williamstown had lost nearly all of its new elms. To McCarthy it was déjà vu. His father, tree warden before him since the 1930s, had supervised the removal of hundreds of Williamstown's legacy elms in the wake of Dutch elm disease.[16]

Nevertheless, there is abundant evidence suggesting that at least two of the Liberty clones are indeed reliably disease-resistant trees. Communities across New England have planted Liberty elms with good results. The American Liberty Elm Project in Damariscotta and Newcastle, Maine, launched in 1986 by the local Rotary Club, has planted nearly two hundred Liberty elms in the neighboring towns. Cared for by tree warden Merle Parise, the trees remain robust and are heading skyward at a blinding clip.[17] New Haven's Project Trees, an initiative of the Garden Club of New Haven, planted a large number of Liberty elms on the Green beginning in 1984; all appear to be in good shape.[18] In the spirit of the great Tree Bee of 1846, the Sheffield Tree Project has planted Liberty elms on the town's streets, mixed in with several other resistant varieties of *Ulmus americana*. All appear to be doing well.[19] So do the Liberty elms set out by Townscape of Lynnfield, Massachusetts, more than a decade ago. "Practically without exception," reports board member Donald Harriss, "these trees have exhibited exceptional and very strong growth."[20]

The Elm Research Institute remains a steadfast advocate of the American Liberty elm, its very image and identity bound to the tree. A dyed-in-the-wool Yankee iconoclast, Hansel dismisses all criticism of his tree, the source of which he identifies as professional rivalry and his refusal to allow commercial nurseries to propagate the variety. At present, Liberty elms can be obtained only from the Elm Research Institute. Predictably, this has led to accusations that the organization is more interested in profit than restoring the elm to the landscape. On the other hand, Hansel has invested a fortune in the development of this tree, and it is not unreasonable for the institute to seek some compensation for its investment. Keeping a tight grip on propagation also enables the institute (in theory at least) to track the fate of every Liberty elm. Each tree comes with its own brass tag and serial number.[21]

Regardless of the controversy, the Liberty elm remains popular with the public. Of the disease-resistant varieties of *Ulmus americana* currently available, none has been more widely planted than the Liberty. According to institute records, more than 250,000 have been planted in some 750 communities across America since the 1980s, mainly through the work of volunteers and Boy Scout troops participating in its "Johnny Elmseed" program. Hansel has been creative in devising strategies to get elms back in the landscape, preferably Liberty elms. Over the years he has promoted Elm Auctions (meant to bring about the "instant elming" of a community); a Liberty Tree Memorial program to commemorate the original Tree of Liberty (and, more recently, to honor the victims of the September 11, 2001, terrorist attacks); and, beginning in 1995, a high-profile effort to "re-elm" U.S. Route 1, the historic highway that threads its way 2,209 miles from the Canadian border to Key West, Florida.

The Liberty elm is by no means the only disease-resistant non-hybrid variety of *Ulmus americana* available today. The "Princeton" variety has actually been around for decades, selected in 1922 by William J. Flemer, a founder of Princeton Nurseries in New Jersey. Flemer chose the tree for its vaselike branching pattern and because it demonstrated resistance to the most notorious elm killer in America prior to 1933—*phloem necrosis*, or elm yellows. Serendipitously, it also turned out that the Princeton elm is extraordinarily resistant to Dutch elm disease. An allée of the trees on Washington Street near Princeton University, planted in the 1930s, flourishes even as all the elms around have succumbed to the pandemic.

Unlike the Elm Research Institute, Princeton Nurseries never filed for a patent on their namesake tree, and so it may be sold legally by anyone.[22] Today one of the most active propagators of the variety is Roger W. Holloway of Atlanta, Georgia. A former Vermont resident and a fifth-generation nurseryman, Holloway is an eclectic soul who studied theater and acting in college during the 1970s. His first encounter with an elm is straight out of *Ethan Frome:* as a young boy his first bicycle ride sans training wheels ended with a face-plant at the base of an elm.[23] Holloway spent his later childhood in Ontario, Canada, where he became acquainted with the tree and the disease that was stalking it. He never forgot the wreckage of the trees that stood outside his grammar school. "Even today I can see those piles in my mind," recalls Holloway; "I was so shocked. I thought something mean was going on."[24] Holloway's college days in elm-rich Putney, Vermont, only added to his passion to bring back this native tree.

Holloway happened upon the Princeton variety quite by accident in 1995 while paging through a Princeton Nurseries catalog. He had been looking for a disease-resistant elm to bring to market and was intrigued by Princeton's neglected champion. But whereas Princeton Nurseries had sat on its elm for decades, Holloway launched an aggressive marketing campaign. He carefully crafted an image for his start-up, one worthy of Madison Avenue. The name he chose, Riveredge Farms, calls to mind a tree-tossed rural idyll, and his Web site invokes nostalgia as it urges visitors to "PLANT A PIECE OF HISTORY." The name is rather ironic, however. As the *New York Times* described it: "There is no river—no farm, either. Mr. Holloway's elms are grown at several nurseries in the South and trucked to a parcel . . . sandwiched between a car lot and a warehouse" in suburban Atlanta.[25] But there is no denying the success of his venture or the beauty of these trees. Holloway uses a proprietary method to help each cutting develop roots of its own—a tedious process, but one that assures a strong and genetically pure sapling.[26] Most of Holloway's orders come from New England, and he can hardly keep up with demand.

If the Princeton variety owes its existence to serendipity, two other rising stars in the elm world—the Valley Forge and New Harmony varieties of *Ulmus americana*—are the fruit of a long-term breeding program at the United States National Arboretum supervised by veteran elm researcher Dr. Alden ("Denny") Townsend. An Oklahoman by birth, Townsend's life has long been filled with trees. His family moved to New Jersey when Townsend was still a boy, and there he began a tiny nursery of gray birches at age fifteen. Townsend later made his way to the old Elm City, where he studied forestry at Yale in the 1960s. He began his career conducting elm improvement studies at the former Shade Tree and Ornamental Plants Laboratory of the United States Department of Agriculture in Delaware, Ohio. Townsend joined the research staff of the National Arboretum in 1984 has been there ever since. The official release, on December 27, 1995, of the Valley Forge and New Harmony elms was the culmination of a lifetime's work in elm research.

In the search for the perfect elm, Townsend inoculated thousands of young trees over the years with aggressive and nonaggressive strains of the fungus that causes Dutch elm disease (the aggressive variety is known as *O. novo ulmi*). In these tests, Townsend used inoculates containing *three million* spores of the fungus—about

30,000 times the number that would be carried by the average elm bark beetle.[27] Valley Forge exhibited the fewest symptoms of Dutch elm disease (typically wilting and discoloration of leaves), followed closely by New Harmony. While the parent tree of the Valley Forge elm was lost years ago to a land clearance project in Ohio, that of the New Harmony variety still stands in the Ohio River valley, in a heavily forested area particularly hard hit by Dutch elm disease. Ironically, this tree, whose issue may well help save the species, is located only 150 miles from the place where Dutch elm disease was first discovered in North America. Commercial nurseries have recently begun raising and selling both varieties of this new American elm.[28]

Just as the Liberty elm has been joined by newer disease-resistant varieties of *Ulmus americana*, the campaign to restore the elm has been joined by a new generation of elm activists dedicated to restoring the tree to its rightful place in the Yankee landscape. Among the most ambitious of these is Tom Zetterstrom, a photographer and environmentalist living in the Berkshires. As the son of an arborist, Zetterstrom has often claimed his love of trees began in utero. Growing up in Connecticut in the 1950s he witnessed firsthand the devastation of Dutch elm disease, and he often helped his father spray DDT into the canopies of Canaan's town trees—most of which later died nonetheless.[29] Zetterstrom spent the Vietnam years as a conscientious objector teaching inner-city children in Washington, D.C., and he later traveled the globe as a photojournalist. His love of photography has become bonded to an even deeper affection for sylva.

Zetterstrom's tree portraits are in the permanent collections of the Metropolitan Museum of Art, the Library of Congress, and the Corcoran Gallery. Reviewing his work in November 2000, the *New York Times* suggested that, in the world of trees, Zetterstrom "has probably done more to promote their beauty and value than Joyce Kilmer."[30] A metaphysician of sorts, Zetterstrom has described trees as "the great deflators of man's hubris." But he has done more than just wax philosophic on the subject. In 1999 Zetterstrom founded a group called Elm Watch. Originally affiliated with the Nature Conservancy, its mission is one of stewardship, preservation, and restoration of the American elm in western New England. Zetterstrom and his Elm Watch volunteers have documented and stabilized some of the last remaining big elms in the Connecticut and Housatonic Valleys—the very landscapes in which the tree first rose to prominence more than two hundred years ago.

The group's Adopt-an-Elm initiative has raised funds to treat exceptional specimens with a systemic fungicide called Arbotect. By contracting this work to professional arborists, Elm Watch has saved elms high-born and low—some tucked on the grounds of prep schools and country clubs, others growing by

Arborists injecting fungicide into the base of an
elm as part of Elm Watch's Adopt-an-Elm
program (Photograph by Tom Zetterstrom)

convenience stores and video rental outlets. All are now part of a "Majestic Elm Trail" running through the Berkshire-Taconic region of Massachusetts, Connecticut, and New York. From preservation, the activities of Elm Watch soon expanded to include restoration using disease-resistant trees. In 2001, Zetterstrom and local science teacher David Moran established an American elm nursery at the Housatonic Valley High School in Falls Village, Connecticut. Moran's students helped plant more than seventy disease-resistant trees that spring as part of a class in horticulture and plant science.[31] The Elm Watch trees at Housatonic Valley High School will ultimately be transplanted to public sites throughout the region. Already, individual saplings have been set out at Tanglewood, the summer home of the Boston Symphony Orchestra; Old Sturbridge Village; and, in a joint effort with the New England Heritage Breeds Conservancy, at Hancock Shaker Village in elm-historic Pittsfield, Massachusetts. In the summer of 2002, Zetterstrom helped plant an American elm sapling in Salisbury, Connecticut, in memory of Susan Getzendanner, a longtime resident who was killed in the terrorist

Students from Dave Moran's plant science class at Housatonic Valley High School in Falls Village tending to their newly planted elms (Photograph by Tom Zetterstrom)

attacks on New York's World Trade Center on September 11, 2001. It was a modest act of remembrance, but one steeped in New England's long-mingled history of elms and cherished souls.

In Acton, Massachusetts, another grassroots activist has been quietly working to restore the elm to its proper place in the landscape. Bruce Carley, an arborist and amateur composer, has been planting disease-resistant American elms in the Nashoba Brook Conservation Area and the Acton Arboretum since the early 1990s. He attends to each sapling like a doting father, posting photos of their growth on his Web site—the most informative on the Internet when it comes to elms. A soft-spoken man with a deep affection for *Ulmus americana*, Carley started out planting Liberty elms, and he is especially optimistic about the same two Liberty clones that prevailed in Eugene Smalley's experiments.[32] More recently Carley has begun to favor the Valley Forge and New Harmony varieties. These, unlike the patented Liberty elm, can be bred by anyone. "I like to propagate my own trees," writes Carley, and "it seems to me that the true spirit of conservation requires that large-scale elm propagation be permissible."[33]

Zetterstrom and Carley are not alone. Elsewhere in New England, activists, grassroots organizations, and progressive municipalities have been effectively campaigning to return the elm to the local landscape. The Farmington Historical

Tom Zetterstrom, American Elm, *1991, gelatin-silver photograph, from his "Portraits of Trees" series (Photograph © Tom Zetterstrom)*

Society in Connecticut has orchestrated the planting of a dozen disease-resistant American elms in town and on the campus of a local boarding school. Officials in Wellesley, Massachusetts, also began planting Valley Forge American elms throughout their town in 2001. New Haven works hard to preserve the dozen or so nineteenth-century elms remaining on its Green, in addition to planting new disease-resistant saplings. Pittsfield, too, has been planting Princeton and Valley Forge saplings in historic Springside Park. Harvard, Massachusetts, even has an "Elm Commissioner" to oversee the community's restoration work. Not far away, in Bristol, Rhode Island, Bill Chittick helped found a group in 1998 called the Bristol Tree Society. Chittick was born in Fitchburg, Massachusetts, and attended high school at Deerfield Academy, a venerable prep school whose campus was a virtual forest of elms until the 1960s. He vividly recalls the great felling of elms in the wake of Dutch elm disease. Chittick urged the Tree Society to consider planting elms again, and while surfing the Web one night came upon Bruce Carley's "Saving the American Elm" site. The two subsequently collaborated to establish a nursery of Valley Forge and other disease-resistant elms at the Blithewold Arboretum. On Arbor Day, April 2001, the society planted its first civic elm, appropriately enough in front of the Bristol Town Hall.[34]

Collectively, these grassroots groups are carrying on the great Yankee tradition of village improvement that was born in the middle of the nineteenth century. Hansel, Zetterstrom, Carley, Chittick, and other campaigners for the restoration of the American elm in New England are the spiritual heirs of the great elm planters of yesterday—men like James Hillhouse of New Haven, Orville Dewey of Sheffield, Massachusetts, or Boston's Nehemiah Adams. These and other long-forgotten visionaries (and everyone who plants a tree is a visionary of sorts) helped forge some of the most salubrious urban environments ever created in America. Today's elm activists, like their forebears, carry on a tradition of sylvan humanism that is as much a part of Yankee heritage as Thanksgiving Day.

Critics are, of course, swift to point out the inherent risks in campaigning for a single and particular tree species. The tragic lesson of Dutch elm disease, after all, was that favoring any one species to excess leads to catastrophe. As Peter Del Tredici has asked, we are right to bring the elm back, but at what density? Certainly we do not want a return to the bloated monoculture that brought about the great pandemic of the 1950s. "If the American elm is to make a return to the modern American landscape," writes Del Tredici, "then it should be on equal footing with other trees, never as an all-encompassing landscape theme."[35] This is sane advice, and no arborist or urban forester would argue with it. Nor would any of the activists campaigning to restore the American elm to the New England landscape.

But then again, had our Yankee forebears exercised such restraint with the trees they planted (they certainly seemed to in nearly every other aspect of life), they would have inadvertently deprived American history of its greenest chapter, and New England of one of its defining symbols. In the economy of the eye, the grace and beauty of the elm-lined street seemed worth any risk. The mantra of urban forestry today is sustainability and species diversity, and it is a wise one indeed. However well intentioned, the Yankee tree planters of the past committed a grave error in planting their cherished elms as far as the eye could see. But what a glorious error it was! And what magic, what magnificence, their recklessness bestowed.

NOTES

Introduction: "The Glory of New England"

1. The "westward transit of New England culture" is from Whitney R. Cross, *The Social and Intellectual History of Enthusiastic Religion in Western New York, 1800–1850* (Ithaca: Cornell University Press, 1950), vii.

2. The first American elm in Oregon was said to have traveled around Cape Horn with a young Yankee missionary named George Atkinson in 1848. The cleric planted the tree "amidst the giant firs" in the parsonage yard. Michael Kammen, *Meadows of Memory: Images of Time and Tradition in American Art and Culture* (Austin: University of Texas Press, 1992), 141.

3. G. H. Collingwood, "A Billion Elms at Bay," *American Forests* 43:5 (May 1937): 212; "Elm Tree Census," *Connecticut Woodlands* 2:2 (May 1937): 8.

4. E. B. White, *One Man's Meat* (Gardiner, Maine: Tilbury House, reprint 1997), 45–46.

5. Charles Dickens, "American Notes," in *Works of Charles Dickens*, (New York: Sheldon, 1865), 2:78.

6. Stephen West Williams, "An Ancient Settler Gone," Deerfield *Gazette and Courier*, August 15, 1853.

7. Ibid.

8. Ibid.

9. Ibid.

10. Thomas J. Schlereth, *Cultural History and Material Culture* (Charlottesville: University Press of Virginia, 1992), 38.

11. Simon Schama, *Landscape and Memory* (New York: Knopf, 1995), 15.

12. The cultural history of trees is immense and largely unexplored terrain. James George Frazer, *The Golden Bough*, is a good introduction, as is Schama, *Landscape and Memory*.

13. Charles Sprague Sargent, "The American Elm," *Garden and Forest*, June 11, 1890, 281.

14. Orville Dewey, *An Address Delivered Under the Old Elm Tree in Sheffield, With Some Remarks on the Great Political Question of the Day* (New York: C. S. Francis, 1856), 5.

15. John R. Stilgoe, "Town Common and Village Green in New England: 1620 to 1981," in *On Common Ground*, ed. Ronald L. Fleming (Cambridge: Townscape Institute, 1982), 26.

16. Charles Joseph Latrobe, *The Rambler in North America*, (New York: Harper and Brothers, 1835), 1:43–44; Henry Ward Beecher, *Norwood, or Village Life in New England* (New York: Fords, Howard, & Hulbert, 1888), 4–5; Henry Ward Beecher, quoted in *Report of the General Superintendent of Parks* (Cambridge: City of Cambridge, 1894), 76f; Nathaniel Parker Willis, "The Elms of New Haven," in *Sacred Poems* (New York: Clark Austin Smith, 1860), 234–235.

17. Henry David Thoreau, *The Journal of Henry D. Thoreau*, 3d ed., ed. Bradford Torrey and Francis H. Allen (Boston: Houghton Mifflin, 1949), 10:89, 142.

18. William Howarth, ed., *Walden and Other Writings* (New York: Modern Library, 1981), xxiv.

19. Robert L. Gale, *A Cultural Encyclopedia of the 1850s in America* (London: Greenwood, 1993), 139–140. The Free Soilers, established in 1848, "adopted a platform with three main planks: no slavery in the territories, no slavery in any new state, and free homesteading rights for public domain settlers. The spirited slogan of the new party— 'Free Soil, Free Speech, Free Labor, Free Men'—gave the party its name."

20. Thoreau, *Journal*, 140–141.

21. Ibid., 116–117, 131–132.

22. Nathaniel Hawthorne, *Our Old Home, and English Note-Books* (Boston: Houghton, Mifflin, reprint 1902), 1:422; Anthony Trollope, *North America* (New York: Harper and Brothers, 1862), 52; Beecher, *Norwood*, 4; "The Old Elms of Northampton: An Appeal for Their Preservation," *Hampshire Gazette*, December 20, 1864.

23. Oliver Wendell Holmes, "Introduction," in Lorin L. Dame, *Typical Elms and Other Trees of Massachusetts* (Boston: Little, Brown, 1890), 8.

24. Oliver Wendell Holmes, *The Autocrat of the Breakfast-Table* (Boston: Houghton Mifflin, reprint 1916), 318–323; Holmes in Dame, *Typical Elms*, 9; Oliver Wendell Holmes, *Elsie Venner: A Romance of Destiny* (Cambridge, Mass.: Riverside, 1891), 56.

25. W. Elmer Ekblaw, *New England Fancies* (Worcester: Achille J. St. Onge, 1935), 35.

26. Jeff Stryker, "They Couldn't Resist: Oh, One Last Thing . . . ," *New York Times*, May 21, 2000.

Chapter 1: A Prospect of Elms

1. John Josselyn, "New England Rarities Discovered," American Antiquarian Society, *Transactions and Collections*, 4 (1860): 139, quoted in Hans Huth, *Nature and the American* (Berkeley: University of California Press, 1957), 5.

2. Le Vicomte de Chateaubriand, *Travels in America and Italy* (London: Colburn, 1828), quoted in Clarence J. Glacken, *Traces on the Rhodian Shore* (Berkeley: University of California Press, 1990), 686.

3. William Wood, *New England's Prospect* (London: John Bellamie, 1634), 16.

4. Thomas Morton, *New English Canaan or New Canaan. Containing an Abstract of New England, Composed in three Bookes* (Amsterdam: Jacob Frederick Stam, 1637), 60, 52.

5. Morton, *New English Canaan*, 54.

6. Timothy Dwight, *Travels in New England and New York* (Cambridge: Belknap Press, reprint 1969), 4:37–38. Also see William Cronon, *Changes in the Land* (New York: Hill and Wang, 1983), 51.

7. Dwight, *Travels in New England and New York*, 4:38.

8. Cronon, *Changes in the Land*, 51.

9. Dwight noted that the Indians "burned such parts" of the forest cover "as they found sufficiently dry." The principal fuel, fallen leaves, was "rarely dry enough for an extensive combustion except on uplands." Dwight, *Travels in New England and New York*, 4:38.

10. Wood, *New England's Prospect*, 16.

11. Morton, *New English Canaan*, 64.

12. The tree gained its Linnaean classification in 1753. Gerald Wilkinson, *Epitaph for the Elm* (London: Hutchinson, 1978), 85.

13. Manasseh Cutler, "An Account of Some of the Vegetable Productions, Naturally Growing in this Part of America, Botanically Arranged," *Memoirs of the American Academy of Arts and Sciences* (1783) (Boston: Adams and Nourse, 1785), 1:425.

14. Charles Sprague Sargent, *The Silva of North America*, (Boston: Houghton Mifflin, 1895), 8:45.

15. H. O. Juel, *Early Investigations of North American Flora* (Uppsala: Almquist and Wiksells, 1920), 66, 67.

16. Sargent, *Silva of North America*, 3:45.

17. Antonio Pace, ed., *Luigi Castiglioni's Viaggio: Travels in the United States of North America, 1785–1787* (Syracuse, N.Y.: Syracuse University Press, 1983), xi-xvi.

18. Luigi Castiglioni, "Observations on Useful Plants," in ibid., 459–460.

19. Howard Ensign Evans, *Pioneer Naturalists: The Discovery and Naming of North American Plants and Animals* (New York: Henry Holt, 1993), 8–9.

20. Reuben Gold Thwaites, ed., *Travels West of the Alleghanies* (Cleveland: Arthur H. Clark, 1904), 11–15. *The North American Sylva* included an additional volume by Thomas Nuttall.

21. F. André Michaux, *The North American Sylva, or A Description of the Forest Trees of the United States, Canada, and Nova Scotia* (Philadelphia: Dobson and Conrad, 1819), 3:83.

22. Michaux, *North American Sylva*, 84–86.

23. Michael Williams, *Americans and Their Forests: A Historical Geography* (New York: Cambridge University Press, 1989), 37; R. H. Richens, *Elm* (London: Cambridge Uni-

versity Press, 1983), 108; Sargent, *Silva of North America*, 3:44; Richens, *Elm*, 108; Frank G. Speck, "Medicinal Practices of the Eastern Algonkians," *Proceedings of the 19th International Congress of Americanists* (1917): 311; Gladys Tantaquidgeon, "Mohegan Medicinal Practices, Weather-lore and Superstitions," *SI-BAE Annual Report* 43 (1928): 264–270, 266; James W. Herrick, "Iroquois Medical Botany," Ph.D. dissertation, State University of New York, 1977, 304. Summer disease was characterized by vomiting, diarrhea, and cramps.

24. Slippery elm, which Linnaeus considered a variety of *Ulmus americana*, was later classified a separate species by Michaux. Wilkinson, *Epitaph for the Elm*, 86.

25. "Pine Trees and Elm Trees," *New England Farmer* 5 (September 15, 1826): 58.

26. Williams, *Americans and Their Forests*, 57.

27. Ibid., 60.

28. Quoted in Richens, *Elm*, 128.

29. Williams, *Americans and Their Forests*, 59.

30. Ibid., 53.

31. Burning was permitted there until 1743, when a Massachusetts law was passed prohibiting such fires—they "impoverished the soil, prevented the growth of wood, and destroyed fences." Daniel White Wells and Reuben Field Wells, *A History of Hatfield, Massachusetts* (Springfield, Mass.: Gibbons, 1910), 36–37.

32. Williams, *Americans and Their Forests*, 60.

33. Ibid., 82. See also Charles F. Carroll, *The Timber Economy of Puritan New England* (Providence: Brown University Press, 1973).

34. Sargent, *Silva of North America*, 3:44.

35. George B. Emerson, *A Report on the Trees and Shrubs Growing Naturally in the Forests of Massachusetts* (Boston: Little, Brown, 1878), 2:329–330.

36. Michaux, *North American Sylva*, 86.

37. C. A. Sheffield, quoted in Donald Culross Peattie, *A Natural History of Trees* (New York: Bonanza, 1966), 243.

38. Sargent, *Silva of North America*, 3:45.

39. "Sheltering Farm Lands," *New England Farmer* 8 (no. 19): 147.

40. "Shade of Trees," *New England Farmer* 14 (August 5, 1835); "Sheltering Farm Lands," *New England Farmer*, 147.

41. *Town Records of Topsfield, Massachusetts*, vol. 1 (Topsfield: Topsfield Historical Society, 1917), 17. Edward F. Johnson, *Abstracts of Early Woburn Deeds* (Woburn, Mass.: News Print, 1895), 71; Harry A. Wright, ed., *Indian Deeds of Hampden County* (Springfield, Mass.: County of Hampden, Massachusetts, 1905); Walter A. Davis, *The Early Records of the Town of Lunenburg* (Fitchburg, Mass.: City Council, 1896).

42. John R. Stilgoe, "Jack O'Lanterns to Surveyors: The Secularization of Landscape Boundaries," *Environmental Review* 1 (Autumn 1976): 14–31. On the use of deeds to reconstruct colonial landscapes, see John R. Stilgoe, "Documents in Landscape History,"

Journal of Architectural Education 30 (September 1976): 15–18.

43. Michaux observed such volunteers on one of his journeys through New England: "In New Hampshire, between Portsmouth and Portland," he wrote, "a great number of young White Elms are seen detached in the middle of pastures." Michaux, *North American Sylva*, 3:85.

44. Ibid., 84–85.

45. Holmes, "Introduction," 12.

46. Joel Barlow, *The Columbiad* (Washington, D.C.: Joseph Milligan, reprint 1825), 26.

47. Adam Hodgson, *Letters from North America* (London: Hurst, Robinson, 1824), 263, 272–273.

48. Charles Joseph Latrobe, *The Rambler in North America* (New York: Harper and Brothers, 1835), 43–44.

49. Una Pope-Hennessy, ed., *The Aristocratic Journey* (New York: G. P. Putnam's Sons, 1931), 80. Margaret Hunter Hall was the wife of Captain Basil Hall, a retired Royal Navy officer and a well-published travel writer who took his family on a tour of the United States in 1827 and 1828. Jill A. Hodnicki, *Arcadian Vales: Views of the Connecticut River Valley* (Springfield, Mass.: Springfield Library and Museums Association, 1981), 16.

50. Thomas Cole, "Essay on American Scenery," in *American Art, 1700–1960: Sources and Documents*, ed. John W. McCoubrey (Englewood Cliffs: Prentice-Hall, 1965), 106.

51. Walter Prichard Eaton, *Green Trails and Upland Pastures* (New York: Doubleday, Page, 1917), 254–255.

52. John Brinckerhoff Jackson, *A Sense of Place, A Sense of Time* (New Haven: Yale University Press, 1994), 99.

53. Roderick Nash, *Wilderness and the American Mind* (New Haven: Yale University Press, 1982), 11.

54. Jackson, *A Sense of Place*, 96.

55. Carl Sauer, "The Settlement of the Humid East," *USDA Yearbook, Climate and Man* (1941): 159, quoted in Cronon, *Changes in the Land*, 173n.

56. Jackson, *A Sense of Place*, 95.

57. Wilkinson, *Epitaph for the Elm*, 106.

58. Richens, *Elm*, 1–4.

59. Bernard Bailyn, *The Peopling of British North America* (New York: Knopf, 1989), 22.

60. Richens, *Elm*, 99, 109, 50–51, 101–102; John Evelyn, *Sylva; or, A Discourse of Forest-Trees* (1664), quoted in Jackson, *A Sense of Place*, 97–98; Richens, *Elm*, 52–53.

61. Ibid., 118–122.

62. Oliver Rackham, *Trees and Woodland in the British Landscape* (London: Dent, 1976), quoted in Wilkinson, *Epitaph for the Elm*, 110.

63. Richens, *Elm*, 112, 50.

64. Wilkinson, *Epitaph for the Elm*, 112.

65. Sargent, "The American Elm," 281.

1. This tree was later known as the Hubbard Elm, one of the celebrated specimens of nineteenth-century Massachusetts. Lorin L. Dame, *Typical Elms and Other Trees of Massachusetts* (Boston: Little, Brown, 1890), 36.

2. Donald Culross Peattie, *A Natural History of Trees* (New York: Bonanza, 1966), 238.

3. J. E. Strong, "Trees as Protectors from Lightning," *New England Farmer* 22 (November 22, 1843).

4. Ernest H. Wilson, *Aristocrats of the Trees* (Boston: Stratsford, 1930), 81.

5. Dame, *Typical Elms*, 29.

6. Clifford H. Lyman, "Northampton in the Days of Jonathan Edwards, 1727–1750," unpublished manuscript (1937), Collections of Historic Northampton.

7. Hannah Gould, quoted in Dame, *Typical Elms*, 47.

8. John Welles, "Remarks on Trees," *New England Farmer* 4 (February 24, 1826): 242–243.

9. Charles Upham Shepard (1838), quoted in Henry Howe, "New Haven's Elms and Green," a scrapbook of his articles from the *New Haven Daily Morning Journal and Courier* (1883–1884), Sterling Memorial Library, Yale University, 11.

10. Nathaniel Hawthorne, *The House of the Seven Gables* (Boston: Ticknor, Reed, and Fields, 1851), 9, 32–33.

11. "Shade Trees," *New England Farmer* 4 (August 5, 1825): 10.

12. Henry David Thoreau, *The Journal of Henry D. Thoreau*, 3d ed., ed. Bradford Torrey and Francis H. Allen (Boston: Houghton Mifflin, 1949), 10:89.

13. Charles Sprague Sargent, "The American Elm," *Garden and Forest*, June 11, 1890, 281.

14. Emma Lewis Coleman, *A Historic and Present Day Guide to Old Deerfield* (Boston, 1912), 105.

15. "Ornamental Trees," *New England Farmer* 4 (May 19, 1826): 341.

16. "Plant Trees" ("Dr. Darlington's address before the Philadelphia Agricultural Society"), *New England Farmer* 23 (December 11, 1844).

17. John R. Stilgoe, *Common Landscape of America* (New Haven: Yale University Press, 1982), 9, 17–18.

18. R. H. Richens, *Elm* (London: Cambridge University Press, 1983), 112.

19. Stilgoe, *Common Landscape*, 18. "Miters, scepters, and maces—perhaps even the patrolman's nightstick—derive from the Christianized pagan symbol of imposed order that dominated the typical late medieval landschaft."

20. When the elm was cut down in 1864, its growth rings revealed a life of 340 years, placing its origins well before European settlement of the area.

21. Morgan Bulkeley, "The Old Elm," *Berkshire Eagle*, December 17, 1968.

22. Allen H. Bagg, "Former Mayor Bagg Tells Thrilling Story of the Old Elm," *Berkshire Eagle*, July 1927.

23. Bulkeley, "The Old Elm."

24. J. E. A. Smith, *The History of Pittsfield* (Boston: Lee and Shepard, 1869), 439.

25. Hawthorne quoted in Kirk Scharfenberg, "Time Runs Short for Park's Elms," *Berkshire Eagle*, September 13, 1975.

26. Smith, *History of Pittsfield*, 440.

27. John Carver, *Sketches of New England* (New York: E. French, 1842), 177–178.

28. C. S. Hayward, "Pittsfield Plans Living Memorial to Men in Service on Site of Famous Elm That Grew in City Hall Park," *Springfield Republican*, April 18, 1943.

29. Stilgoe, *Common Landscape*, 251.

30. *A Handbook of New England* (Boston: Porter E. Sargent, 1917), 402.

31. W. R. Plunkett, "The 'Old Elm' Sun-Dial," *Berkshire Eagle*, n.d.

32. June Sprigg and Paige Savery, "Pittsfield's Precious Plates," article (n.d.), Collection of the Berkshire Athenaeum; Amanda E. Lange, "The Story of the Pittsfield Elm Platter," brochure, Berkshire Botanical Garden 36th Annual Antiques Show (July 1996).

33. William H. Phillips quoted in Bagg, "Former Mayor Bagg."

34. Herman Melville, *Moby-Dick*, ed. Harrison Hayford and Hershel Parker (New York: W. W. Norton, 1967), 110.

35. Smith, *History of Pittsfield*, 35–36. Some accounts erroneously place its felling in 1861.

36. Samuel Sass, "Sylvanus Grant and the Pittsfield Elm," *Berkshire Eagle*, October 18, 1984; Hayward, "Pittsfield Plans Living Memorial."

37. Arthur M. Schlesinger, "Liberty Tree: A Genealogy," *New England Quarterly*, December 1952, 435.

38. Ibid.

39. The boot was "emblematic of the Earl of Bute, First Lord of the Treasury." Ibid., 437–438.

40. Ibid.

41. Quoted in Frederick Fitch Hassam, *Liberty Tree, Liberty Hall* (Boston: privately published, 1891), 1.

42. Schlesinger, "Liberty Tree," 439.

43. Esther Forbes, *Paul Revere and the World He Lived In* (Boston: Houghton Mifflin, 1942), 101–102, 115–117.

44. Inscription on obelisk by Paul Revere, quoted in Elbridge Henry Goss, *The Life of Colonel Paul Revere* (Boston: J. G. Cupples, 1891), 35–43. Revere's illuminated obelisk was intended to be placed beneath the Liberty Tree, a phallic counterpoint to the tree itself. But it caught fire on the Common and was destroyed. The symmetry of obelisk and elm was a subject of great interest to Joel Barlow—author of the celebrated *Columbiad* of 1787—who speculated on the pagan heritage of the Liberty Elm. Barlow argued that the Boston tree should be understood as part of a long tradition of phallus worship dating back to antiquity. In an unpublished essay from 1796, entitled "Genealogy of the Tree of Liberty," he recounted the legend of Osiris, the Egyptian god who was killed in a battle with Typhon, the victor tossing the genitals of the defeated into the Nile. The vanquished god's organs endowed the river with supernatural power, and it thus became the

source of all life—and vegetation—in Egypt. "To commemorate the tragical death of Osiris and the great benefit that resulted . . . from the posthumous power of his organs," wrote Barlow, "a solemn feast was instituted in which the phallus in a posture of strong erection was carried in procession." According to Barlow, the story of Osiris made its way through the lands of antiquity, subtly changing form. In Greece, it emerged in the myth of Bacchus, whose memory was celebrated by "the procession of a Phallus" accompanied by "the most extravagant scenes of debauchery." These nocturnal bacchanals became so associated with "freedom and licentiousness," he speculated, that during the Roman era Bacchus himself acquired the name Liber Deus, or God of Liberty. Thus the phallus eventually became linked with *libertas*, or freedom. To Barlow, the Maypole tradition in England was yet another manifestation of the ancient rite of penis worship, though to the unsuspecting villagers it meant little more than "the liberty of a frolic." The poet concluded that the Liberty Tree itself was heir to this venerable legacy, a theory evinced by Revere's illuminated obelisk. Barlow hardly seemed disturbed by the pagan sexuality of such precedent. The freedom bid absolved the Sons' totem of such heathen parentage, for it was "planted in the ground as a solid emblem of *political Liberty*." Joel Barlow, "The Genealogy of the Tree of Liberty," unpublished manuscript (1796–1797), BMS Am 1448, Notebook 13, Houghton Rare Book Library, Harvard University.

45. Harriet S. Tapley, *Salem Imprints, 1768–1825* (1927), 14, quoted in Schlesinger, "Liberty Tree," 444.

46. Samuel Eliot Morison, *Three Centuries of Harvard* (Cambridge: Harvard University Press, 1936), 133.

47. Schlesinger, "Liberty Tree," 444.

48. Ibid., 441–448.

49. Ibid., 448–449.

50. Hassam, *Liberty Tree*, 2.

51. Nehemiah Adams, *Boston Common, or Rural Walks in Cities* (Boston: George H. Light, 1838; Bostonian Society edition), 13–14.

52. Schlesinger, "Liberty Tree," 453. For Paine's poem ("Liberty Tree"), see Moncure Daniel Conway, ed., *The Writings of Thomas Paine*, (New York: G. P. Putnam's Sons, 1896), 4:484–485.

53. Quoted in Hassam, *Liberty Tree*, 3.

54. Ibid., 3–9.

55. Douglas Kendall, "In the Shadow of the Great Elm: Wethersfield, Connecticut in Transition, 1850–1940," Ph.D. dissertation, Boston University, 1994.

56. At its prime the tree was 26 feet in circumference and held aloft a crown 140 feet in width.

57. *A Handbook of New England*, 309. Photographs of the tree were proudly displayed at both the Chicago and the St. Louis world's fairs.

58. James R. Simmons, *The Historic Trees of Massachusetts* (Boston: Marshall Jones, 1919), 134; Henry Smith Chapman, *History of Winchester* (Winchester, Mass.: Town of Winchester, 1936), 176–177.

59. Alain C. White, *The History of the Town of Litchfield* (Litchfield, Conn.: Enquirer, 1920), 171–172.

60. Wells and Wells, *A History of Hatfield*, 37. The tree had apparently earlier played a role in the native American landscape; a cut in its trunk, several feet from the base, was said to have been made by Indians to record the high-water mark of the Connecticut River. *New England Farmer* 4 (November 25, 1825): 142.

61. Gerard Chapman, "Sheffield's Big Elm," *Berkshire Eagle*, June 11, 1985. The Sheffield Elm was one of the largest elms in Massachusetts. In 1844, George B. Emerson measured it at twenty-two feet in girth at the base. George B. Emerson, *A Report on the Trees and Shrubs Growing Naturally in the Forests of Massachusetts* (Boston: Little, Brown, 1878), 2:328. When the tree was finally removed in 1926, its age was determined to be four hundred years. Gerard Chapman, "The Great Elm," *Berkshires Week*, September 13, 1985.

62. "The Elms of Old Sheffield," *Berkshire Courier*, June 18, 1896.

63. Actually, two big elms competed for this honor, the "center of the state" being a rather imperfect geography. Each tree had a set of adherents. Simmons, *Historic Trees of Massachusetts*; Lyman P. Powell, *Historic Towns of New England* (New York: Knickerbocker, 1899), 103. Although the old Central Tree is gone, a young heir now grows in its place. The landmark is also preserved in the name of the street, Central Tree Road.

64. *Leslie's*, July 19, 1856. This tradition seems to have begun around 1800.

65. Morison, *Three Centuries of Harvard*, 249–250.

66. Thoreau, *Journal*, 10:88–89.

67. Mircea Eliade, *The Sacred and the Profane* (New York: Harcourt Brace, 1959), 20–31.

68. Ibid., 31.

69. Stilgoe, *Common Landscape*, 57.

Chapter 3: The Witness Tree

1. This did not prevent, however, a certain longing for things European, and for the approval of European society in general.

2. David Lowenthal, *The Past Is a Foreign Country* (New York: Cambridge University Press, 1985), 109.

3. Leo Marx, *The Machine in the Garden* (New York: Oxford University Press, 1964), 36–47.

4. Ibid., 55.

5. Johann Wolfgang von Goethe, "Die Vereinigten Staaten," English trans. by Stephen Spender, quoted in Hans Huth, *Nature and the American* (Berkeley: University of California, 1957), 49–50.

6. William Tudor, *Letters on the Eastern States* (New York: Kirk and Mercein, 1820), 271–272.

7. Ibid., 272.

8. Quoted in Perry Miller, *Errand into the Wilderness* (Cambridge: Belknap Press, 1964), 205–206.

9. Orville Dewey, *An Address Delivered Under the Old Elm Tree in Sheffield, with Some Remarks on the Great Political Question of the Day* (New York: C. S. Francis, 1856), 5.

10. Nehemiah Adams, *Boston Common, or Rural Walks in Cities* (Boston: George H. Light, 1838; Bostonian Society edition), 16.

11. Andrew Jackson Downing, *Rural Essays*, George W. Curtis, ed. (New York: George A. Leavitt, 1869), quoted in Jeanne Goode, "Andrew Jackson Downing on Trees," *Arboricultural Journal* 12 (1988): 191.

12. Charles Joseph Latrobe, *The Rambler in North America* (New York: Harper and Brothers, 1835), 43.

13. The writer was referring to the ancient Endicott pear tree in Danvers, Massachusetts. From a letter to the *Boston Times* reprinted in the *New England Farmer* 20 (October 27, 1841): 136.

14. Quoted in Herbert Gutman, *Work, Culture, and Society in Industrializing America* (New York: Knopf, 1976), 29. Michael Kammen, *Meadows of Memory: Images of Time and Tradition in American Art and Culture* (Austin: University of Texas Press, 1992), 143–145.

15. Adams, *Boston Common*, 16.

16. Oliver Wendell Holmes, "Introduction," in Lorin L. Dame, *Typical Elms and Other Trees of Massachusetts* (Boston: Little, Brown, 1890), 8.

17. "The Elms of Court Square," *Springfield Union* (Summer 1898).

18. James R. Simmons, *The Historic Trees of Massachusetts* (Boston: Marshall Jones, 1919), 133–134.

19. John Hill Hewitt, "The Old Elm Tree: A Patriotic Ballad" (Baltimore: G. Willig Junior, 1842).

20. Dame, *Typical Elms*, 51.

21. Nathaniel B. Shurtleff, *A Topographical and Historical Description of Boston* (Boston: Noyes, Holmes, 1872), 336, 334. Shurtleff suggested that after the Tree of Liberty was removed, the Great Elm may have even been called "Liberty Tree"; at least one map, from 1784, marked it as such.

22. J. C. Warren, *The Great Tree on Boston Common* (Boston: John Wilson and Son, 1855), 6.

23. Shurtleff, *Topographical and Historical Description of Boston*, 332.

24. J. W. Hamilton, *Memorial of Jessie Lee and the Old Elm* (Boston: J. P. Magee, 1875), 47.

25. Quoted in ibid., 49.

26. Warren, *The Great Tree*, 17.

27. For a refutation of the Henchman claim, see ibid., 10–15.

28. M. A. DeWolfe Howe, *Boston Common* (Cambridge: Riverside, 1910), 20. The notorious Tyburn hanging tree, which grew in a corner of London's Hyde Park (and may well have been an elm), was used as a place of execution from about 1100 to 1783.

29. Warren, *The Great Tree*, 7.

30. Ibid., 7–9.

31. Shurtleff, *Topographical and Historical Description of Boston*, 333.

32. "The Boston Elm: The Famous Tree Succumbs to the Gale," *Boston Herald*, February 16, 1876.

33. Dame, *Typical Elms*, 49.

34. "The Boston Elm," *Boston Herald*.

35. "Affidavit Tells of True Scion of Boston Old Elm," *Boston Herald*, January 10, 1910.

36. Donald Culross Peattie, *A Natural History of Trees* (New York: Bonanza, 1966), 239.

37. The phrase is from Kammen, *Meadows of Memory*, 150.

38. Samuel Adams Drake, *Historic Mansions and Highways Around Boston* (Boston: Little, Brown, 1906), 268.

39. Mary Perkins Quincy (1901), quoted in Alain C. White, *The History of Litchfield, Connecticut* (Litchfield, Conn.: Enquirer, 1920), 170.

40. Simmons, *Historic Trees*, 27.

41. Ibid., 79–82.

42. Ibid., 101.

43. Ibid., 61–62.

44. Henry Howe, "New Haven's Elms and Green," a scrapbook of his articles from the *New Haven Daily Morning Journal and Courier* (1883–1884), Sterling Memorial Library, Yale University, 5–6.

45. Ibid., 8, 9.

46. Wells and Wells, *A History of Hatfield*, 223.

47. Letter from Thomas A. Dickinson in the Framingham *Tribune*, quoted in Simmons, *Historic Trees*, 54–55.

48. Simmons, *Historic Trees*, 85–86.

49. James Russell Lowell, "Under the Old Elm," *Poems* (Cambridge: Riverside, 1890), 4:74–89.

50. "Diary of Dorothy Dudley," quoted in Samuel F. Batchelder, "The Washington Elm Tradition," *Publications of the Cambridge Historical Society*, vol. 17 (Cambridge: Cambridge Historical Society, 1931), 50.

51. John Langdon Sibley in "The Washington Elm, Cambridge," *Old Time New England*, vol. 14 (Boston: Society for the Preservation of New England Antiquities, 1924), 143.

52. Eric Hobsbawm, "Inventing Traditions," in *The Invention of Tradition*, ed. Eric Hobsbawm and Terence Ranger (Cambridge: Cambridge University Press, 1983), 1–4.

53. Lucius R. Paige, *History of Cambridge* (Boston: H. O. Houghton, 1877), 452.

54. Batchelder, "The Washington Elm Tradition," 54.

55. Quoted in Miller, *Errand into the Wilderness*, 205.

56. Ralph Waldo Emerson, "Nature," quoted in Alfred Kazin, *A Writer's America: Landscape in Literature* (New York: Knopf, 1988), 50.

57. Sibley in "The Washington Elm," 143–144.

58. Washington Irving, *Life of George Washington* (New York: G. P. Putnam, 1855), 318.

59. Samuel Eliot Morison, "Proposed Tablet Under Washington Elm," unpublished manuscript, Cambridge Historical Commission (October 27, 1949).

60. Drake, *Historic Mansions and Highways*, 268.

61. The tablet is extant, located on Cambridge Common adjacent to the former site of the elm.

62. Dame, *Typical Elms*, 27.

63. Simmons, *Historic Trees*, 15.

64. Erle Kauffman, "The Elm—America's Tree of Glory," *American Forests* 42 (May 1936): 222.

65. J. Gardner Bartlett in *The Cambridge Tribune* (November 3, 1923), reprinted in "The Washington Elm, Cambridge," *Old Time New England*, 145–146. The Cambridge Cow Common originally extended as far west as Linnaean Street. The Washington Elm, located at the present intersection of Mason and Garden streets, was the first of the six elms. The second gained fame in association with George Whitefield, one of the firebrands of the Great Awakening. From its shade in 1745, Whitefield preached to a crowd on the Common, blasting the Harvard Unitarians as "close Pharisees, resting on head knowledge" (Van Wyck Brooks, *The Flowering of New England*, 33). Known as the Whitefield Elm—and often confused with its more famous neighbor—the tree was felled in 1871. Several of the other elms, located at five-hundred-foot intervals along Garden Street, survived well into the twentieth century, becoming neighborhood landmarks as the area developed.

66. Lt. Colonel E. M. Harris to John B. Atkinson, May 4, 1949, unpublished letter, Cambridge Historical Commission.

67. Washington quoted in Batchelder, "The Washington Elm Tradition," 73.

68. Ibid., 56–57. Washington was thus the *second* commander of the American army—a point, Batchelder allowed, that was "not generally appreciated." Oliver Wendell Holmes was later born in the house that served as Ward's headquarters.

69. Batchelder, "The Washington Elm Tradition," 73–75.

70. Simmons, *Historic Trees*, 15.

71. "The Washington Elm, Cambridge," *Old Time New England*, 143.

72. "Some Interesting Work About the Famous Washington Elm," n.d., unpublished affidavit, Cambridge Historical Commission.

73. "Washington Elm Finally Topples," *Cambridge Chronicle*, October 27, 1923.

74. Charles M. Sullivan to Gary Griffith, September 25, 1996, unpublished letter, Cambridge Historical Commission.

75. "A Tribute to the Washington Elm," *Cambridge Chronicle*, July 4, 1925.

76. Quoted in Lowenthal, *The Past Is a Foreign Country*, 323.

77. "Washington Elm Is Cut Up and Stored," *Cambridge Chronicle*, November 3, 1923.

78. "Mayor Curley Makes Offer to Cambridge," *Cambridge Chronicle*, November 10, 1923.

79. A later medallion still marks the spot, though it is indistinguishable from a manhole cover.

80. Lt. Colonel E. M. Harris to John B. Atkinson, May 4, 1949, unpublished letter, Cambridge Historical Commission.

81. Frank A. K. Boland to Hon. Michael J. Neville, December 28, 1949, unpublished letter, Cambridge Historical Commission.

82. The bas-relief was later stolen and had to be recast from a plaster model now located in the lobby of the Sheraton Commander Hotel. Eliot B. Spaulding, "Stolen Bronze Memorial Recast for April 19," *Cambridge Chronicle*, March 20, 1975.

83. "Many Interested in Historic Elm," *Cambridge Chronicle*, December 1, 1923.

84. "A Tribute to the Washington Elm," *Cambridge Chronicle*, July 4, 1925.

85. Batchelder, "The Washington Elm Tradition," 47.

Chapter 4: A Surfeit of Leaves

1. William Tudor, *Letters on the Eastern States* (New York: Kirk and Mercein, 1820), 266.

2. Alain C. White, *The History of Litchfield, Connecticut* (Litchfield, Conn.: Enquirer, 1920), 168; Chard Powers Smith, *The Housatonic, Puritan River* (New York: Rinehart, 1946), 302.

3. Walter Prichard Eaton, "Ancestral Shade," *Berkshire Eagle*, May 29, 1946.

4. White, *History of Litchfield*, 168–170.

5. Margaret French Cresson, *The Laurel Hill Association, 1853–1953* (Pittsfield: Eagle Printing, 1953), 11; Emma Lewis Coleman, *A Historic and Present Day Guide to Old Deerfield* (Boston: Plimpton Press, 1907), 105; Solomon Clark, "The Henshaw Elms of Northampton—Something About Their Early History," reprinted in C. H. Lyman, "C. H. Lyman Writes on the Henshaw Elms," *Northampton Gazette*, August 7, 1936; Arthur Percy Fitt, *All About Northfield* (Northfield, Mass.: Northfield Press, 1910), 83.

6. Basil Hall, *Travels in North America in the Years 1827 and 1828* (Edinburgh: Cadell, 1829), 1:128–129.

7. Ibid., 2:92.

8. Ibid., 1:106–107.

9. Ibid., 2:92–95.

10. Charles Joseph Latrobe, *The Rambler in North America* (New York: Harper and Brothers, 1835), 43–44.

11. Nathaniel Parker Willis, "Connecticut Valley, From Mount Holyoke," *American Scenery* (London: James S. Virtue, 1857), 1:117.

12. Nathaniel Parker Willis, *Life, Here and There* (New York: Baker and Scribner, 1850), 133–134.

13. Quoted in Hans Huth, *Nature and the American*, 17. Although Collin was primarily concerned with "timber for fuel and domestic uses," he also urged a "*treatise on ornamental* planting."

14. Ironically, many of these poets—Coleridge and Byron in particular—had themselves been influenced by earlier accounts of nature in the New World by the Bartrams, St. John de Crèvecoeur, and others. Alfred Kazin, *Writer's America: Landscape in Literature* (New York: Knopf, 1988), 24–28.

15. Richard Tarnas, *The Passion of the Western Mind* (New York: Ballantine, 1991), 366–369.

16. Ralph Waldo Emerson, "Nature," quoted in Kazin, *A Writer's America*, 50.

17. Thomas Cole, "Essay on American Scenery," in *American Art, 1700–1960: Sources and Documents*, ed. John W. McCoubrey (Englewood Cliffs: Prentice-Hall, 1965), 100.

18. Stephen E. Burrall, quoted in Richard Berenberg, "Village Improvement Societies in New England, 1850–1900: The Rural Ideal in an Age of Rural Depopulation and Urban Growth," Ph.D. dissertation, Harvard University, 1966, 18.

19. John R. Stilgoe, "Town Common and Village Green in New England: 1620 to 1981," in *On Common Ground*, ed. Ronald L. Fleming (Cambridge: Townscape Institute, 1982), 26.

20. Susan Fenimore Cooper, "A Plea for American Tress," reprinted from *Rural Hours* in *The Horticulturalist* 5 (1850): 138.

21. *Monitor*, January 3, 1798, quoted in White, *History of Litchfield*, 168.

22. Catherine Beecher, *Autobiography*, vol. 2, quoted in White, *History of Litchfield*, 168–169.

23. The *New England Farmer* began publication in 1822.

24. "Shade Trees," *New England Farmer* 4 (August 5, 1825): 10.

25. "Ornamental Trees," *New England Farmer* 4 (May 19, 1826): 341. In an age before enclosed vehicles, the microclimate of roads and highways was critically important to the comfort and safety of travelers.

26. Reprinted in "Shade Trees," *New England Farmer* 4 (May 18, 1827): 340.

27. "Trees," *New England Farmer* 9 (June 1, 1831): 365. The precise line of demarcation between public and private was often vague. In this case, it is unclear whether setting out trees on the "public road" meant planting them on private land bordering the road, or in the shared common space of the corridor itself. In towns, the issue of public/private ownership of road margins was similarly vague. It was drawn into focus only later in the century, as modernization introduced new infrastructure to the street corridor and forced a more systematic approach to its management.

28. "Ornamental Trees," *New England Farmer* 4 (May 6, 1835).

29. David Lowenthal, *The Past Is a Foreign Country* (New York: Cambridge University Press, 1985), 109.

30. "Trees," *New England Farmer* 8 (June 25, 1830): 387.

31. Andrew Jackson Downing, "Shade Trees in Cities," *The Horticulturalist* 8 (August 1, 1852): 346–347.

32. Tudor, *Letters on the Eastern States*, 280.

33. Ibid. Waterhouse also offered the first lectures in natural history at Harvard.

34. Colonel Robert Carr, "Introduction of the Lombardy Poplar into America," *Gardener's Monthly*, January 1861, 9. As William Bartram's nephew, Carr (then "the oldest American horticulturalist") had the credentials to back his claim. The *Monthly* described him as "the last living representative of the great Bartram family."

35. W. R. Prince, "Introduction of the Lombardy Poplar," *Gardener's Monthly*, March 1861, 80.

36. Samuel Eliot Morison, *Three Centuries of Harvard* (Cambridge: Harvard University Press, 1936), 172.

37. Spiro Kostof, *America by Design* (New York: Oxford University Press, 1987), 169; Nathaniel B. Shurtleff, *A Topographical and Historical Description of Boston* (Boston: Noyes, Holmes, 1872), 326.

38. Charles W. Brewster, *Rambles About Portsmouth* (Portsmouth, N.H.: C. W. Brewster & Son, 1859), 343–344.

39. Walter T. Swingle, "The Early European History and the Botanical Name of the Tree of Heaven, *Ailanthus Altissima*," *Journal of the Washington Academy of Sciences* 6 (August 19, 1916). D'Incarville also introduced golden-rain tree *(Koelreuteria paniculata)* and arborvitae *(Thuja orientalis)* to the West. Richard Peigler, "A Defense of Ailanthus," *American Horticulture* 72 (February 1993): 42.

40. Allen Chamberlain, *Beacon Hill: Its Ancient Pastures and Early Mansions* (Boston: Houghton Mifflin, 1925), 269. Andrew Jackson Downing claimed that the tree arrived in New England directly from China, imported under the name Tillou tree. Downing, *Landscape Gardening and Rural Architecture* (New York: Dover, reprint 1991), 204.

41. W. R. Prince, "Introduction of the Lombardy Poplar," 80.

42. *New England Farmer* 12 (October 9, 1833): 101.

43. Birdsey Grant Northrup, *Rural Improvement* (New Haven: Tuttle, Morehouse & Taylor, 1880), 25.

44. "Trees," *New England Farmer* 8 (June 25, 1830): 387.

45. "A correspondence from Otis Turner, Medina, Orleans County," *New England Farmer* 11 (November 21, 1832): 150.

46. "Ornamental Trees," *New England Farmer* 4 (May 6, 1835).

47. "Trees," *New England Farmer* 8 (June 25, 1830): 387.

48. Brewster, *Rambles About Portsmouth*, 344.

49. Sylvester Judd, *History of Hadley* (Northampton, Mass.: Metcalf, 1863), 430.

50. Shurtleff, *Topographical and Historical Description*, 326.

51. The house was his birthplace, on the present site of Harvard Law School. Oliver Wendell Holmes, "The Gambrel-Roofed House," in *The Cambridge of Eighteen Hundred and Ninety-Six*, ed. Arthur Gilman (Cambridge: Riverside, 1896), 43–44.

52. Andrew Jackson Downing, "Shade Trees in Cities," 345–346.

53. Ibid., 346–347; italics in original.

Chapter 5: The Verdant Village

1. "The Elms of Old Sheffield," *Berkshire Courier*, June 18, 1896.

2. Ibid.

3. Mary Dewey to Chas. O. Dewey (Orville Dewey's son), reprinted in ibid.

4. Ibid.

5. Orville Dewey, *Autobiography and Letters of Orville Dewey*, ed. Mary E. Dewey (Boston: Roberts Brothers, 1883), 156–157.

6. His daughter wrote: "Mr. Bryant and my father were about of an age. They had known each other almost from boyhood, and their friendship had matured with time." Ibid., 53n.

7. The Sketch Club was also known as the Club of the Twenty-one, Club XXI, or the Artists' Club. It later became the Century Club of New York. Ibid., 86.

8. Ibid., 76, 85–86.

9. Orville Dewey to W. C. Bryant, February 25, 1850, in ibid., 215; W. C. Bryant to Orville Dewey, March 29, 1850, in *The Letters of William Cullen Bryant* ed. William C. Bryant II and Thomas G. Voss (New York: Fordham University Press, 1975), 3:12.

10. "Pastoral Landscape," exhibited at the National Academy in 1849, was inspired by Bryant's poem "Green River," as was "Landscape, Scene from 'Thanatopsis.'" *Letters of William Cullen Bryant*, 118.

11. Gerard Chapman, "Sheffield's Big Elm," *Berkshire Eagle*, June 11, 1985.

12. Dewey, *Autobiography and Letters*, 184.

13. Orville Dewey, *An Address Delivered Under the Old Elm Tree in Sheffield, With Some Remarks on the Great Political Question of the Day* (New York: C. S. Francis, 1856), 3. Also see *Reply to Dr. Dewey's Address, Delivered at the Elm Tree* (Charleston, S.C.: privately published, 1856).

14. Dewey, *Autobiography and Letters*, 188.

15. Dewey, *Address Delivered Under the Old Elm Tree*, 25–26.

16. See "Chapter XLI of the Revised Statutes of the Commonwealth of Massachusetts," in B. F. Atkinson, *A Short History of the Amherst Improvement Association* (1937), unpublished manuscript, Jones Library, Amherst, Massachusetts, 18–19.

17. Walter Prichard Eaton, "Second Fiddle?" *Berkshire Eagle*, August 13, 1941.

18. Margaret French Cresson, *The Laurel Hill Association* (Pittsfield: Eagle Printing, 1953), 14–15.

19. Ibid., 15–16.

20. Parris Thaxter Farwell, *Village Improvement* (New York: Sturgis and Walton, 1913), 18–19.

21. Cresson, *Laurel Hill Association*, 16, 34.

22. Ibid., 34–35.

23. Farwell, *Village Improvement*, 14–15.

24. Atkinson, *Short History of the Amherst Improvement Association*, 7.

25. Richard Berenberg, "Village Improvement Societies in New England, 1850–1900: The Rural Ideal in an Age of Rural Depopulation and Urban Growth," Ph.D. dissertation, Harvard University, 1966, 49; Warren H. Manning, *The History of Village Improvement in the United States* (Syracuse, N.Y.: Mason Press, 1904), 9.

26. Downing perished when the steamer *Henry Clay* burned on the Hudson River in 1852.

27. Berenberg, "Village Improvement Societies," 15–16. "No such group," writes Berenberg, "would have failed to have read Downing, in those years." An address delivered at the Anniversary Day exercises in 1855 included several references to his writings, and a later one included "an interesting biography of the lamented Andrew Jackson Downing." Ibid.

28. David Schuyler, *Apostle of Taste: Andrew Jackson Downing, 1815–1852* (Baltimore: Johns Hopkins University Press, 1996).

29. Andrew Jackson Downing, "On the Improvement of Country Villages," *The Horticulturalist* 3 (June 1849): 545–546; italics in original.

30. Ibid.

31. Ibid.

32. Andrew Jackson Downing, "Trees in Towns and Villages," *The Horticulturalist* 1 (March 1847): 394.

33. Andrew Jackson Downing, "On Planting Shade-Trees," *Rural Essays*, George William Curtis, ed. (New York: Da Capo, reprint 1974), 300.

34. Downing, "Trees in Towns and Villages," 396.

35. Ibid., 395.

36. Downing, "On the Improvement of Country Villages," 548–549.

37. Ibid., 546.

38. Downing, "Trees in Towns and Villages," 394.

39. Ibid., 395.

40. Ibid; italics in original.

41. "Report of the Rockingham Farmers' Club," in *The Horticulturalist* 4 (December 1849).

42. H. F. Wilson, *Hill Country*, quoted in Dona Brown, *Inventing New England* (Washington: Smithsonian Institution Press, 1995), 138.

43. Dewey, *Autobiography and Letters*, 28.

44. Berenberg, "Village Improvement Societies," 72.

45. Brown, *Inventing New England*, 8–9.

46. Berenberg, "Village Improvement Societies," 3.

47. Henry David Thoreau, *The Journal of Henry D. Thoreau*, 3d ed., ed. Bradford Torrey and Francis H. Allen (Boston: Houghton Mifflin, 1949), 8:139–140.

48. Henry D. Thoreau, "Autumnal Tints," *Excursions* (Boston: Ticknor and Fields, 1863), 233–234.

49. Ibid.

50. Ibid.

51. Henry Ward Beecher, *Plain and Pleasant Talk About Fruits, Flowers, and Farming* (New York: Derby & Jackson, 1859), 116–117.

52. Henry Ward Beecher, *Norwood; or, Village Life in New England* (New York: Charles Scribner, 1868), 3.

53. Ibid., 4–5.

54. Henry James, *The American Scene* (New York: Charles Scribner's Sons, 1946), 38–39.

55. Ibid.

56. Ibid., 39.

57. Ibid., 40–41, 43.

58. Nathaniel Parker Willis, *Life, Here and There* (New York: Baker and Scribner, 1850), 130.

Chapter 6: City of Elms

1. Charles W. Brewster, *Rambles About Portsmouth* (Portsmouth: C. W. Brewster, 1859), 345; "Arboreal Springfield," *Progressive Springfield* 2 (June 1891): 12.

2. William E. Buckley, *A New England Pattern* (Chester, Conn.: Pequot Press, 1973), 112.

3. "Trees," Portland *Yankee*, July 23, 1828, 240.

4. Quoted in Salma Hale, *Annals of the Town of Keene* (Keene, N.H.: J. W. Prentiss, 1851), 117. The "unknown profligate" was supposedly an "instrument of feminine malice," but the meaning of this is unclear. Ibid., 120.

5. Keene History Committee, *Upper Ashuelot: A History of Keene, New Hampshire* (Keene, N.H.: City of Keene, 1968), 88.

6. S. G. Griffin, *A History of the Town of Keene* (Keene, N.H.: Sentinel Printing, 1904), 451.

7. "How Our Park Was Made," *The May Flower* (Keene, N.H.: Sentinel Printing, 1873), 41.

8. Ibid., 42.

9. Ibid.

10. James O. Lyford, ed., *History of Concord, New Hampshire* (Concord, N.H.: Rumford Press, 1903), 50–51.

11. Howard M. Cook, *Wayside Jottings; or, Rambles Around the Old Town of Concord, New Hampshire* (Concord, N.H.: E. C. Eastman, 1910), 131.

12. Flora Graves Phelps, "Living Room Tales—Springfield Justly Called a City of Trees," *Springfield Sunday Republican*, April 1924.

13. M. A. DeWolfe Howe, *Boston Common: Scenes from Four Centuries* (Cambridge, Mass.: Riverside, 1910), 29.

14. Nathaniel B. Shurtleff, *A Topographical and Historical Description of Boston* (Boston: Noyes, Holmes, 1872), 326.

15. Mason A. Green, *Springfield, 1636–1886* (Springfield, Mass.: C. A. Nichols, 1888), 404–406.

16. Lyford, ed., *History of Concord*, 51.

17. Brewster, *Rambles About Portsmouth*, 344.

18. "Ornamental Trees," *Eastern Argus* 27 (May 17, 1831): 2.

19. "Arboreal Springfield," *Progressive Springfield*, 12.

20. Jared Eliot, "Essay on Tree Planting" (1884), quoted in George Dudley Seymour, *New Haven* (New Haven: privately printed, 1942), 82.

21. Henry Howe, "New Haven's Elms and Green," a scrapbook of his articles from the *New Haven Daily Morning Journal and Courier* (1883–1884), Sterling Memorial Library, Yale University, 1.

22. Seymour, *New Haven*, 84. This motion was likely a response to appeals by Hillhouse himself.

23. James Hillhouse, "Subscription to Set Trees—upon Green," April 6, 1786, James Hillhouse MSS No. 117 Box 1 Folder D, New Haven Colony Historical Society.

24. Howe, "New Haven's Elms and Green," 3.

25. Seymour, *New Haven*, 84.

26. Howe, "New Haven's Elms and Green," 7–8. Baldwin was nominated by Andrew Jackson in 1830 and served on the courts of John Marshall and Roger B. Taney.

27. Seymour, *New Haven*, 87.

28. Howe, "New Haven's Elms and Green," 2.

29. Christopher Tunnard, *The City of Man* (New York: Charles Scribner's Sons, 1970), 240–243.

30. Henry W. Lawrence, "The Origins of the Tree-Lined Boulevard," *Geographical Review* 78 (October 1988): 356–360.

31. Ibid.

32. Ibid., 360–361.

33. Ibid., 361–363.

34. Ibid., 355–358, 365, 374.

35. R. H. Richens, *Elm* (London: Cambridge University Press, 1983), 112.

36. The elm avenue noted by John Eveyln at Nonsuch Palace, and that at Longford Castle, may have dated to the late sixteenth century. Ibid.

37. Batty Langley, *A Sure Method of Improving Estates* (London: Francis Clay and Daniel Browne, 1728), 52, 62.

38. Lawrence, "Origins of the Tree-Lined Boulevard," 370–371.

39. Ibid., 373–374.

40. Robert W. Miller, "The History of Trees in the City," in *Shading Our Cities: A Resource Guide for Urban and Community Forests*, ed. Gary Moll and Sara Ebenreck (Washington, D.C.: Island Press, 1989), 33.

41. Quoted in Spiro Kostof, *The City Shaped: Urban Patterns and Meanings Through History* (Boston: Little, Brown, 1991), 145–146.

42. Exactly when Philadelphia received its first street trees is not clear. Peter Kalm, who described the city in 1748, made no note of trees flanking the public thoroughfares. Since he recorded with considerable detail such items as the pavement and the presence of trees "planted about the houses and in gardens" (and having made careful note of the street trees in New York on the same journey), it may safely be inferred that Philadelphia had not yet planted trees on its streets in 1748. Peter Kalm, *Travels in North America* (London: 1772), 1:24.

43. John M. Duncan, *Travels Through Part of the United States and Canada* (Glasgow: Wardlaw and Cunninghame, 1823), 188–189.

44. William Newnham Blane, *Travels Through the United States and Canada* (London: Baldwin, 1828), 24.

45. James Silk Buckingham, *America: Historical, Statistic, and Descriptive* (New York: Harper and Brothers, 1841), 329. Buckingham was a keen observer; he noted that those trees on the north side of the street flourished, as they had the benefit of the sun throughout the day; those on the south appeared to lag comparatively, as they received "only the beams of the rising and setting sun, and that only when he is north of the equator."

46. Kalm, *Travels in North America*, 1:193–194. The following year Kalm visited Albany, where he also observed tree-lined streets.

47. Andrew Burnaby, *Travels Through the Middle Settlements in North America in the Years 1759 and 1760* (New York: A. Wessels, reprint 1904), 111–112.

48. Henry Bradshaw Fearon, *Sketches of America* (London: Longman, Hurst, Rees, Orme, and Brown, 1818), 11.

49. Portland Town Records (1799), in "A Street's History" (1899), Post Scrapbook, Maine Historical Society, 187.

50. "Twenty Dollars Reward," *Portland Gazette*, October 20, 1800.

51. Edward H. Elwell, *Portland and Vicinity* (Portland, Maine: Loring, Short & Harmon, 1881), 60.

52. Quoted in Lucius R. Paige, *History of Cambridge* (Boston: H. O. Houghton, 1877), 236.

53. Lewis M. Hastings, *The Streets of Cambridge: An Account of Their Origin and History* (Cambridge, Mass.: City of Cambridge, 1921), 27–28.

54. Shurtleff, *Topographical and Historical Description*, 330.

55. Nehemiah Adams, *Boston Common, or Rural Walks in Cities* (Boston: George H. Light, 1838; Bostonian Society edition), 51. Adams went on to point out that "there is something repugnant in the figure which represents a common, or parks, as the *lungs* of a city; but it will at least be congruous (if this be any apology) with that figure, to say, that every superfluous tree in the centre of the Common is a *tubercle*."

56. Many of the 150 trees set out by the city that year were maples, a reaction to a canker worm attack on the elms the year before. Seymour, *New Haven*, 87.

57. Fifteen years later, the last of these trees died, the result of poisoning from leaky gas lines under the street. *Manchester: A Brief Record of Its Past and a Picture of Its Present* (Manchester, N.H.: John B. Clarke, 1875), 67–68.

58. George Dudley Seymour referred to the 1839 action as "the last considerable planting." Seymour, *New Haven*, 87.

59. Henry C. Binford, *The First Suburbs: Residential Communities on the Boston Periphery, 1815–1860* (Chicago: University of Chicago Press, 1985), 12.

60. T. C. Amory, *Old Cambridge and New* (Boston: J. R. Osgood, 1871), 21.

61. Hastings, *The Streets of Cambridge*, 35, 24.

62. Ibid., 28–29.

63. James Hayward, *Report of the Survey of the Roads in Cambridge* (Cambridge, Mass.: Metcalf, Torry & Ballou, 1838), 3.

64. Ibid., 6–7.

65. Ibid., 10, 8.

66. City of Cambridge, *Mayor's Address . . . [and] Annual Reports made to the City Council* (Cambridge, Mass.: Allen and Farnham, 1862), 16.

67. Hayward, *Report*, 14.

68. Ibid., 14.

69. Hayward quoted in Hastings, *The Streets of Cambridge*, 28–29.

70. Hayward, *Report*, 15.

71. City of Cambridge, *Address of the Mayor, Upon the First Organization of the City Government* (Cambridge: Andrew Reid, 1846), 10–11.

72. City of Cambridge, *The Mayor's Address at the Organization of the City Government, and Reports of the Committee on Finance, and the School Committee of the City of Cambridge* (Cambridge: John Ford, 1847), 9–10.

73. City of Cambridge, *Mayor's Address* (Cambridge: John Ford, 1848), 4–5.

74. Ibid., 7–8.

75. City of Cambridge, *Mayor's Address* (Cambridge: John Ford, 1851), v.

76. City of Cambridge, *Mayor's Address* (Cambridge: Riverside, 1869), 18; City of Cambridge, *Mayor's Address* (Cambridge: Riverside, 1871), 26.

77. "Public Improvement," *Daily Advertiser*, May 29, 1833.

78. William F. Fox, *Tree Planting on Streets and Highways* (Albany, N.Y.: J. B. Lyon, 1903), 206–207.

79. *Report of the General Superintendent of Parks* (Cambridge: City of Cambridge, 1894), 71–72.

80. Ibid.

81. Ibid., 72–73.

82. Ibid., 73.

83. Ibid., 72.

84. Ibid., 74.

85. Ibid., 75–77.

86. Frank J. Scott, *The Art of Beautifying Suburban Home Grounds*, 3d ed. (New York: American Book Exchange, 1881), 317.

87. "American Elm," *The Horticulturalist* 2 (September 1847): 117.

88. Fox, *Tree Planting On Streets and Highways*, 193.

89. Charles Sprague Sargent, "An Avenue of Elms," *Garden and Forest*, April 19, 1893, 172.

Chapter 7: Yankee Elysium

1. Thomas Jefferson, *Notes on Virginia*, in *The Life and Selected Writings of Thomas Jefferson*, ed. Adrienne Koch and William Peden (New York: Modern Library, 1972), 280.

2. David Schuyler, *The New Urban Landscape: The Redefinition of City Form in Nineteenth-Century America* (Baltimore: Johns Hopkins University Press, 1986), 24.

3. Ibid.

4. Perry Miller, *Errand into the Wilderness* (Cambridge: Belknap Press, 1964), 207.

5. Morton and Lucia White, "The American Intellectual Versus the American City," in *American Urban History*, ed. Alexander B. Callow (New York: Oxford University Press, 1969), 353.

6. James L. Machor, *Pastoral Cities: Urban Ideals and the Symbolic Landscape of America* (Madison: University of Wisconsin Press, 1987), 5, 3.

7. Michael H. Cowan, quoted in Thomas Bender, *Toward an Urban Vision: Ideas and Institutions in Nineteenth-Century America* (Baltimore: Johns Hopkins University Press, 1982), 14; Bender, ibid.

8. Machor, *Pastoral Cities*, 9–13.

9. For examples, see Bender, *Toward an Urban Vision*, 12–17; Machor, *Pastoral Cities*, 3–16.

10. Nehemiah Adams, *Boston Common, or Rural Walks in Cities* (Boston: George H. Light, 1838), 23.

11. Ibid.

12. Ibid., 7, 11–12.

13. Ibid., 19.

14. Frederick Noble Evans, *Town Improvement* (New York: D. Appleton, 1919), 173.

15. Adams, *Boston Common*, 7, 11–12.

16. James Hillhouse, "Subscription to Set Trees—upon Green," April 6, 1786, James Hillhouse MSS No. 117 Box 1 Folder D, New Haven Colony Historical Society.

17. "Records of the Proprietors of the New Burying Ground in New Haven," 1796, Grove Street Cemetery MSS No. 74 Box 1 Folder K, New Haven Colony Historical Society, 1.

18. James Hillhouse, Philadelphia, to Henry Lloyd, London, February 2, 1793, Hillhouse Papers, Sterling Memorial Library, Yale University.

19. James Silk Buckingham, *America: Historical, Statistical, and Descriptive* (New York: Harper and Brothers, 1841), 2:286.

20. Edward T. Coke, *A Subaltern's Furlough* (New York: J. & J. Harper, 1833), 190–191.

21. A. M. Maxwell, *A Run Through the United States* (London: Henry Colburn, 1841), 85.

22. "Arboreal Springfield," *Progressive Springfield* 2 (June 1891): 11.

23. Flora Graves Phelps, "Living Room Tales—Springfield Justly Called a City of Trees," *Springfield Sunday Republican*, April 1924.

24. John Neal, *Account of the Great Conflagration in Portland* (Portland, Maine: Starbird & Twitchell, 1866), 81.

25. William Willis, *The History of Portland from 1632 to 1864* (Portland, Maine: Bailey & Noyes, 1865), 728. The character of this urban pastoral was largely lost in 1866, when fire ravaged Portland and destroyed hundreds of the city's finest elms. Neal, *Account of the Great Conflagration*, 81.

26. David T. Pottinger, "I, Too, in Arcadia," in *Cambridge Historical Society Publica-*

tions, vol. 35, *Proceedings for the Years 1953–1954* (Cambridge: Cambridge Historical Society, 1955), 113.

27. Not all praise was unreserved. Edward T. Coke, writing in the 1830s, appreciated the beauty of the elms but deplored the way their canopy kept the streets "exceedingly wet and dirty." Coke, *A Subaltern's Furlough*, 157.

28. Nathaniel Parker Willis, "The Gothic Church, New Haven," *American Scenery* (London: James S. Virtue, 1857), 2:9.

29. Nathaniel Parker Willis, quoted in W. E. Decrow, *Yale and "The City of Elms,"* (Boston: W. E. Decrow, 1885), 85.

30. Willis, "The Gothic Church, New Haven," 9.

31. Quoted in Ezekiel Porter Belden, *Sketches of Yale College* (New York: Saxton & Miles, 1843), 67–68.

32. Lady Emmeline Stuart Wortely, *Travels in the United States* (New York, 1851), quoted in George Dudley Seymour, *New Haven* (New Haven: privately printed, 1942), 77–78.

33. Charles Dickens, "American Notes," in *Works of Charles Dickens*, (New York: Sheldon, 1865), 2:78. Dickens was immensely popular when he toured the United States in 1842, and his *American Notes* sold briskly in both American and England. His New York publisher sold fifty thousand copies within two days, and the three thousand copies sent to Philadelphia were gone in less than an hour. Allan Nevins, *America Through British Eyes* (New York: Oxford University Press, 1948).

34. William Smith, *A Yorkshireman's Trip to the United States and Canada* (London: Longmans, Green, 1892), 151.

35. Seymour, *New Haven*, 78.

36. Henry Howe, "New Haven's Elms and Green," a scrapbook of his articles from the *New Haven Daily Morning Journal and Courier* (1883–1884), Sterling Memorial Library, Yale University, 1.

37. Luigi Castiglioni, "Observations on Useful Plants," in *Luigi Castiglioni's Viaggio*, ed. Antonio Pace (Syracuse, N.Y.: Syracuse University Press, 1983), 459–460.

38. Walter Prichard Eaton, *Green Trails and Upland Pastures* (New York: Doubleday, Page, 1917), 253.

39. Charles Sprague Sargent, "An Avenue of Elms," *Garden and Forest*, April 19, 1893, 172.

40. Bruno Zevi, *Architecture as Space* (New York: Horizon, reprint 1974), 24.

41. Robert Geddes, *The Forest Edge* (New York: St. Martin's, 1982), 13–16.

42. Nathaniel Hawthorne, *The English Note Books*, ed. Randall Stewart, reprint 1962, 390. Hawthorne was quoting from Milton's *Paradise Lost*, 9:1107.

43. Kenneth Clark, *The Gothic Revival: An Essay on the History of Taste*, 3d ed. (London: John Murray, 1995), 11.

44. Calder Loth and Julius Trousdale Sadler, Jr., *The Only Proper Style: Gothic Architecture in America* (Boston: New York Graphic Society, 1975), 42–43.

45. William Cullen Bryant, "A Forest Hymn," *Poems* (Philadelphia: A. Hart, 1850), 130.

46. Adams, *Boston Common*, 14–15.

47. Henry Wadsworth Longfellow, *Journal* (December 12, 1849), quoted in *Report of the General Superintendent of Parks* (Cambridge, Mass.: City of Cambridge, 1894), 77n.

48. Henry Wadsworth Longfellow, "Hawthorne," *Tales of a Wayside Inn* (Boston: Ticknor and Fields, 1863).

49. Henry Ward Beecher, quoted in *Report of the General Superintendent of Parks* (Cambridge: City of Cambridge, 1894), 76f.

50. "The Old Elms of Northampton: An Appeal for Their Preservation," *Hampshire Gazette*, December 20, 1864.

51. Oliver Wendell Holmes, *Elsie Venner: A Romance of Destiny* (Cambridge, Mass.: Riverside, reprint 1891), 55–56.

52. John Maass, "'Sylvan Temples,' Dead Ends in the Gothic Forest," *Landscape Architecture* 61 (October 1970): 50.

53. M. C. Meigs, letter, in *Architectural Review and American Builder's Journal*, August 1870. Published for only three years (1868 to 1870), this was apparently the first architectural magazine in America. Maass, "Sylvan Temples."

54. Swormstedt quoted in Howe, "New Haven's Elms and Green," 1; Smith, *A Yorkshireman's Trip*, 151; Richard Upton Piper, *The Trees of America* (Boston: William White, 1855), 6; Howe, "New Haven's Elms and Green," 4.

On the ecclesiastical origins of the New Haven plan, see John Archer, "Puritan Town Planning in New Haven," *Journal of the Society of Architectural Historians* 34 (May 1975): 140–149.

55. Nathaniel Parker Willis, quoted in Howe, "New Haven's Elms and Green," 1.

56. Nathaniel Parker Willis, "The Elms of New Haven," *Sacred Poems* (New York: Clark, Austin & Smith, 1860), 233–235.

57. Charles Sprague Sargent, "The American Elm," *Garden and Forest*, June 11, 1890, 281.

Chapter 8: Boulevard of Broken Trees

1. "The Old Elms of Northampton: An Appeal for Their Preservation," *Hampshire Gazette*, December 20, 1864.

2. Blake McKelvey, *The Urbanization of America, 1860–1915* (New Brunswick, N.J.: Rutgers University Press, 1963), 92.

3. George A. Cromie, "An Unusual Case of Electrical Injury to Street Trees: Some Peculiar Cases Observed at New Haven, Conn.," *Scientific American* Supplement No. 1985 (January 17, 1914): 36.

4. "Replacing the Ancient Elms," *Hampshire Gazette*, February 9, 1886.

5. McKelvey, *The Urbanization of America*, 108.

6. Paul V. Hayden, "Neglected and Undesirable Trees Responsible for Many Power Failures in Recent Storm," *Connecticut Woodlands* 18:1 (January 1953): 31.

7. David Anderson, "Tree Man Says U.S. Needs Big Pruning," *New York Times*, August 3, 1953.

8. Pruning trees and repairing lines damaged by falling limbs cost utility companies millions of dollars annually, prompting at least one conspiracy theory suggesting that linemen were instructed to spread Dutch elm disease along company corridors in the 1950s, an effort to hasten the disappearance of the problematic trees. The allegation, however enticing, has never been proven.

9. Clay McShane, *Down the Asphalt Path: The Automobile and the American City* (New York: Columbia University Press, 1994), 64, 58.

10. Ibid., 58–65.

11. *Report of the General Superintendent of Parks* (Cambridge, Mass.: City of Cambridge, 1894), 72–73.

12. George Dudley Seymour, *New Haven* (New Haven: privately printed, 1942), 93–115.

13. Andrew S. Fuller, "The Passing of the Elm—A Tree Culturist Who Is Glad to Have It Go," *New York Tribune*, September 23, 1890.

14. Clarence Moores Weed, "The Passing of the Elm," *Craftsman*, July 1913, 452–453.

15. John C. Devlin, "Disease Dooming American Elms," *New York Times*, March 12, 1957; Francis W. Holmes, "Seven Dutch Women Scientists Whose Early Research Is Basic to Our Knowledge of the 'Dutch Elm Disease,'" *Dutch Elm Disease Research: Cellular and Molecular Approaches* (New York: Springer-Verlag, 1993), 9. *Dutch Elm Disease: Perspectives After Sixty Years* (Ithaca: Cornell University Agricultural Experiment Station, 1978), 13.

16. *Dutch Elm Disease: Perspectives After Sixty Years*, 5–10.

17. The geographic origin of the pathogen has never been proven, although based on the natural resistance of certain Asian varieties of elm, it is likely that it originated in Asia. The pathogen eventually made its way to Europe, possibly via the Dutch East Indies during the late nineteenth century.

18. F. A. Bartlett, "The Dutch Elm Disease," *American Landscape Architect* 3:2 (August 1930): 40–41.

19. R. Kent Beattie, "The Threat of the Dutch Elm Disease," *American Forests* 37:8 (August 1931): 489.

20. Bartlett, "The Dutch Elm Disease," 42.

21. E. P. Felt, *The Dutch Elm Disease and Its Control* (Stamford, Conn.: Bartlett Tree Research Laboratories, 1933), 4.

22. Curtis May, "Outbreaks of the Dutch Elm Disease in the United States," USDA Circular No. 322 (August 1934), 1–4.

23. Devereux Butcher, "Watch Your Elms!" *American Forests* 47:5 (May 1941): 246.

24. Felt, *Dutch Elm Disease*, 5. A second insect vector was the native elm bark beetle *Hylurgopinus rufipes* Eichloff. *Dutch Elm Disease: Perspectives After Sixty Years*, 5.

25. E. P. Felt, *Our Shade Trees* (New York: Orange Judd, 1938), 162–163.

26. Walter O. Filley, "Status of Dutch Elm Disease," *Connecticut Woodlands* 1:3 (September 1936): 14.

27. Bartlett, "The Dutch Elm Disease," 42.

28. Howard Mansfield, "Elm Street Blues," *American Heritage* 37:6 (October–November 1986): 99.

29. Felt, *Dutch Elm Disease*, 10.

30. "American Elm Faces an Emergency," *American Forests* 40:11 (November 1934): 534.

31. "Dutch Elm Disease Shows Alarming Gains," *American Forests* 40:9 (September 1934): 420.

32. Elvin McDonald, "How to Save the Elm," *House Beautiful* 110:6 (June 1968): 148.

33. "American Elm Faces an Emergency," *American Forests*, 534.

34. "$527,000 to Fight Dutch Elm Disease," *American Forests* 41:1 (January 1935): 31; "P.W.A. Funds for Elm Protection," *American Forests* 41:1 (January 1935): 33.

35. "Dutch Elm Disease Control Work Makes Progress," *American Forests* 41:3 (March 1935): 132.

36. "Looking Ahead for the Elms," *American Forests* 41:3 (March 1935): 118.

37. "$2,500,000 for Dutch Elm Disease Control," *American Forests* 41:8 (August 1935): 382.

38. "Wallace Asked to Clarify Charge Elms Are Doomed," *American Forests* 42:3 (March 1936): 132.

39. "Fight on Elm Disease Gaining Ground," *American Forests* 42:8 (August 1936): 376.

40. "The Elm's Rendezvous with Death," *American Forests* 42:5 (May 1937): 221; "Dutch Elm Disease Funds Reduced," *American Forests* 44:8 (August 1938): 374.

41. Joseph Edgar Chamberlain, "To Arms for the American Elm," *American Forests* 40:5 (May 1934): 230.

42. Bernard L. Gordon, "Metamorphosis of the '38 Hurricane," in *Hurricane in Southern New England: An Analysis of the Great Storm of 1938*, ed. B. L. Gordon (Watch Hill, R.I.: Book and Tackle Shop), 8–10.

43. Everett S. Allen, *A Wind to Shake the World: The Story of the 1938 Hurricane* (Boston: Little, Brown, 1976), 95.

44. E. P. Felt, "Hurricane Damage to Shade Trees," *American Forests* 45:1 (January 1939): 20.

45. Quoted in Allen, *A Wind to Shake the World*, 95–96.

46. David Morton, *In the Wake of the Hurricane* (Amherst, Mass.: Carpenter and Morehouse, 1938).

47. E. P. Felt, "Hurricane Damage," 20.

48. Gordon T. Woods, "New England Hurricane Benefits Wildlife," *American Forests* (September 1940): 402.

49. *Dutch Elm Disease: Perspectives After Sixty Years*, 13.

50. "Dutch Elm Disease Funds Reduced," *American Forests* 44:8 (August 1938): 374.

51. Russell R. Whitten, "Protecting Against Dutch Elm Disease," USDA Central States Forest Experiment Station, Miscellaneous Release 10 (March 1956), 5.

52. William P. Wharton, "Are the Elms Being Saved?" *American Forests* (December 1938): 545–546.

53. Filley, "Status of Dutch Elm Disease," 14; E. G. Brewer, "The Elms and the War," *American Forests* 49:2 (February 1943): 75–76.

54. Brewer, "The Elms and the War," 75.

55. Carol H. Woodward, "The Elms of America: What Is to Be Their Fate?" *Journal of the New York Botanical Garden* 49:579 (March 1948): 57.

56. Brewer, "The Elms and the War," 75; "The Case of the Elms," *American Forests* 47:1 (January 1941): 31.

57. George H. Plumb, "The Dutch Elm Disease Problem in Connecticut," *Connecticut Woodlands* 15:1 (March 1950): 13.

58. Judith A. Bellafaire, *The Army Nurse Corps: A Commemoration of World War II Service* (Washington, D.C.: U.S. Army Center of Military History, 1993), 26.

59. Rachel Carson, *Silent Spring* (Boston: Houghton Mifflin, reprint 1987), 20–21.

60. "Rachel Carson: A Scientist Alerts the Public to the Hazards of Pesticides," Online Ethics Center for Engineering & Science, 2000 (www.onlineethics.org).

61. "Fights Elm Tree Disease," *New York Times*, October 24, 1946; "To Fight Elm Beetle," *New York Times*, May 5, 1947.

62. Woodward, "Elms of America," 3.

63. Ibid; italics in original.

64. Malcolm A. McKenzie and W. B. Becker, "What Can I Do to Protect My Elms?" Massachusetts Forest and Park Association Bulletin No. 172 (March 1950), 4.

65. *Dutch Elm Disease Survey for Massachusetts* (Boston: Massachusetts Forest and Park Association, January 1948), 4; A. W. Hurford, "Save the Elms Program Increasingly Effective," *Connecticut Woodlands* 17:1 (March 1952): 5; Victor Jarm, "The Control Program for Dutch Elm Disease in Hartford," *Connecticut Woodlands* 21:6 (November 1956): 104.

66. Carson, *Silent Spring*, 23.

67. "DDT Controversy Erupts in Detroit," *New York Times*, September 16, 1962.

68. Ibid.

69. Walter Sullivan, "News of the Week in Science: Elm Blight," *New York Times*, April 4, 1965.

70. Carson, *Silent Spring*, 107–108.

71. Ibid., 105.

72. Bob McCarthy, Williamstown, Massachusetts, conversation with author, August 20, 2002.

73. "Use of DDT to Fight Elm Fungus Attacked by Audubon Society," *New York Times*, September 25, 1964.

74. "DDT Ban Takes Effect," EPA Press Release, December 31, 1972.

75. Walter Sullivan, "The Vanishing American Elm," *New York Times*, August 18, 1968.

76. Jane E. Brody, "Tests Hint Gain on Dutch Elm Disease," *New York Times*, January 27, 1970.

77. "An Ally To Protect Elms?" *Conservationist*, February–March 1970.

78. Nancy Cass, "Famed Wethersfield Elm Goes," *Hartford Times*, May 29, 1953.

79. Sullivan, "The Vanishing American Elm."

80. Syracuse, New York, lost most of its twenty-two thousand maples in this way. Mansfield, "Elm Street Blues," 101.

81. Quoted in Phil McCombs, "Making a Stand," *Washington Post*, July 30, 2001.

82. Mansfield, "Elm Street Blues," 4–5.

Epilogue: Return of a Native

1. Peter Del Tredici, "The Ecology and Economics of Elm Replacement in Harvard Yard," *Arnoldia* 58:1 (1998).

2. John P. Hansel, copy from Elm Research Institute brochure, 2002.

3. Joan Lee Faust, "Hope for a Vanishing American," *New York Times*, June 28, 1970.

4. John P. Hansel, conversation with author, August 20, 2002.

5. Ibid. Hansel recalls an ERI meeting during the 1970s which took place in a high-rise residence hall on the Syracuse University campus. The conference room windows afforded a stunning view of the city, from which Hansel and his colleagues literally watched as city arborists took down elm after elm in the streets below.

6. Ibid.

7. Ibid.

8. Elm Research Institute, "Elm tree Named Independence," 1988, Plant Patent number 6,227.

9. Kathleen Hickey and Matthew Petitjean, "Elms," *City Trees: The Journal of The Society of Municipal Arborists* 34:4 (July 1998).

10. Five of the six were derived from the controlled pollinations of 1969–1971, while the sixth (known as M-8) "was the single survivor of about 1,000 inoculated seedlings obtained from Kansas in 1957." E. P. Smalley, R. P. Guries, and D. T. Lester, "American Liberty Elms and Beyond: Going from the Impossible to the Difficult," *Dutch Elm Disease Research: Cellular and Molecular Approaches* (New York: Springer-Verlag, 1993), 27.

11. Ibid., 27, 29.

12. Ibid., 34.

13. Plant Patent 3,780 (1975) was for a variety of Siberian elm *(U. pumila)*; 5,335 (1984) was derived varieties of *U. pumila* and *U. carpinifolia.*

14. Smalley, Guries, and Lester, "American Liberty Elms," 43.

15. Ibid., 35.

16. Bob McCarthy, Williamstown, Massachusetts, conversation with author, August 20, 2002.

17. "Legacy of Rotary Elm Project Keeps Growing," *Lincoln County News*, July 11, 2002.

18. Peter Tyrell, New Haven, Connecticut, conversation with author, September 19, 2002. The low incidence of Dutch elm disease on the Green is also likely due to a vigorous sanitation campaign.

19. Tom Zetterstrom, conversation with author, August 4, 2002.

20. Donald Harriss, Lynnfield, Massachusetts, to Elm Research Institute, Westmoreland, New Hampshire.

21. Hansel, conversation with author, August 20, 2002.

22. William J. Flemer and William Flemer III did file a patent for a somewhat mysterious "Elm Tree" in December 1969, described as a "selected seedling of an unnamed and unidentified variety of the species *Ulmus americana*." But this was a different variety than the Princeton elm. Treesearch, "Elm Tree," 1972, Plant Patent number 3108.

23. Roger Holloway, Atlanta, Georgia, communication with author, September 16, 2002.

24. Quoted in Anthony DePalma, "The Star of Elm Street Stages a Comeback," *New York Times*, July 11, 2002.

25. Ibid.

26. Grafting leads to structural weakness, while growing the trees from seed would open the genetic floodgates and cause the disease-resistant pedigree to be lost.

27. Quoted in Anne Raver, "Once Devastated, Elms Start to Rebound," *New York Times*, January 13, 2002.

28. Alden Townsend, National Arboretum, communication with author, September 20, 2002.

29. Tom Zetterstrom, conversation with author, September 19, 2002.

30. Eleanor Charles, "Portraits of Trees," *New York Times*, November 12, 2000.

31. Jane Gordon, "A High School Class Tries to Restore the Elm," *New York Times*, July 8, 2001.

32. Bruce Carley, Acton, Massachusetts, conversation with author, September 6, 2002.

33. "Saving the American Elm" (www.elmpost.org).

34. Bill Chittick, Bristol Tree Society, conversation with author, September 17, 2002.

35. Del Tredici, "Ecology and Economics of Elm Replacement."

SELECTED BIBLIOGRAPHY

A Handbook of New England. Boston: Porter E. Sargent, 1917.

Adams, Henry. *The Education of Henry Adams.* Boston: Houghton Mifflin, 1918.

Adams, Nehemiah. *Boston Common, or Rural Walks in Cities.* Boston: George W. Light, 1838.

Allen, Everett S. *A Wind to Shake the World: The Story of the 1938 Hurricane.* Boston: Little, Brown, 1976.

American Forestry Association. *The American Elm: Its Glorious Past, Its Present Dilemma, Its Hope for Protection.* Washington D.C.: American Forestry Association, 1937.

Arnold, Henry F. *Trees in Urban Design.* New York: Van Nostrand Reinhold, 1980.

Batchelder, Samuel F. "The Washington Elm Tradition." *Publications of the Cambridge Historical Society,* vol. 17. Cambridge, Mass.: Cambridge Historical Society, 1931.

Beecher, Henry Ward. *Norwood; or, Village Life in New England.* New York: Charles Scribner, 1868.

Belden, Ezekiel Porter. *Sketches of Yale College.* New York: Saxton & Miles, 1843.

Bender, Thomas. *Toward an Urban Vision: Ideas and Institutions in Nineteenth-Century America.* Baltimore: Johns Hopkins University Press, 1982.

Berenberg, Richard. "Village Improvement Societies in New England, 1850–1900: The Rural Ideal in an Age of Rural Depopulation and Urban Growth." Ph.D. dissertation, Harvard University, 1966.

Binford, Henry C. *The First Suburbs: Residential Communities on the Boston Periphery, 1815–1860.* Chicago: University of Chicago Press, 1985.

Brooks, Van Wyck. *The Flowering of New England.* New York: Modern Library, 1941.

Brown, Dona. *Inventing New England: Regional Tourism in the Nineteenth Century.* Washington, D.C.: Smithsonian Institution Press, 1995.

Bryant, William Cullen. "A Forest Hymn." *Poems.* Philadelphia: A. Hart, 1850.

————. *The Letters of William Cullen Bryant.* Edited by William C. Bryant II and Thomas G. Voss. New York: Fordham University Press, 1975.

Buckingham, James Silk. *America: Historical, Statistic, and Descriptive.* New York: Harper and Brothers, 1841.

Burnaby, Andrew. *Travels Through the Middle Settlements in North America in the Years 1759 and 1760.* New York: A. Wessels, reprint 1904.

Carroll, Charles F. *The Timber Economy of Puritan New England.* Providence, R.I.: Brown University Press, 1974.

Carson, Rachel. *Silent Spring.* Boston: Houghton Mifflin, reprint 1987.

Carver, John. *Sketches of New England.* New York: E. French, 1842.

City of Cambridge. *Address of the Mayor, Upon the First Organization of the City Government.* Cambridge, Mass.: Andrew Reid, 1846.

————. *Report of the General Superintendent of Parks.* Cambridge, Mass.: City of Cambridge, 1894.

Clark, Kenneth. *The Gothic Revival: An Essay on the History of Taste*, 3d. ed. London: John Murray, 1995.

Coke, Edward T. *A Subaltern's Furlough.* New York: J. & J. Harper, 1833.

Cole, Thomas. "Essay on American Scenery." In *American Art, 1700–1960: Sources and Documents*, ed. John W. McCoubrey, 98–110. Englewood Cliffs, N.J.: Prentice-Hall, 1965.

Coleman, Emma Lewis. *A Historic and Present Day Guide to Old Deerfield.* Boston: 1912.

Cook, Howard M. *Wayside Jottings; or, Rambles Around the Old Town of Concord, New Hampshire.* Concord: E. C. Eastman, 1910.

Cresson, Margaret French. *The Laurel Hill Association, 1853–1953.* Pittsfield: Eagle Printing, 1953.

Cronon, William. *Changes in the Land.* New York: Hill and Wang, 1983.

Dame, Lorin L., and Henry Brooks. *Typical Elms and Other Trees of Massachusetts.* Boston: Little, Brown, 1890.

Davis, Richard C. *North American Forest History: A Guide to the Archives and Manuscripts in the United States and Canada.* Santa Barbara: Forest History Society, 1977.

Dewey, Orville. *Autobiography and Letters of Orville Dewey.* Edited by Mary E. Dewey. Boston: Roberts Brothers, 1883.

DeWolfe Howe, M. A. *Boston Common: Scenes from Four Centuries.* Cambridge, Mass.: Riverside, 1910.

Dickens, Charles. *Works of Charles Dickens.* New York: Sheldon, 1865.

Downing, Andrew Jackson. *Landscape Gardening and Rural Architecture.* New York: Dover, reprint 1991.

————. *Rural Essays.* Edited by George W. Curtis. New York: George A. Leavitt, 1869.

Dutch Elm Disease: Perspectives After Sixty Years. Ithaca: Cornell University Agricultural Experiment Station, 1978.

Dutch Elm Disease Research: Cellular and Molecular Approaches. New York: Springer-Verlag, 1993.

Dwight, Timothy. *Travels in New England and New York.* Cambridge, Mass.: Belknap Press, reprint 1969.

Eaton, Walter Prichard. *Green Trails and Upland Pastures.* New York: Doubleday, Page, 1917.

Ekblaw, W. Elmer. *New England Fancies.* Worcester, Mass.: Achille J. St. Onge, 1935.

Eliade, Mircea. *The Sacred and the Profane.* New York: Harcourt Brace, 1959.

Emerson, George B. *A Report on the Trees and Shrubs Growing Naturally in the Forests of Massachusetts.* Boston: Little, Brown, 1878.

Evans, Howard Ensign. *Pioneer Naturalists: The Discovery and Naming of North American Plants and Animals.* New York: Henry Holt, 1993.

Fearon, Henry Bradshaw. *Sketches of America.* London: Longman, Hurst, Rees, Orme, and Brown, 1818.

Frazer, James George. *The Golden Bough: A Study in Magic and Religion.* New York: Macmillan, 1922.

Geddes, Robert. *The Forest Edge.* New York: St. Martin's, 1982.

Glacken, Clarence J. *Traces on the Rhodian Shore.* Berkeley: University of California Press, 1967.

Green, Mason A. *Springfield, 1636–1886: History of Town and City.* Springfield, Mass.: C. A. Nichols, 1888.

Griffin, S. G. *A History of the Town of Keene.* Keene, N.H.: Sentinel Printing, 1904.

Gronovius, J. F., and Johannes Clayton. *Flora Virginica, exhibens plantas, quas nobilissimus vir D. J. Claytonius in Virginia crescentes observavit atque collegit.* Leiden: Cornelium Haak, 1739.

Hall, Basil. *Travels in North America in the Years 1827 and 1828.* Edinburgh: Cadell, 1829.

Hamilton, J. W. *Memorial of Jessie Lee and the Old Elm.* Boston: J. P. Magee, 1875.

Harrison, Robert P. *Forests: The Shadow of Civilization.* Chicago: University of Chicago Press, 1992.

Hassam, Frederick Fitch. *Liberty Tree, Liberty Hall.* Boston: privately published, 1891.

Hastings, Lewis M. *The Streets of Cambridge: An Account of Their Origin and History.* Cambridge, Mass.: City of Cambridge, 1921.

Hawthorne, Nathaniel. *The House of the Seven Gables.* Boston: Ticknor, Reed, and Fields, 1851.

————. *Our Old Home, and English Note-Books.* Boston: Houghton Mifflin, reprint 1902.

Hayward, James. *Report of the Survey of the Roads in Cambridge.* Cambridge, Mass.: Metcalf, Torry & Ballou, 1838.

Herrick, James W. "Iroquois Medical Botany." Ph.D. dissertation, State University of New York, 1977.

Hobsbawm, Eric. "Inventing Traditions." In *The Invention of Tradition*, ed. Eric Hobsbawm and Terence Ranger. Cambridge: Cambridge University Press, 1983.

Hodgson, Adam. *Letters from North America.* London: Hurst, Robinson, 1824.

Holmes, Oliver Wendell. *The Autocrat of the Breakfast-Table.* Boston: Houghton Mifflin, reprint 1916.

————. *Elsie Venner: A Romance of Destiny.* Cambridge, Mass.: Riverside, 1891.

Hornby, E. B. *Under Old Rooftrees.* Jersey City, N.J.: privately published, 1908.

Huth, Hans. *Nature and the American.* Berkeley: University of California Press, 1957.

Jackson, John Brinckerhoff. *A Sense of Place, A Sense of Time.* New Haven: Yale University Press, 1994.

James, Henry. *The American Scene.* New York: Charles Scribner's Sons, 1946.

Juel, H. O. *Early Investigations of North American Flora.* Uppsala, Sweden: Almquist and Wiksells, 1920.

Kalm, Peter. *Travels in North America.* London, 1772.

Kammen, Michael. *Meadows of Memory: Images of Time and Tradition in American Art and Culture.* Austin: University of Texas Press, 1992.

Kazin, Alfred. *A Writer's America: Landscape in Literature.* New York: Knopf, 1988.

Kostof, Spiro. *America by Design.* New York: Oxford University Press, 1987.

Langley, Batty. *A Sure Method of Improving Estates.* London: Francis Clay and Daniel Browne, 1728.

Latrobe, Charles Joseph. *The Rambler in North America.* New York: Harper & Brothers, 1835.

Loth, Calder, and Julius Trousdale Sadler, Jr. *The Only Proper Style: Gothic Architecture in America.* Boston: New York Graphic Society, 1975.

Lowell, James Russell. "Under the Old Elm." *Poems.* Cambridge, Mass.: Riverside, 1890.

Lowenthal, David. *The Past Is a Foreign Country.* New York: Cambridge University Press, 1985.

Machor, James L. *Pastoral Cities: Urban Ideals and the Symbolic Landscape of America.* Madison: University of Wisconsin Press, 1987.

Marx, Leo. *The Machine in the Garden: Technology and the Pastoral Ideal in America.* New York: Oxford University Press, 1964.

McKelvey, Blake. *The Urbanization of America, 1860–1915.* New Brunswick, N.J.: Rutgers University Press, 1963.

Michaux, F. André. *The North American Sylva, or, A Description of the Forest Trees of the United States, Canada, and Nova Scotia.* Philadelphia: Dobson and Conrad, 1819.

Miller, Perry. *Errand into the Wilderness.* Cambridge, Mass.: Belknap Press, 1964.

Morton, Thomas. *New English Canaan or New Canaan: Containing an Abstract of New England, Composed in Three Bookes.* Amsterdam: Jacob Frederick Stam, 1637.

Nash, Roderick. *Wilderness and the American Mind.* New Haven: Yale University Press, 1982.

Northrup, Birdsey Grant. *Rural Improvement.* New Haven: Tuttle, Morehouse & Taylor, 1880.

Pace, Antonio, ed. *Luigi Castiglioni's Viaggio: Travels in the United States of North America, 1785–1787.* Syracuse, N.Y.: Syracuse University Press, 1983.

Peattie, Donald Culross. *A Natural History of Trees.* New York: Bonanza, 1966.

Piper, Richard Upton. *The Trees of America.* Boston: William White, 1855.

Powell, Lyman P. *Historic Towns of New England.* New York: Knickerbocker, 1899.

Richens, R. H. *Elm.* London: Cambridge University Press, 1983.

Rogers, Julia Ellen. *The Tree Book*. New York: Doubleday, Page, 1906.

Sandroff, Ivan. *More Massachusetts Towns*. Barre, Mass.: Barre Publishers, 1965.

Sargent, Charles Sprague. *The Silva of North America*. Boston: Houghton Mifflin, 1895.

Schama, Simon. *Landscape and Memory*. New York: Knopf, 1995.

Schlereth, Thomas J. *Cultural History and Material Culture: Everyday Life, Landscapes, Museums*. Charlottesville: University Press of Virginia, 1992.

Schuyler, David. *The New Urban Landscape: The Redefinition of City Form in Nineteenth-Century America*. Baltimore: Johns Hopkins University Press, 1986.

Scott, Frank J. *The Art of Beautifying Suburban Home Grounds*, 3d ed. New York: American Book Exchange, 1881.

Shurtleff, Nathaniel B. *A Topographical and Historical Description of Boston*. Boston: Noyes, Holmes, 1872.

Simmons, James R. *The Historic Trees of Massachusetts*. Boston: Marshall Jones, 1919.

Smith, Chard Powers. *The Housatonic, Puritan River*. New York: Rinehart, 1946.

Smith, J. E. A. *The History of Pittsfield*. Boston: Lee and Shepard, 1869.

Smith, William. *A Yorkshireman's Trip to the United States and Canada*. London: Longmans, Green, 1892.

Stilgoe, John R. *Common Landscape of America, 1580–1845*. New Haven: Yale University Press, 1982.

———. "Town Common and Village Green in New England: 1620 to 1981." In *On Common Ground*, ed. Ronald L. Fleming. Cambridge, Mass.: Townscape Institute, 1982.

Sundberg, Jane M. "The Role of the American Elm and Dutch Elm Disease in the Urban Environments of the United States." Master's thesis, University of Chicago, 1969.

Thoreau, Henry David. *Excursions*. Boston: Ticknor and Fields, 1863.

———. *The Journal of Henry D. Thoreau*. Edited by Bradford Torrey and Francis H. Allen. Boston: Houghton Mifflin, 1949.

Trollope, Anthony. *North America*. New York: Harper and Brothers, 1862.

Tudor, William. *Letters on the Eastern States*. New York: Kirk and Mercein, 1820.

Tunnard, Christopher. *The City of Man*. New York: Charles Scribner's Sons, 1970.

Warren, J. C. *The Great Tree on Boston Common*. Boston: John Wilson and Son, 1855.

Wells, Daniel White, and Reuben Field Wells. *A History of Hatfield, Massachusetts*. Springfield, Mass.: Gibbons, 1910.

Wilkinson, Gerald. *Epitaph for the Elm*. London: Hutchinson, 1978.

Williams, Michael. *Americans and Their Forests: A Historical Geography*. New York: Cambridge University Press, 1992.

Willis, Nathaniel Parker. *American Scenery*. London: James S. Virtue, 1857.

———. "The Elms of New Haven." *Sacred Poems*. New York: Clark, Austin & Smith, 1860.

Wilson, Ernest H. *Aristocrats of the Trees*. Boston: Stratsford, 1930.

Wood, William. *New England's Prospect*. London: John Bellamie, 1634.

INDEX